Hope, Grit and Gratitude

AN INSPIRING JOURNEY OF TURNING ADVERSITY INTO JOY

Leigh Caldwell

Copyright © 2022 by Leigh Caldwell.

This work depicts actual events in the life of the author as truthfully as recollection permits. While all persons within are actual individuals, some names and identifying characteristics have been changed to respect and protect their privacy.

All rights reserved. No part of this publication may be reproduced, distributed or transmitted in any form or by any means, including photocopying, recording, or other electronic or mechanical methods, without the prior written permission of the publisher, except in the case of brief quotations embodied in critical reviews and certain other non-commercial uses permitted by copyright law. For permission requests, write to the publisher, addressed "Attention: Permissions Coordinator," at the address below.

Leigh Caldwell C/- Intertype Publish and Print
Unit 45, 125 Highbury Road
BURWOOD VIC 3125
www.intertype.com.au

Ordering Information:
Quantity sales. Special discounts are available on quantity purchases by corporations, associations, and others. For details, contact the "Special Sales Department" at the address above.

Hope, Grit and Gratitude/ Leigh Caldwell. —1st ed.
ISBN 978-0-6455754-5-3

Contents

Life Can Change in a Heartbeat. 11

A Whole New World 17

Choosing Positive 23

Adjusting to Our New 'Normal.' 31

Behind the Smile 39

Crikey! She's a Beauty! 47

Ashley's Party - What a Blast! (Literally) 55

Soaring High with Sir Richard Branson 61

A Star is Born... Reluctantly! 73

A New Beginning 79

Serendipity 91

Where's That To-Do List? 97

Flashback 103

Believe and You Can Achieve 113

A Dream Comes True 117

Watching Flowers Bloom 121

A Glimpse Behind Closed Doors 129

A Great Excuse to Shine. 137

Preparing for More Than a Concert. 143

Another Star is Born... In Fact, Lots of Them! 151

Million Dollar Memo 159

New Legends at the Cowboys Stadium 169

Meeting The Wiggles... 177

Sharpening the Saw.. 185

Making a Difference 193

Dodging a Bullet... 199

Reliving the Horror... 203

Celebrating Two Years of Wow.. 207

Another Magical Night Full of Surprises 211

Hang on, is That in My Job Description? 215

Performing with Guy Sebastian - A Crazy Idea! 221

The Special Olympic Games: The Journey Begins. 231

Being Strong When Your Heart is Breaking. 235

The Special Olympic Games: Adventure of a Lifetime 245

Sheer Terror in the Grand Canyon.. 265

We'll Keep Dancing for Lany 277

Remind Me Why I Do This? 285

Another Incredible Guy Sebastian Experience 293

In the Blink of an Eye 301

Life is like a Box of Chocolates.. 305

Carols by Candlelight 311

Australia Day 2017 321

Pressing the Pause Button.. 327

You've Got the Wrong Person! 329

The Dance for Daniel Ball - Take 2... 335

Ride Like a Girl 343

Meeting an Aussie Icon 349

The Mayor's All Stars Concert.. 353

Born To Try... 361

That's a wrap.. 387

ACKNOWLEDGMENTS 389

'Things work out best for those who make the best of the way things work out.'

—JOHN WOODEN

DEDICATION

A huge thank you to my wonderful family for all your love and support while I made a dream come true. Thank you also for allowing me to believe that even though I look old, I don't have to act old!

This book is dedicated to my amazing parents, John & Bette Grady. They taught me to care for others and a valuable lesson that with just a little bit of effort, you can make a big difference in other peoples' lives.

Steve Price OAM.
NQ Radio Superstar

'I've not met anyone quite like Leigh Caldwell.

Always looking on that bright side of life, always finding the best in someone, and in the most extraordinary ways.

Truly a guiding light in life, though her own has been a battle, yet never dwelling on it, always showing the smile, the kind and positive words, the goal of a better life, not for her, a better life for others.

I know, because I've had the absolute honour of seeing it first-hand...and feet for that matter, or should I say Happy Feat.

If I could show the world, and especially those in need of confidence and joy, one night of the smiles and laughs at a Happy Feat gathering, it would soothe and lift many a soul. I have been there many many times and wish I could share it, a most illuminating experience.

Created by this incredible lady, she along with the volunteers, has truly lifted the lives of those who are known as Happy Feat. I know these members, I know many of the backgrounds, and when you see them together and the joy they give others, it's a living blessing. I've talked to the mums, watched them cry with joy at a concert, I've seen a Townsville crowd of thousands stand and applaud, you see these wonderful Happy Featers would never have had this opportunity without Leigh, and we would never have had the opportunity of looking deeply into our own lives too.

Inspirational yes, but more so when you watch Leigh, its Enlightenment.'

OFFICE OF THE MAYOR

TOWNSVILLE CITY COUNCIL
ADMINISTRATION BUILDING
103 WALKER STREET

PO BOX 1268, TOWNSVILLE
QUEENSLAND 4810

TELEPHONE 07 4727 9201

enquiries@townsville.qld.gov.au
townsville.qld.gov.au

19 September 2022

Happy Feat Testimonial

Happy Feat is a joyful and inclusive community organisation which empowers people of all abilities through the wonders of dance.

Leigh Caldwell, as the founder of Happy Feat, takes the members on a journey, giving them all a chance to let their light shine as they step on stage.

Their dedication, commitment and mantra of no labels, and certainly no limitations, gives these amazing dancers the opportunity to grow and flourish.

Happy Feat not only changes the lives of those directly involved in the dance group, but the organisation continues to change the way people in our community perceive those with special needs.

I look forward to seeing all Happy Feat accomplishes in the years ahead.

Cr Jenny Hill
Mayor of Townsville

CHAPTER 1

Life Can Change in a Heartbeat.

Have you ever found yourself coasting along the highway of life, getting caught up in the constant hustle and bustle? Believing all those daily tasks and responsibilities are a top priority and must get done urgently?

Then a monumental event takes you into the crash zone and your world is suddenly on a detour through some terrifying, uncharted territory?

That happened to our family on the 5th of November 2005.

Our wonderful, strong, happy, and healthy-looking 14-year-old son, Ashley, was diagnosed with Acute Lymphoblastic Leukaemia - an aggressive type of cancer of the blood and bone marrow.

The week before, he'd mentioned that the glands in his neck were swollen. As both my husband and daughter had just had throat infections, I told him it was probably the same thing, and that we'd keep an eye on it. His glands were still enlarged a couple of days later, so we went for what I thought would be just a routine check-up at the doctors.

When I noticed the doctor being unexpectedly thorough with his examination for a sore throat, things suddenly became very serious for me.

He asked if Ash had been getting bruises and my heart stopped. I froze with fear.

"Oh, my goodness, he's checking for Leukaemia!" I realised. When I was a child, I lost my cousin (and best friend) to Leukaemia. I knew what the doctor was looking for.

He went on to explain that it was probably just a throat infection, but to come back in three to four weeks if his glands were still up.

I put it in my diary to check every two days!

After my first check, Ashley seemed to be getting better. Then alarm bells loudly clanged. An active teenage boy, he had been out riding his motorbike all afternoon. He was doing all sorts of fancy tricks that no mother should know about; wheelies, endos (riding on the front wheel only), and tearing around the place at an ungodly speed. Later at dinner, he mentioned that his swollen glands were annoying him. Feeling them, my blood ran cold.

I didn't say a word. I finished serving the roast dinner. Then I quietly took the patio chair out into the middle of the yard and fell to pieces. When Geoff came looking for me, he was shocked at the state I was in. We'd been married for over 20 years, and he'd never seen me this distressed.

I was shaking from head to toe and said, "Geoff, you might think taking a seemingly healthy 14-year-old to Emergency on a Saturday night is crazy, but I know we have to go."

Geoff told Ash what we were doing, explaining that "it will put Mum's mind at rest and stop her worrying". Arriving at the hospital, I stepped up to the triage nurse, looked her in the eye, and told her the situation.

I explained that this was very serious. There was a moment where the nurse and I just looked at each other, and no further words were necessary.

To our relief, we didn't have to wait long and were soon with the doctor in the emergency ward. He examined Ash and concluded, as our GP had done, that it was probably a throat infection. He asked what we wanted to do from there. My wonderful husband said, "I know this sounds crazy, but we came to the hospital to get a blood test, so we'd still like to go ahead with it."

While we waited, Ash had us in fits of laughter with his quirky sense of humour as he blew up the rubber gloves that he'd helped himself to. An hour went by and there was no news. Then another hour.

At 11:45pm, the doctor returned looking shattered as he slumped into a chair. His body language had already delivered the news.

"Your son has an abnormality in his blood," he said gravely. "I'll speak to the oncologist in the morning."

Words no parents ever want to hear. They shattered our world on that long November night. We sat there speechless, motionless, feeling like deer caught in headlights. The doctor told us to go home, get some sleep, and said they would call us in the morning.

It was a slow walk back to the car. Ash and Geoff talked about not worrying about anything until we knew more. Remembering everything my family and I had gone through with my cousin, I felt sick to the core. My stomach was churning, and my heart was pounding.

Back home, Geoff, Ash and I had a cuppa out under the stars and just sat quietly. We always loved to sit under the stars. It usually brought a sort of peace to the soul. That was something else that changed that night. I didn't enjoy sitting under the stars again for many years, as each time I'd gaze at the stars, it took me back to that dark, devastating and traumatic moment in our lives.

Sleep was a complete waste of time that night, so instead I sat at the computer researching Leukaemia. The more I learned, the more terrified I became. Just after 6:00am the next morning, I couldn't wait any longer to ring my parents. What a difficult phone call that was to make. As always, Mum and Dad were incredibly strong, supportive, and ready to help in any way they could.

At 8:00am, Geoff rang the doctor we'd spoken to the night before.

"Come straight to the hospital," he instructed.

It was such a short sentence, but the impact was colossal. How do you get any teenager up at that time of the morning, let alone to break the news that we had been summoned to the hospital? But Ashley was incredible, taking it all very calmly.

What followed that morning seemed a blur. Waiting, medical examinations, waiting, more blood tests. And yes, more waiting.

Eventually we were summoned to a little room with two doctors. They broke the news that Ashley had been diagnosed with Acute Lymphoblastic Leukaemia (ALL) and told us they were sending him to Brisbane for treatment immediately. That is, as soon as it could be arranged.

Even though Ash was 14 years old, the doctors chose to put him through the children's ward as they felt he would get the best treatment available there. This meant travelling to the Royal Children's Hospital in Brisbane for treatment – over 1,300kms away.

A jumble of questions flooded my mind: What was ahead for our son? What would his treatment involve? What about Stacey? How could we leave her? It was her 16th birthday in three days' time?! How could we kiss her goodbye and tell her we didn't know when we would see her again? When we came home, would we be bringing our son home with us? How long would we be away? What would happen to our family home building business?

The one question we didn't ask was, "Why us?" We knew that there was nothing a question like that could do to help the situation.

Even Ashley seemed determined to remain positive. Only half an hour after Ash heard his diagnosis, he said to me, "Don't worry, Mum. We'll make a difference in this world just by the way we are. When we get to that hospital in Brisbane, we'll cheer them up."

It doesn't happen very often, but I was speechless. What could I say? Here was a 14-year-old teenager who had just been diagnosed with a serious life-threatening disease, and all he could think of were others!

We were expected at the Royal Children's Hospital in Brisbane first thing the next morning. For now, they had put Ashley on a drip in the Townsville Hospital.

It was time to let our family know and to prepare for our stay in Brisbane.

That afternoon as I numbly threw random clothes in a suitcase, a bizarre and bone-chilling thought came to me: "I don't even know when I'll be home again."

I simply couldn't face the thought of having to tell our friends individually. Besides, I just didn't have the mind space – or the time. There were far more urgent things to think about. I sent out a text message to all our friends and family. It wasn't the ideal way to break the news, but drastic times called for drastic measures. We were now in survival mode.

CHAPTER 2

A Whole New World

I can't even begin to explain how difficult and heart-wrenching it was to leave our daughter behind when we made the trip down to Brisbane. Even now, many years later, it is something that still brings me to tears every time I think of it. With her brother seriously ill and her family leaving during a sensitive time for her, Stacey was just heartbroken. Instead of being able to help and comfort her, we had to leave.

I've heard of the expression 'counter-intuitive' (which means 'contrary to what seems intuitively correct') and this phrase certainly describes the situation. Every one of my instincts was telling me to stay and comfort my daughter – and yet I had leave, not knowing how long I was leaving her for, or when I would see her again.

My wonderful mum and dad came to stay at our place so that Stacey had at least some small sense of 'normal.' She had her horses to look after, and she was in the middle of her end of year exams. We wanted to protect and shelter her from this horror as much as possible – it was horrendous enough for us to go through. Looking back, we still wonder how on earth we got through it all.

At 6:00am, Geoff, Ashley, and I flew from Townsville to Brisbane the very next morning. I remember sitting on the plane, looking at the cannula in Ashley's hand. I remembered it was only two days ago that he was doing tricks on his motorbike. Here we were on a whole new journey, going to live in an unfamiliar city. During the flight we laughed, joked, and spoke positively. The outside world would never have guessed the grave situation we were facing.

By 8:00am that morning, less than 24 hours since Ashley's diagnosis, Geoff, Ashley, and I were sitting in the children's ward of the Royal Children's Hospital. The three of us must have looked stunned as we took in the sights around us.

We saw frail young children, sitting quietly as drips pumped chemicals into their delicate little bodies, cosy beanies covering their bare little heads. We heard babies screaming as nurses attempted procedures on them. It all seemed very alien to us. We were not only in a new city; we were living in whole new world.

Our family has always believed that living life to the fullest is about having a positive attitude and a sense of humour – making the most of every situation and keeping a strong sense of family. When Ash was diagnosed, I reminded them of that philosophy.

Everyone has choices in life. We could choose to go around with long faces and have a 'pity party', or we could choose to be happy and positive. I certainly knew which option I was choosing and hoped the others would also make good decisions. Every family has its challenges. There is always someone having a worse day than you so you shouldn't complain.

Having just been ripped away from our daughter, our wider family, our friends, our home and our work, our entire life had changed in a heartbeat. We were in a surreal environment, totally lost and terrified to the core, but our tight-knit, little family was up for the challenge.

Our first hospital encounter was with a counsellor who had been appointed to us. She introduced herself and after chatting for ten minutes, declared that with our positive thinking and attitudes, we should be the counsellors, not her. She then asked us to promise something.

Not having known her for very long I was hesitant to agree, but we listened to what she had to say. She said that we would have a lot to deal with and asked us not to speak with the other families in the hospital system. She said this would stop us taking on their troubles and would help us keep our positive attitude.

I was dumbfounded. As a social butterfly who loves being with people, I couldn't believe that she was asking us not to speak with anyone! If we didn't feel totally alone and isolated before, we certainly did now! That meeting was the first, last and only counselling session we experienced during the whole three and a half years of treatment that followed.

Eventually Geoff and I met with Ashley's doctor who oversaw the whole children's oncology ward, Doctor Helen. Huddled in a little room with her, we learned just how serious it was. She explained that as Ashley was 14 years old and male, he fell into the high-risk category. There was a 75% recovery rate.

When you are trying to take in information like that, it's so terrifying; your thoughts go straight to the 25%. But then you take control and realise that at 75%, the odds are still definitely in your favour.

Dr Helen advised us that we had a decision to make. There was a study underway that was seeking to establish the best treatment for Ashley's disease. If we joined the study, we would be randomly allocated a treatment path, which would carry a 50% chance of receiving the current best treatment, and a 50% chance of receiving the alternative being tested, which they believed would be slightly better.

Up until now, we had faith in the experts and were willing to follow their advice. But this changed things. Now we had to make a decision that could affect our son's life. And there was no right answer.

Geoff and I were so traumatised by the whole situation that we both went into shock and felt chilled to the bone. A nurse came in with blankets to wrap around us as we sat there, trembling uncontrollably. As we huddled together, I did something very out-of-character.

I got angry. I think my exact words were, "You are the medical professionals with years and years of training, medical degrees, and knowledge and here you are, asking us the parents, to decide on a treatment to save our son's life! I can't believe you're asking us to do this!"

Doctor Helen was very empathetic and said that we didn't have to decide immediately. We could sleep on it and give them our decision in the morning.

From that moment to the early hours of the following day, Geoff and I waded through every bit of information the medical team provided on treatments, medications, side effects, and the worst possible outcomes. In the end, we concluded two things.

Firstly, there was no definitive right or wrong answer. If we decided to put Ashley into the study, he would either get the current best proven treatment or a treatment the medical experts believed would be even more effective. If we chose not to include him in the study, he would still get the current best treatment.

Secondly, the only reason there is such a good survival rate is because studies have previously been done. We believed that even though it was uncomfortable to expose him to some degree of 'unknown', we had a moral responsibility to participate and do our bit in these ongoing studies.

While we were completing various bits of paperwork, it got to the point where I just couldn't take any more and returned to our room exhausted – emotionally, mentally, and physically.

I fell asleep immediately. When I awoke, I felt a new resolve and made a conscious decision that from that moment on I was not going to cry.

I'm not exactly sure why. It could have been that crying takes energy and I knew I needed every bit of energy to get through the next minute (let alone the next 3½ years). It could have been that subconsciously I was concerned that if I started crying, I may not be able to stop. So, from that day on, even though I had my moments, it became rare for me to cry.

Even though I'd only had a few hours' sleep, I felt as if I'd recharged the batteries and put some fuel in the tank. I was ready to take whatever was going to hit me that day.

Geoff and I had made our decision and we advised the medical team. It was another 24 hours before we heard which treatment the study had allocated us, and it turned out that Ashley had been allocated the current best method. Learning this news, various thoughts and feelings went through me.

The first was slight disappointment because, perhaps, the new treatment would turn out to be better. This was quickly followed by some sense of relief. If things didn't work out for the best, we needn't hold ourselves responsible because he was on the same treatment he would have had if we had chosen not to participate.

Now it was time for the treatment protocol to begin. A planned 3 ½ years of various chemotherapies, lumbar punctures, steroids, blood tests, injections, and lots of other 'character-building' stuff.

The crazy thing was that Ashley didn't appear to be sick and didn't even feel sick. We had to 'make him sick' by effectively putting poison – chemotherapy – into his body to make him better. How bizarre is that? Once again, that word 'counter-intuitive' pops up.

From the trauma of abandoning Stacey when she needed me, to the new ongoing waves of fresh stress and horror, I was reeling from one blow after another. As the gruelling treatment began, our decision to be positive in whatever we faced, and my new resolve not to cry, was about to be tested on every level during the long journey ahead.

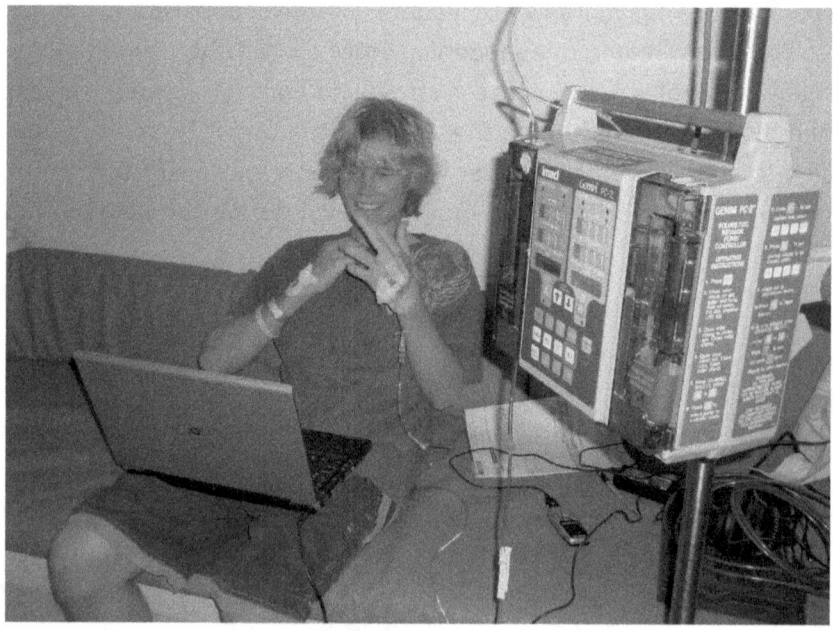

CHAPTER 3

Choosing Positive

Just a couple of weeks into his treatment, Ashley developed pneumocystis pneumonia. He would vomit every time he moved even so much as an eyelid. Our beautiful 14-year-old boy was painfully fragile, weighing a mere 46kg, bald, and frighteningly pale and weak. I remember looking at my distraught husband and seeing the pain in his eyes.

"At least he's not in intensive care," I said. "That's got to be a good thing." Geoff and I both smiled and even chuckled at how desperate this comment sounded.

It took a great deal of energy to keep such a positive attitude, and there were times when we struggled. Just when we thought things couldn't get any worse, they did.

Ash was going downhill rapidly, and the decision was made to operate and insert a PICC (peripherally inserted central catheter) line in his arm. This enabled nutrition to be pumped directly into his vein.

Watching Ash deteriorating made me feel so helpless. I needed every bit of energy to get through the next minute – and I didn't know how I would get through the next hour, day, or week.

During these very dark times, I went 'off air'. This meant turning my phone off and not having any contact with the outside world. I honestly had nothing left for connecting with family and friends – and everyone knew that when Leigh went off air, things were dire.

It was during this agonising time that one of the doctors tried to take a blood sample, making several unsuccessful attempts. This doctor admired Ashley and thought so highly of him, that every time she went to carry out a procedure, she would try too hard and get nervous. Things never went to plan. Watching her cause even more pain for our son was the breaking point for me. I snapped at her and left the room.

Retreating to the parents' room, I broke down and sobbed my heart out. I was watching my son slowly slipping away and it felt like my heart was being ripped out. Sometime later, that same doctor sought me out and sat down quietly beside me.

Even though I didn't really associate with any of the other families in the children's ward (on that initial advice from the counsellor), I had overheard some mothers talking about a new drug that had helped their children with nausea. I asked the doctor if they'd considered it for Ash yet. How could we stop him from going further downhill?

Pleading with her, I said, "I've never begged for anything in my life, but I'm now begging you to help save our son's life!"

She squeezed both my hands and quickly left. I don't think she quite made it out of the room before bursting into tears herself.

Not long after, I regained my composure and put on my happy face again. When I returned to Ashley's bedside, a group of doctors arrived and were examining him. They administered medication and wrote copious notes. There was a whole lot happening, but this already big day was about to get a lot bigger.

Looking up from Ashley's bedside I saw the most wonderful sight ever. Mum, Dad and my brother, Bruce, walked into the room. It was like seeing the most brilliant rainbow. My rainbow! I nearly knocked them over with my hugs.

As I'd been 'off air' for some time, they'd decided to just book tickets and come to Brisbane to be with us for a couple of days. Even if there was nothing they could do, they wanted to be with us and share the burden. I'd been trying to protect them, but there was no escaping it as they now saw and experienced the horror of Ash's condition for themselves.

Welcome to our world.

When you're going through such a momentous roller coaster of emotions, it's difficult for friends and family to know what to say and do to help. For us, it was the little things that helped us through the nightmare. We were so lucky to have such wonderful, supportive family and friends. Not all the families we saw in the hospital were as fortunate as we were, and we certainly felt extremely blessed.

I was also very fortunate that a very special friend would regularly send crazy, random texts and emails just to make us smile, laugh, brighten our day or to say she was thinking of us. Not many people realise that for us, even going through such trauma, it was a welcome relief to have something to take our mind off the situation and probably escape the nightmare, even if it was only for a fleeting moment. If there were times when we weren't up to these messages, we would just revisit them when we were ready again. Now I try to share the joy these messages brought us. Whenever I hear of someone in a difficult situation, I also look for things to make them smile and make their day.

After the doctors changed the medication and plan of attack, Ashley was able to start moving slowly and weakly without vomiting constantly. Just to be able to move his head without vomiting was truly exciting. Perhaps we'd turned the corner and could at last see a glimmer of light at the end of the tunnel!

It was only a few days later that the alarm bells started ringing. Ash had developed pain at the site of the PICC line, and an ultrasound revealed that he had developed a blood clot. Dispersing it required twice-daily injections of Clexane (blood thinner). This was OK now, but what were we to do when we were away from the hospital?

My choices were: I must give the injections myself – or take him to the hospital for each one.

My first thought was, "There's no way I can push a needle into my own son, let alone do it every day for six months!" I had specifically chosen not to become a nurse because I couldn't bear the thought of giving needles. Now here I was with no choice but find a way to get used to them.

I had already learned how to gown up to give Ash cytotoxic needles through an Insuflon (a type of cannula) in his leg when he was able to stay with us at Ronald McDonald House. This was different. This was injecting into my son directly.

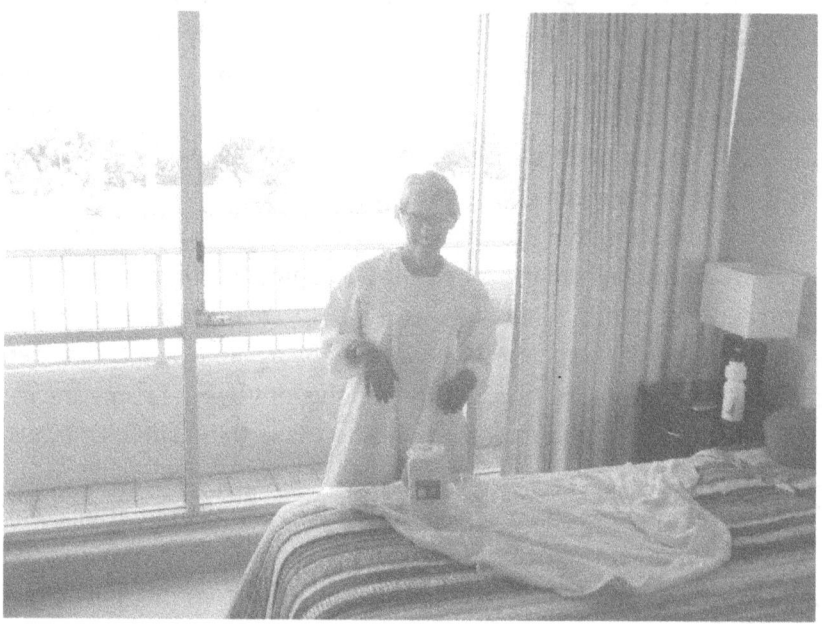

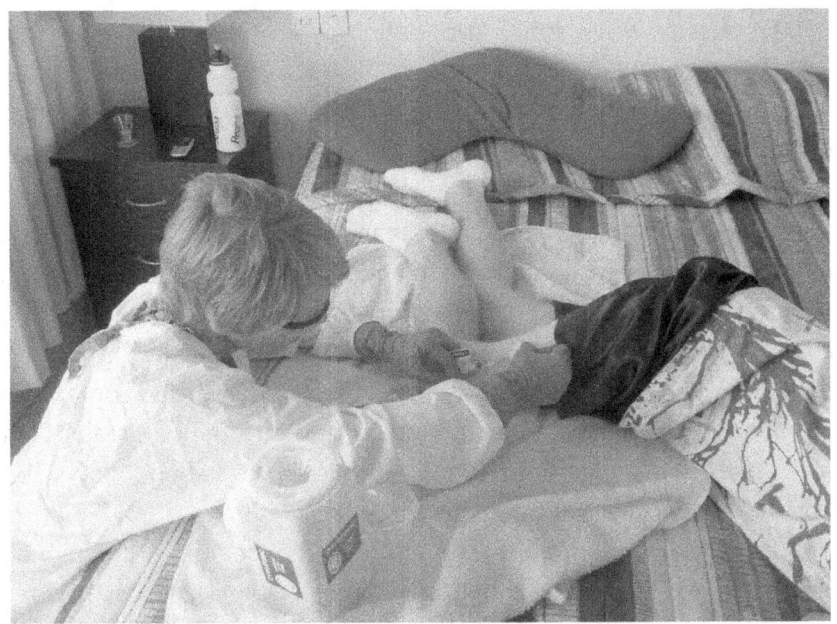

Every time I gave the Clexane injection, I would have to cause pain to my child – and the thought tore me apart. Unfortunately, it had to be done, and the old Nike 'Just do it' attitude kicked in. OK, Leigh. Smile, put on your happy face again, and get on with it.

This doesn't mean that even after five and three-quarter months of giving daily injections, I was remotely OK with it! I hated and dreaded giving every single injection. We had the added challenge of Stacey's needle phobia. On any trips home, we had to make sure she wasn't around when I gave the injections, or it would only add to the already stressful situation. The syringes and needles themselves had to be hidden in the fridge and the sharps container kept out of sight. Yes, these were certainly 'character-building' times!

The persistent blood clot also meant that Ashley was very restricted in what he could and couldn't do, which is never an easy thing for a teenage boy. I'll never forget the meeting we had with Doctor Helen when Ash asked the dreaded question – whether he could still ride his motorbike when he returned home.

The answer was a stern, "No, definitely not! If you ride your motorbike, you could die."

It was as simple as that. She explained that if Ash were to injure or cut himself while on the Clexane, a blood thinner, he could bleed to death.

How was I going to keep a 14-year-old occupied for the next six months when he wasn't allowed to have his favourite adrenaline rush – riding his motorbike, water-skiing, fishing, or snorkelling? He couldn't even do something as simple as ride his pushbike.

Our family used to joke that there's always Plan B, and sometimes we even got to Plan Z when trying to find alternative ideas. Right from the start, it was Geoff's and my mission to keep Ashley in his positive headspace. But even I secretly struggled!

After racking my brain, I came up with the idea of getting him an Xbox with different action-packed games. Other kids had owned Xboxes for years, but our kids had been too busy getting out doing things and just didn't find the need for one. Ashley couldn't go out to play, but now he could race and explore using this gaming console. Yes, this was the answer.

So, it was off to the shops to buy an Xbox, which I knew absolutely nothing about but was soon to discover. I bought some crazy car-racing games and the sort of games that I knew would get his adrenaline racing. That night, I gleefully watched as Ashley annihilated Geoff in a car-racing duel.

After Ashley's PICC line was eventually removed because of the blood clot, they decided to try him with a nasogastric tube to get some much-needed nutrition into his extremely frail body. A plastic tube was to be inserted through his nose, past the throat and down into the stomach so a high protein mixture could be pumped straight into his stomach.

The wonderful young nurse who was to carry out this procedure thought the world of Ashley and wanted to cause him the least possible discomfort. But as we witnessed many times, even with the best intentions in mind, things didn't always go to plan.

We knew it wasn't going to be a pleasant experience and just wanted to get it over and done with. I held and comforted Ash as the nurse began inserting the tube down his nose. This was one of the many times when all I wanted was to take the pain away. How I wished it were me instead of him.

Down the tube went, but to our horror, it became kinked! Oh no, this meant it would have to be taken out and inserted again! The nurse was devastated and close to tears. She understood that this poor kid had been through more pain and suffering in a few short months than anybody should go through in a lifetime. The last thing she wanted to do was add to it.

Thankfully the second attempt worked, and Ashley's nasogastric tube was able to pump vital nutrition into his skeletal body. I gently squeezed the nurse's arm, looked her in the eye, smiled and thanked her. Looking extremely relieved, she cleaned up all the equipment, bursting into tears as she bustled out of the room.

Our time in hospital was like a non-stop roller coaster ride, with one sharp scary turn after the other. It was a time of facing fear and pushing us way out of our comfort zone. We were on our own, and yet surrounded by a medical team fighting for us too. At times, it was hard to make the best of things, and to be so grateful for the friends and family supporting us from home. Everything Ashley and I loved seemed just so far away.

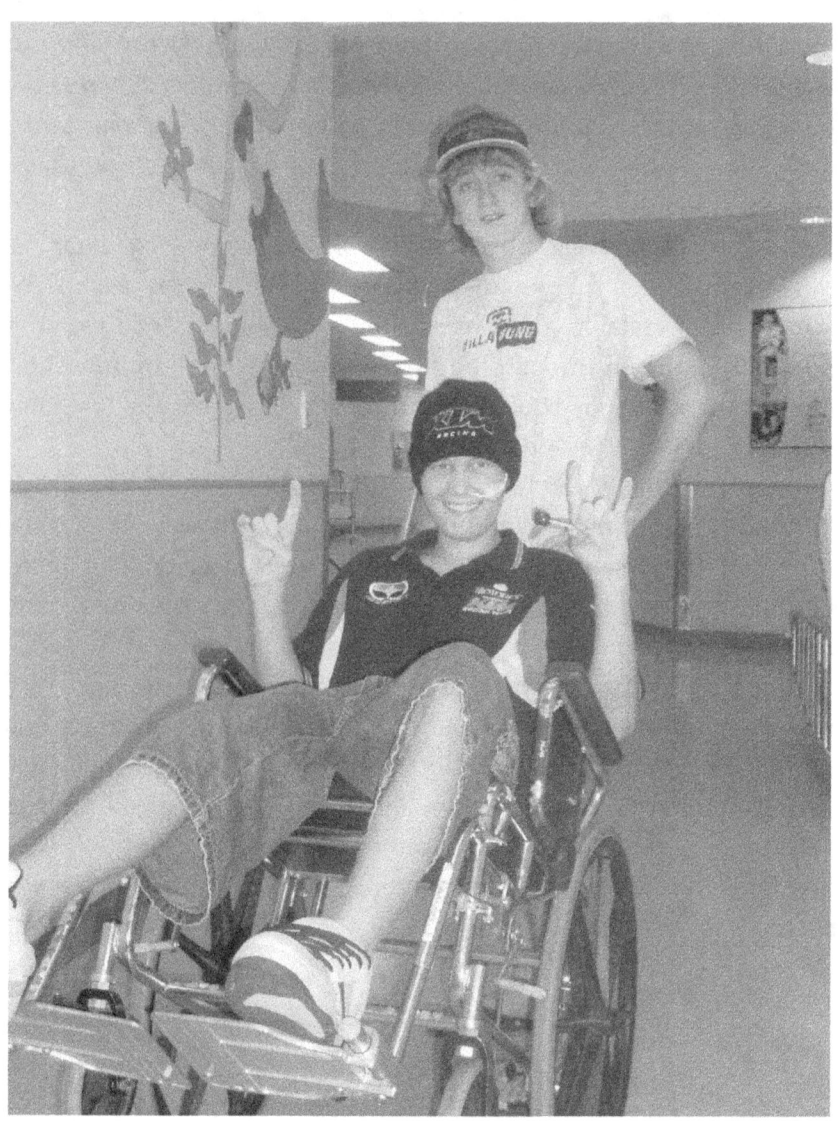

CHAPTER 4

Adjusting to Our New 'Normal.'

We desperately wanted to go home and escape this nightmare. With no end in sight, this was one period where we struggled to keep up our positivity.

Because of our business back in Townsville, Geoff was soon summoned home to take care of things. He reluctantly flew home, leaving Ashley and I to face to this ordeal alone. We had so far been lucky to be able to go through this together.

Many families had just one parent dealing with their sick child, while the other had to keep working to keep income, siblings, and bills sorted. It's difficult to explain, but the minute the partner is back in the home environment, it's easy for them to feel disconnected from the horrific hospital world. Even regular phone calls couldn't seem to bridge the gap and the feeling of isolation and separation grew stronger.

Some of this imposed isolation came from Ashley's illness itself. For most of his treatment, Ashley was 'neutropenic', which meant he had no immune system. Catching a cold or even having a cut or minor scratch could be life-threatening. He couldn't be with anyone who wasn't 100% well, and certainly wasn't allowed to be among crowds. This didn't help the constant struggle of feeling totally alone and it exacerbated the craving for our past 'normal' life back in Townsville.

After what seemed like an eternity, there was some discussion about letting us go home! Several setbacks had delayed this, and the disappointment of not being able to be with Stacey and the rest of the family was unbearable. I remember feeling totally shattered on one such occasion when we were told, once again, that we still couldn't go home. I snapped at the nurse and walked out. Shortly after, I returned to apologise for my behaviour, but apparently, I'd done it in such a nice manner that the nurse hadn't even noticed I was at breaking point.

It was a long, sad walk back to our unit at Ronald McDonald House. We prepared ourselves for a further indefinite period of being away from our family and of our usual routines. Times like these made you wonder how you were going to get through it all.

When we were finally allowed to go back home, I had to visit the pharmacy to stock up on all the medications to take with us. Imagine my horror when they wheeled out a whole pallet laden with Ashley's special preparation for his nasogastric tube! I was flabbergasted! How on earth was I going to fit all this in our luggage to cart back on the plane?

As if that wasn't enough, I was bombarded with all the instructions for the different medications: this one could only be taken two hours after food (and at least half an hour before his next meal); each mouth wash had three steps and needed to be given four times a day; some medication was cytotoxic and came with a strict procedure for administering it. On it went. I remember standing at the pharmacy feeling a combination of sheer terror and anxiety. I felt absolutely shell-shocked – I wanted the floor to open and swallow me.

My instinct was yelling to me to run away and hide, and I could picture myself running out the door... and keeping on running! Yet again I must have looked like a deer caught in the headlights! So many thoughts were going through my head: How on earth am I going to cope and remember all this? Is this a terrible nightmare that I'll soon wake up from? Stop the world, I want to get off!

Luckily, sanity and common sense eventually prevailed. Geoff came up with the brilliant idea of programming various reminders into my phone for what medication was required and when. This was a lifesaver and gave me peace of mind that I wouldn't forget anything. In fact, I am extremely proud of the fact that in the three and a half years of Ash's illness, I never once forgot a medication. Mind you, our whole family was fed up with my phone ringing constantly with all the reminders for so many years!

After what seemed like an eternity, how can I explain the feeling of driving from the airport, back to our place that first time? I would get to see our daughter again, hold her in my arms and hug her to pieces.

The sight of the kangaroos (our beloved skippies), our beautiful property in the bush, the birds, the patio where we like to eat outside, our own bed...home. It was like opening my heart and letting a rainbow into a place that had been very dark for a long time.

But that moment was just as terrifying as it was euphoric. How on earth was I going to cope with all the medication, injections, and mouth washes – having the total responsibility of keeping our son alive? I no longer had the comfort of a whole medical team; *I* was the whole medical team! Again, it was about facing the fear and finding a way.

Some days later, if you could believe it, I was so happy to be home again that I was cleaning my oven, a job that I hate with a vengeance. I sang out to Geoff, "I'm so excited to be cleaning my oven because it means I'm in my own home again."

They say it's the simple things in life, but that was just ridiculous!

After we returned home to Townsville on a more permanent basis, life started to get into its own rhythm and routine. Our new Normal. There were still many trips we had to make back to Brisbane for tests and treatment.

These long days would start with a 3:00am alarm so I could get up and cook Ashley a big breakfast. He had to fast from 4.00am, followed by a quick shower, and we'd drive to the airport by 5.00am. If we were lucky, we'd get a return flight the same day. That way we'd be home again by 10:30pm and be able to sleep in our own beds.

I needed to be stronger in ways I never thought I'd need to be. I'll never forget arriving at the airport at 5:00am one morning only to hear that our flight had been cancelled due to mechanical problems. It was important that Ashley get to Brisbane for his regular lumbar puncture and treatment. There just wasn't any other option. I joined the queue of another airline.

As I waited patiently, hoping for a miracle, a fellow pushed past me to get to the front of the line. He barged up to the counter. He was in the process of asking the check-in staff for the first available seat when my protective motherly instinct kicked in big time. I stood in front of him (feeling ten feet tall and bullet proof) demanding that he go to the back of the line because we were there first. I'm not a violent person (and I'm barely five feet tall) but I was ready to take him on there and then. I even surprised myself! The man sheepishly conceded his place.

When we flew into Brisbane that morning, I mused with a big smile on my face, on the fact that Ashley would not miss his treatment after all — even if I had to fly him there on the back of my broomstick!

While exhausting, making the return trip to Brisbane in one day was a better option by far than living in Brisbane for the whole three and a half years of treatment. When we first arrived in Brisbane, we'd had no time to search for accommodation and the only option available to us was to stay at Ronald McDonald House. Whenever Ashley was given the luxury of getting out of hospital (even for an hour or two), he had to be close by in case an emergency arose, and Ronald McDonald House was an acceptable distance. We felt guilty taking another family's accommodation and looked around to rent something close by but there just wasn't anything else available.

There is accommodation at the Leukaemia Foundation, but it was full the whole time Ashley was on treatment. This was truly unfortunate for us, as the Leukaemia Foundation understands the importance of critical care when these young people are neutropenic. Viruses, colds and anything else contagious, could be life-threatening for patients with Leukaemia. Patients staying at Ronald McDonald

House have such a variety of illnesses that if Ash was allowed out of hospital, we had to retreat to our room and keep to ourselves.

This only exacerbated the loneliness and isolation we felt. Donating to Ronald McDonald House in the past, I had no idea we would ever be in a situation where they would rescue our family. We were extremely grateful to have these amazing facilities so close to the hospital, and I encourage everyone to support this incredible organisation. You never know if it will be your family needing it.

During Ashley's treatment where we were allowed to stay at home and do the regular trips to Brisbane, it didn't matter how many times I'd go to the children's oncology ward, or how much time I'd spend there, it always absolutely shattered me to pieces. I'm super tough and super brave but being in that ward rocked me to the core. Smiling brightly at the littlies hooked up to drips, pale and weak as they received their treatment, totally gutted me. These children should be out playing in their backyards.

One day, waiting in the recovery ward for Ashley to return from yet another lumbar puncture I noticed a young mum. She was nursing her four-day-old baby while trying to comfort her four-year-old son. Nurses were trying to administer his chemo and the young boy was crying out, "Somebody help me. I'm dying here."

Fighting back the lump in my throat, I approached the desperate young mum, saying, "Here, I'll hold bubby so you can look after your little man."

That mum should have been relaxing and enjoying her brand-new baby, not having to endure this horror. As I rocked that gorgeous little bub, I fought back tears thinking how I'd like to take all their pain away so they could be a normal family again.

Maybe that counsellor was right about not speaking with any other families.

I really hate to admit it, but this incident made such an impression on me that it still brings tears to my eyes every time I think of it. I saw the family again in the children's ward some years later and that gorgeous little baby girl was running around the ward as though it was her second home, and the nurses were like her aunties. How we all adjust!

After getting home from our regular tips to Brisbane, I would really struggle to pick myself up and be bright and chirpy again. It was one of those mornings, not long after I'd met that young mum, that I broke down in tears while having a morning cuppa with my hubby. It was rare for me to cry before Ashley's diagnosis and rarer still after my resolution to be strong.

I told Geoff I had seen the look in that young mum's eyes and could feel every bit of pain, hurt and helplessness she was feeling – probably because deep down, I was feeling the same. I said to Geoff, "I'm Mighty Mouse so this shouldn't affect me so much. Why does it still shatter me every time? It shouldn't, I'm tough, I'm tough, I'm tough!"

Then Geoff said something that changed everything for me. He said that it was understandable for me to feel the way I did. I needed to acknowledge how I felt and accept my feelings.

Gee! It was OK for me to feel like this? Wow! It was amazing the difference this piece of wisdom made to my life. When you are so used to being emotionally bulletproof – for your children, for your family, and yourself – you forget that you're only human and can only take so much.

I even found that on future trips to the children's ward I felt so much stronger. Mums were coming to me to talk, and get some encouragement, and positive thoughts. I don't know whether I was emanating positive vibes or whether it was something else, but those trips were definitely easier than they had been in the past.

Another memorable trip to hospital happened when Ashley's treatment required him to be admitted to hospital for four days. During those days in hospital, he was regularly given blood tests, the results of which determined when he could return home. We were also getting regular reports of a large cyclone that was lurking around home in North Queensland. Everyone was busy preparing. While Ashley spoke to all his friends on MSN (there was no social media at that time), he felt as if he was missing all the excitement and build up that comes before a cyclone.

We had our return flight home booked for 6:15pm on the fourth day, but the airline called to say that our flight had been cancelled because of the cyclone threat. I kept checking the internet that day to see if they'd added another flight – maybe they had to fly SES workers to Townsville. And bingo! Our original flight reappeared. Would Ashley's blood results allow us time to catch that flight? They weren't due until 5:00pm.

I didn't tell Ash about the flight being available again because I didn't want to disappoint him if his results didn't allow us to leave. Waiting patiently and holding my tongue was very difficult, but at 5.03pm the all-clear came that we could leave the hospital. Telling Ashley about the possibility of the 6:15pm flight (we weren't necessarily on it because they had cancelled our original booking), I asked if he wanted to try to catch it.

"Hell yeah!" was the enthusiastic reply.

The nurses and everyone else in the ward got caught up in the excitement. His Port-acath was de-accessed (it's probably more accurate to say it was ripped out) and was still bleeding at the site, but that didn't stop Ashley. I threw all our gear into the suitcase, and we literally ran to the taxi rank. As I climbed into the taxi, I looked up to Ashley's ward and saw all the nurses, parents and even a few patients at the window, waving us off and wishing us good luck catching the plane!!

We explained to the driver how desperately we needed to catch the plane to be with our family during the cyclone and the trip that followed was like a car chase scene from a movie. We tore along at 110km/h (in an 80km/h zone) while Ash and I giggled as we held on tightly in the back seat. Jumping out, I sprinted to the check-in counter and Ashley wasn't far behind, dragging the suitcase. I was catching my breath when the check-in employee promptly stated that the flight had been closed.

They didn't know who they were dealing with. I was on a mission, and we were going to catch that plane.

I explained the urgency and asked to speak with a supervisor. Once again, he repeated, "The flight has been closed."

This was not stopping me. I said that my son had just got out of hospital, but that was a wrong move. Where was his clearance to fly? I opened the suitcase in the middle of the floor and proceeded to pull out the paperwork. (Phew! Luckily, I had thought of that earlier in the day.)

Time was ticking and we were holding up the check-in queue. Other passengers were gathering to see what the commotion was about, and in the end, the supervisor just wanted to get rid of us. He made some phone calls and told us to run to Gate 17.

I held Ashley's urgent medication in my handbag, so we didn't even care if our luggage didn't make it, so long as we were on that plane! Speed records were broken, and we reached the plane just as they were about to close the doors. We fell into our seats, huffing and puffing, exhilarated that we'd made it. As I began to calm down, I realised that nobody at home even knew we were on that flight. After a quick text to Geoff, we relaxed at last.

That flight home was exhilarating. We laughed and giggled, thrilled at our narrow escape. A song came over the loudspeakers and Ash and I locked eyes, looking at each other in disbelief. It was Bon Jovi's 'Welcome to Wherever You Are'. The first time we'd heard it was in the ward a couple of days after arriving in Brisbane for Ash's first treatment, and we had immediately adopted it as 'our song'.

It has the lines, 'Welcome, you gotta believe that right here, right now, you're exactly where you're supposed to be!'

Throughout our journey, there were so many times when we wanted to escape. This song reassured us that there was a reason for us to be here right here, right now. We were exactly where we were supposed to be. This was our new normal.

Chapter 5

Behind the Smile

We were finally home. Life could get back to normal now, right?

Life continued to be 'character-building' and kept throwing multiple challenges at us. It was relentless – 24 hours a day, seven days a week, every week of the year for several years straight. Leukaemia just doesn't give you a break. It wasn't just dealing with our own emotions, our own fatigue and trying to keep our family and business running. While we were fighting the disease, we were also coping with the impacts of both the side effects and the drugs were having on Ashley – and by extension, Stacey.

While Ashley was receiving treatment for Acute Lymphoblastic Leukaemia every day for three and a half years, he had countless 'special needs' and challenging behaviour. We too, strived and nearly turned ourselves inside out to make him feel included, and just like every other kid. Many parents will understand how hard that can be to achieve.

When Ashley first began chemo, I asked him to let me know if at any time he wanted to get his hair cut or shaved. If he wanted a wig, I would organise it in a heartbeat. It was agonising to see his hair in clumps in the bathroom, bedroom and on the floor. In fact, his hair was all over the unit where we were staying in at Ronald McDonald House. He soon decided to get it shaved off and wear a beanie. I fought back tears as I watched his beautiful blond hair falling to the floor. I had to be strong for him as I knew how shattering this was. Not only was this a blow to his self-worth as a cool and proud teenager, but he was also losing an aspect of his identity.

After lunch one Friday afternoon, he mentioned he'd like to have a look at wigs. I had never driven in Brisbane before and the thought terrified me, but I was on a mission, and nothing would stop me. I'd work it out. Luckily, my parents had bought us a satnav for the car, so we programmed in the address and went off into the busy Friday afternoon city traffic. To say this country girl was terrified was an understatement - but there was no way I was going to let on to Ashley how I was feeling!

We arrived safely at the shopping centre, found the wig shop, and met the two lovely shop assistants. Ashley wasn't eating much at that stage, so when he mentioned he wanted an iced coffee, I set off to find him one before racing back. When I walked in, I had to catch my breath.

I had my Ashley back! Amazingly, the ladies had found a wig very similar to his natural hairstyle, and with the addition of a cap, he could still be 'Ashley with the trendy hair'. The cap was very important as it made the wig look more like natural hair. Ash now had his identity back and could feel like the other teenagers again - but our solution didn't come without its own challenges! While being back at school brought some normality to Ashley's life, the changes to his body brought out some hard emotional changes for Ashley to struggle with too.

His school was wonderfully understanding and allowed Ash to wear the cap to school, notifying as many teachers as possible about his situation. Inevitably, though, there would be a supply teacher or someone who hadn't got the message, who would give Ash a hard time and try to make him take the cap off. When Ashley refused, it invariably led to a confrontation. The poor teachers were mortified when they learned of the circumstances and would then apologise to Ashley! Talk about awkward!

Then there were the kids who would have a go at Ash for wearing a cap and try to take it off him. This was extremely stressful, because the thought of anyone other than his family seeing his pale, bald head was inconceivable. Not even Grandma and Grandad saw Ash without the wig!

There were also swimming carnivals where Ash wouldn't be able to participate for several reasons. He wouldn't take his wig and cap off for starters, and he certainly wouldn't take his shirt off. He didn't want anyone to see how skeletal his body had become due to the chemo, nor the sight of his Port-acath (a catheter installed beneath the skin with a port that connects to a vein allowing drugs to be administered and blood samples taken with less discomfort than constant injections). Ashley had to be content with sitting on the sidelines, cheering the others on.

Then there was the challenge of 'sports' at school. So often during the time of his illness, Ashley was neutropenic (having no immune system), which meant that even the smallest cut or graze could get infected and become life-threatening. During these times, Ashley wasn't allowed to do anything that might put him in danger. This included team sports and manual arts lessons at school, as well as his favourite things at home: riding his motorbike or even his push bike, water-skiing and fishing. Again, he had just to sit on the sidelines and watch. This was challenging and frustrating for an active teenager!

Likewise, if Ashley was neutropenic for any planned events such as parties, weekends away and family gatherings and someone had a cold or virus, Ashley was unable to attend. I must admit, there was one time I had a catch up planned with friends who were visiting Townsville and who I hadn't seen for several years. I was really looking forward to seeing them, but my excitement quickly turned to disappointment when one of their family members caught a cold. I couldn't risk seeing any of the family in case I caught the virus, because if I did, I would have to move out of the house to prevent spreading it with Ash. Impossible in my role as his in-house medical team! Devastated, I had to ring my friends to say I couldn't see them. I was so upset that I escaped to the seclusion of our creek with a huge glass of wine for some much-needed time-out from this nightmare.

It always seemed to be during school holidays that Ash would end up back in hospital - just when he thought he'd be able to have fun like all the other kids. Despite being back home, it was painfully evident that our life was far from normal.

There were times when the doctors would allow Ashley to have 'home IV' instead of keeping him in hospital because they knew how difficult it was for him. This meant he had to wear a little machine 24 hours a day that pumped antibiotics straight into his port-a-cath. Each day, a nurse would visit, or we'd go to the hospital to get the IV bag replaced. He preferred this method instead of staying in hospital.

Ashley's wish was to just be like all the other kids at school. One time he had a mouth full of ulcers from the chemo. Trying to get Ashley to visit the doctor was challenging at the best of times, and when the doctor gave orders to admit him to hospital immediately and began instructing the nurses to draw up morphine to be administered, Ashley strongly objected. He politely informed the doctor that he had to get back to school as he had a group assignment to present after lunch. The doctor was astounded - not only at his pain threshold but also his grit and determination.

I knew how much he hated hospital and would have done anything I could to keep him out and happy. I agreed to do the intense mouth treatment procedure at home. This meant very little sleep for the next two to three days and nursing him constantly, but it was worth it to see him achieve his goal to participate in the assessment. Little did the kids at school know how much pain he was in as he gave his part of the presentation. I certainly gave him a high distinction for that assignment!

Another challenge presented itself every month when he had to take Dexamethasone (or the 'Dreaded Dex' as we called it). He was on it for five days every month and he didn't sleep for most of those five days. The drug also had the capability to make him angry and short tempered, which was totally out-of-character for Ashley.

I've lost count of the incidents that occurred during these times, and we could be guaranteed there would be dramas. There were times when Geoff and I were out searching our property for him at 11:00pm at night, worried sick when he took off on his motorbike in a Dreaded Dex rage. Imagine our horror when our normally beautifully natured son punched a hole in his bedroom wall and had to present at the hospital with a broken hand as well! Aggressive behaviour was a side effect of this horrific medication.

During one Dreaded Dex moment, Ashley headed out the door in a rage to get on his motorbike. The rule was that when he was neutropenic, he wasn't allowed on his motorbike. As the doctor had said, if he fell and wounded himself, he could die. I reminded Ashley of the rule and the severe consequences of disobeying it, but he continued out the door. I heard his motorbike roar off up the road.

I was overcome by a mixture of fury, desperation, and terror. What consequences could I give him that would match this blatant disregard of the rules? I decided to completely strip his room. That's right, I dragged his double bed and mattress out the door and down the hallway with a mighty strength I didn't know I possessed. I then emptied his room of his computer and every other item – not just his games and equipment, everything. I threw a pillow on his bare floor and prayed for his safe return.

After what seemed like a lifetime, he walked through the door with a smug look on his face and when I didn't react, he must have thought, 'Mmmm, I got away with that!' as he continued to his room. Years later he recalled to me the feeling of standing in the doorway aghast at seeing his room completely stripped.

Despite his shock he thought with a grin, "Good one, Mum, you won that battle!"

He had to earn back every single item, which meant sleeping on the bare floor for several nights with nothing but a pillow! It was a drastic action, but these were drastic times.

His angry outbursts would have been unimaginable if he wasn't on the Dreaded Dex, and this made it even more difficult to understand and predict. I even had the local police on speed dial just in case we couldn't find him if he went off in a rage. Luckily, he also had wonderful and sympathetic teachers at school, who regularly prevented situations from getting out of hand there.

What people didn't realise was that Ashley was on chemo treatment every single day for three and a half years. Even if he went for a sleepover or a party, we had to juggle his oral medication and at one stage, his daily Clexane injections as well. Just one of the daily medications required him to fast for two hours before taking it then to wait another 30 minutes before being able to eat again. And I won't even mention what was required for his daily mouthwashes! Just a normal day in the Caldwell household.

As with a lot of children with special needs, Ashley had a sibling as well who always seemed to get a totally raw deal. We'd had to relocate to Brisbane within 24 hours of Ashley being diagnosed - and this happened to be three days before Stacey's 16th birthday. Prior to everything happening, we had a water-skiing party organised for the following Saturday. I said to Geoff that no matter what happened, we needed to make sure Stacey's birthday party went ahead.

The day after Ashley was diagnosed and we'd gone to Brisbane, Stacey went to school and discovered that the school administration had already organised counsellors. Not only were there counsellors for the students, but also for the teachers who were devastated by the news about Ashley.

I was blown away by their empathy and understanding. All that week, kids and teachers were crying about Ashley's news. The situation was already extremely traumatic for our amazing daughter, having her whole family torn away. Now she also had to cope with everyone else's grief in addition to her own. By the time her birthday arrived on the Wednesday, celebrating was the last thing on her mind.

Even many years later, this memory can leave me with tears streaming down my face. Thinking of what Stacey had to endure, and not being there and able to comfort her, is something I've never fully recovered from.

We were extremely fortunate that several special friends helped with the birthday preparations. Geoff flew back for the weekend and the party went ahead. Having to stay in Brisbane and not being able to be part of Stacey's 16th birthday celebrations was another extremely challenging and distressing aspect of that horrific first week. I remember disappearing and sitting all alone in a little playground just outside Ashley's hospital ward. Feeling totally devastated and overwhelmed, I sobbed my heart out.

It was wonderful for Stace to have her dad home for a little taste of normal life again, even if only for a very brief time.

When school finished for the year, Stace was itching to come to Brisbane to be with us. By this stage, I was living at the hospital with Ashley 24 hours a day, seven days a week and it was a horrific time. There was an 'Empower You' program for young adults running in Sydney at the same time, which promotes motivation and positive mindset. We thought it would be a better option for Stacey to do the program in Sydney than having to spend her holidays in an oncology ward in Brisbane.

After the program finished, Stacey was to fly back and stay with us in Brisbane, but in the end that wasn't to be. With all the stress she was going through, she developed a throat infection and as Ashley's health was extremely precarious at that time, we couldn't risk him being exposed to it.

It was one of most devastating moments of our life as a family. After several weeks of being apart, we couldn't wait to be with our daughter again. Instead, we had to send our sick daughter back home to Townsville to her grandparents and uncle. It was too dangerous to have her stay with us. When Geoff returned from the airport that day, we both escaped to the parent's room at the hospital to hide our feelings completely. We felt utterly shattered.

Most people describe me as a happy, bubbly, outgoing and positive person. Actually, I'm a very private person, who keeps a lot of things close. I don't feel comfortable being vulnerable. During Ashley's treatment, I felt even more so. I simply couldn't let anyone see how much it was taking out of me. To be honest, I don't know if I knew at the time myself. It was like being hit by a constant wave after wave, one thing after another after another! Thank heavens I had something wonderful that helped to ground me and recharge the near-empty batteries.

Chapter 6

Crikey! She's a Beauty!

Being able to live surrounded by an abundance of wildlife and nature has been instrumental to our wellbeing and happiness. It's provided much-needed 'bush therapy' for me and my family – serving at times as an escape from reality, and at other times, a recharging station.

For nearly 20 years, we've had a family of Eastern Grey Kangaroos (fondly referred to as our 'skippies') live on our property and have had the pleasure of watching them raise countless joeys and robust males duelling for the female's affections. A colony of bettongs has also taken up residence among the bush and regularly visit when we're dining on the patio at night. We refer to them as our 'teenagers' because they turn up, bring all their friends, eat enthusiastically, fight among themselves, then disappear until they're hungry again!

We've also been wildlife carers for many years, rescuing, raising, and releasing many orphaned and injured skippies as well as several bettongs.

Two very devoted Tawny Frogmouth owl parents also return each year to raise their ridiculously cute bundles of fluff. Having the privilege of watching their brood grow up and learn to fly makes us feel like proud grandparents every time.

There have also been several occasions where we've rescued our little owl family.

One such occasion was when we were looking out our bedroom window to see what wildlife was waiting, when Geoff gasped in horror.

He quickly rushed out of the room to grab the ladder and gloves, yelling, "One of the baby owls is on the ground!"

He gently approached the little bundle of feathers and attitude that was sitting on the ground and went to gather it in his hands. The baby owl spread its wings and made a pathetic effort to sound scary. Tenderly, Geoff picked it up and climbed the ladder.

By this time, the mother owl was upset and scary, flapping about when Geoff reached the top of the ladder. He returned the baby owl as close to the nest as possible however, with the mother making such fuss, the bubby was left balancing precariously on the side of the nest.

As we sat having our cuppa, we watched anxiously as the chick attempted to get back inside. After a final, successful leap, it landed in the nest and jostled for position as it snuggled up to Mum. I'm not sure who was more thrilled to have him back in the nest!

Our home has a reputation for its surprise visitors, but none was surprising as the frilled neck lizard I met in the toilet! One morning while I was sitting on the throne, Geoff appeared in the doorway, and it took me a few seconds to register that he was holding a frilled neck lizard as long as his forearm. A panicked shrill rang out and I asked why on earth had he brought it into the toilet?! Geoff began to explain.

Spotting the frilly in our yard, he crept outside to take a photo just as the frilly escaped up the tree. Being in a hurry to capture the moment, Geoff had left the door open into the house. When the frilly had had enough of being photographed, it jumped to the ground and headed straight for the open door at the speed of lightning.

Beating Geoff hands down, the frilly ran inside and retreated behind the stereo system. OK, so how do you remove a frilled neck lizard from inside your house? Geoff gently picked it up with a towel -

and thought he'd show it to me while he had it in his hands. That's why it ended up in our toilet!

Going outside to release the stunned creature, I decided to capture it on video. Geoff gently placed the frilly on the ground, but it didn't move. We started to think there was something wrong when we realised the frilly was playing dead. Geoff cautiously lifted its tail and the frilly went as stiff as a board. Our amusement soon turned to fright, as when Geoff went to touch it again, it flared its frill and came running at me at lightning speed!

I screamed at the top of my lungs but kept the video going as it took off towards the open door of the house once again. Oh no! We made a mad dash to get the door shut and managed just in time. Changing direction, the frilly headed around the corner. Oh no, it's going inside the garage! Fortunately for the frilly, the garage door was closed so it made a mad dash out of sight where I'm sure it gave a huge sigh of relief.

Our wildlife and surprise visitors have provided more entertainment than the Netflix channel, not to mention lots of memories...not all of them fond memories!

One such occasion looked like a normal day in the life of the Caldwells. We were having our morning cuppa on the patio, laughing at the funny antics of our resident skippies. There an unfamiliar huge male Eastern Grey having a good old scratch of his testicles - that's probably way too much information!

For some reason, that morning when I went out to feed our skippies, I felt uncomfortable about this new male skippy. There was something about him that I didn't trust, so I put the macropod pellets out, stepped back and made sure I kept my distance as I walked around him.

Geoff was inside the yard, wondering why I was acting so weird. Suddenly, the enormous kangaroo leaped forward, grabbed my shoulders from behind and began kicking me with his two massive feet! Screaming with fright, I thought, "When is he ever going to stop?!" Geoff immediately yelled at the top of his voice and ran straight at the aggressive skippy. Luckily the big fella released me, and I made a speedy exit, trembling with fear.

Gingerly taking off my shirt, I discovered scratch marks on the back of my neck and shoulders, but thankfully nothing too dramatic. Geoff smothered the scratches with Betadine. Ash and I were all packed to travel to Brisbane for another few of days of treatment, so I changed all my summer outfits to hide the abrasions.

Sitting on the plane I struggled to get comfortable but ignored it as I was too busy thinking about what lay ahead for us that day. For a treat, if we didn't have to stay in hospital overnight, I sometimes booked accommodation in the city.

After a gruelling round of treatment, we arrived at the hotel that night and I went for a long-awaited shower. I let out a squeal when I glimpsed my reflection in the full-length mirror and saw the back of my legs. From my knees up, they were black and purple with shocking bruising. I'd been so busy and concerned about Ashley that I'd blocked out the pain.

Hearing my scream, Ashley was immediately at the door checking I was OK. Doubled over from laughter, I reluctantly opened the door and revealed my war wounds. We made an immediate call and text to Geoff so I could 'bare' my battle scars, but it wasn't to end there.

In the middle of the night, I awoke in fright with the image before me of that ghastly skippy scratching his testicles before tearing into me with those same claws. Eww! I bounced out of bed and doused the wounds with another splash of Betadine to kill any nasty germs. When Geoff rang in the morning, we both had a chuckle when I shared my nightmare and urgent midnight medical application!

Being surrounded by our wonderful wildlife has not only provided much entertainment, but it has also helped heal, restore, and soothe our souls. It's my escape away from the world. A special place to recharge from the emotional toll this was taking on me – and I wasn't the only one it helped heal.

CHAPTER 7

Ashley's Party - What a Blast! (Literally)

Something special was coming up: Ashley's 15th birthday. We decided to have a combined birthday party at our place for Ash and his friend, Jarrod. As often happens when people get together to plan things, big ideas started flying everywhere. Suddenly, we were planning a 'Survivor' party that would match anything seen on TV. The kids were to go on the orienteering adventure of a lifetime.

Preparations began. Geoff and I set off through our property with a compass in hand and a notebook. We found and wrote orienteering clues that would take them on different routes through the fifty-three acres on which we live. I made up coloured 'Survivor' bandanas, and Jarrod's dad, Noel, was to dress in camouflage clothes and make pig noises, scaring the kids as they hiked through the creek in the dark. Then, when they gathered by the dam at the end of the course, Noel was to have the smoke machine set up to add to the suspense of the grand finale.

What we hadn't planned was having over 50mm of rain the night before, plus continuous rain on the day of the party.

"The Survivor' course will have to be cancelled. Someone could fall over and get hurt," Geoff announced.

I was gutted but determined to find a way. So much time and effort had gone into making the party exciting, different, and fun for all the kids. I mentioned it to Kerry, Jarrod's mum, when she arrived, and she agreed with me that it should still go ahead.

When the kids began arriving, Kerry and I greeted them, armed with clipboards and pens to get their parents' permission for their child to participate in the course - and mobile numbers, just in case. Nobody would ever have thought we were about to hold a birthday party as we stood in our raincoats, still getting drenched and looking like very daggy parking officials!

When everyone had arrived, we told them about the 'Survivor Orienteering Adventure' we had planned. There were cries of 'Awesome!' 'Unreal!' 'How cool is that!' Everyone was so excited. As I couldn't get hold of fifty raincoats that day, we issued everyone with the next best thing... garbage bags! Then, out came the bandanas - each with the Survivor logo. The kids were thrilled and there were whoops of 'How fun is this!'

Each group had to come up with a team name and was issued with a compass, torch, walkie-talkie, and a list of clues. It was great to see how enthusiastic they all were. For once, they could just have fun and not have to act like cool teenagers.

Off they went into the darkness and rain. There were more whoops of excitement and delight and we quickly lost sight of them. When they radioed in at strategic points, Geoff warned them of the 'very wild pigs' we had on the property (Noel, playing his part!) and we could hear girls squealing in the background as they clocked the warning. Well, I think it was just the girls!

I made my way down to the dam with a wheelbarrow filled with soft drink cans, two large bamboo candles, and a huge Survivor banner I'd made. I lost count of how many times the wheelbarrow got bogged in the mud, and the noise from the rain and the cane toads added to the drama of the game. Over the next half hour or so, the groups began to arrive at the dam, laughing and sharing stories.

When everyone was gathered, there was a moment when they realised just how eerie this setting was. The noise from the toads was near deafening, there was mist wafting across the water, and it was still lightly drizzling. It was like a scene from a horror film and the kids looked a little uneasy. I added to the drama by asking Geoff what was happening on the other side of the creek and pretended to be scared.

The next minute stopped us all in our tracks. Our grand finale surprise was supposed to be a loud noise like a firecracker going off, to signal the end of the course - but it ended up being the biggest boom you could imagine! Because of the low clouds, instead of the noise escaping into the sky, the sound hit the clouds and kept reverberating for miles. After their initial shock, when the kids realised that it was all planned, you should have heard them. 'Awesome!' 'I can't believe it!' 'This is the best party I've ever been to!' On it went as we made our way back to the shed for dinner.

That was the end of the planned excitement, but little did we know there was more to come. As we were laughing and the kids were recapping their adventures, we noticed a truck coming up the driveway. As it got closer, we wondered why a fire truck would be turning up on a wet Saturday night. The firemen jumped out of the truck, noticeably irate. They had been called out by an 'explosives expert' who had notified them of a bomb exploding in the area!

Oops! This wasn't good. The kids gathered around and were listening intently. Geoff and I explained that it was us, and it had been planned for our son's birthday party. Unfortunately, this did nothing to defuse the situation. We were informed that making an explosion was a criminal offence and that we could go to jail!

As the conversation went on, my hubby and the firemen were getting even more fired up (pardon the pun!) so I stepped in to explain that we'd organised a 'Survivor' party because we wanted to make Ashley's birthday special...as he was going through treatment for Leukaemia. I didn't want to have to bring this up, but it was important for them to understand. It worked, this calmed the situation and the firemen cooled off slightly. They realised we were totally naïve and had no intention of causing any trouble. Eventually, they climbed into their truck and drove off.

I went inside to ring our daughter. She was staying with my parents overnight as she had important final exams coming up and needed to study in peace.

"You won't believe it Stace, the fire brigade arrived and everything. You should have heard the boom!" My voice quivered as I whispered anxiously, "Hang on hon, I'm going to have to ring you back. I think the police have just pulled up."

I hurried out to greet the police and started rabbiting on about all the safety precautions we'd taken: the preparation; parents' approval; noting mobile numbers; and the fact that the source of the boom was nowhere near the kids. To my disbelief, the policewoman turned and said, "Yes, I know. My daughter is a guest at the party. I loved the invitation."

Hang on, what did she just say? One minute we were practically heading to jail and the next we were discussing Ashley's birthday invitation. I couldn't believe it. We laughed with relief, then Geoff suggested we pretend the police were going to take him away in the patrol car. It was an opportunity too good to pass up, as the kids had come out to see what was happening.

Geoff asked in a loud voice, "Do you think I'll be able to come home tonight?"

The policeman replied sternly, "Well, that depends on the night staff, and I suppose it depends on your attitude as well!"

I wish I could have filmed the looks on the kids' faces as they loaded Geoff into the patrol car and drove off with lights flashing.

The kids were devastated, "Is this for real?" "I can't believe it!" On they went, standing in the rain in disbelief.

I faked crying and said, "Everything's all right. Don't worry."

We turned to walk back into the shed, the kids in a state of shock, when Geoff appeared running up the road, laughing. Once again, there were loud, excited squeals of delight. We did have a lot of explaining to do, though, when the parents arrived to take them home and were greeted by stories of the near sonic boom, then the arrival of the fire brigade and police!

This adventure is the epitome of our family's beliefs and life values. During dark and stormy times, by having a positive attitude, determination to make the most of things, (and yes, a little stubbornness), can make a huge difference with not only the outcome, but the journey as well.

If we'd lived in town, on a suburban block, surrounded by more houses and streets, we couldn't have had such an amazing party. It was such a fantastic break for Ashley from hospitals and sickness.

They still talk about the birthday party to this day. What a blast! We'd made it such an amazing memorable adventure – it was unthinkable that anything could possibly top it!

Until we did ...

CHAPTER 8

Soaring High with Sir Richard Branson

Not long after Ashley was diagnosed with Leukaemia, he was asked if he had a wish.

Surprising everyone, he replied, "I'd like to meet Richard Branson. He seems like a cool guy; he has a good attitude and treats everyone really well."

Ashley rarely asked for anything so, knowing how important this must be to him, I added this wish to the top of my To-Do list.

Then it happened. On the way to Brisbane for another of Ash's treatments, I was checking in online for our Virgin flight, when a picture of Richard Branson popped up. Investigating further, I learned that Richard Branson and Brett Godfrey, CEO of Virgin Australia, would be in Brisbane a few weeks later for the 2008 Virgin Hangar Ball.

I couldn't believe that there might be an opportunity for Ash to meet Richard Branson and we didn't have to take him to the other side of the world to do it! I was so determined to make this happen for Ash that I didn't for one minute consider how slim the chances were of him saying yes.

I immediately went to work sending emails to various people at Virgin Blue. A week passed: no reply. Anxiously, I suggested to Geoff that we buy tickets for a table of ten and just go to the ball. At least Ash would be in the same room as Richard Branson, and we would have family and friends to share the night with.

Knowing that Ashley's dream was to meet Richard, I couldn't give up so easily. Wearing my invisible Sherlock Holmes cape, I was determined to contact Virgin Airlines. Finding out the names of Richard's key staff, I sent dozens of emails, hoping that miraculously one would arrive in the correct Inbox. I had certainly 'put it out there' and wondered anxiously if the Universe would deliver.

On Saturday morning as I casually checked my emails, I couldn't believe what I was seeing. I let out a cheer and squealing loudly, danced around the house. I had received a reply email from CEO Brett Godfrey, letting me know they were organising something special for Ashley. I had a chuckle when he'd borrowed my signature signoff phrase 'You have a 'peachy' weekend also.'

After I let Brett know that I could get Ashley to Brisbane any time, he replied asking if we could keep it "Mum's the word for Ashley."

They must get inundated with requests, but they'd chosen Ashley and were excited to organise something memorable for him.

The day of the ball arrived, and we were waiting in the Townsville airport departure lounge. Glancing at my ringing phone, I had to quickly move away from the group.

"Hello, this is Heather, Richard Branson's assistant. I just wanted to run our plan past you and make sure it's OK to go ahead. Richard is set to go on stage, acknowledge the dignitaries and speak about Earth Hour. Then he's going to say a special hello to Ashley. We'll have the cameras set up on your table and when they zoom in on Ashley, he will be on the giant screens all around the hangar. Is that OK with you? Richard and Brett have asked for it to be kept secret from Ashley."

My heart was hammering with excitement. What could I say? This was so much more than Ashley could ever have dreamed. How was I going to sit quietly in the plane when I wanted to shout and dance all over the place? The anticipation was incredible, and it took all my might to fake being calm and collected.

I couldn't even share the news with Geoff as he was already in Brisbane waiting for us, having attended a football game the night before.

Outside the hotel that afternoon, we were dressed and waiting for our maxi taxi. Our group watched in awe as a stretch limousine arrived. While everyone was admiring and gushing over it, I surprised them with the news that this was in fact our 'maxi taxi'. Many whoops of excitement and plenty of photos later, we all scrambled into the magnificent car. Perhaps not with as much class as others who had travelled before us!

The Virgin hangar had been transformed into a magnificent party venue, and we were soaking in the atmosphere when Richard Branson arrived. To keep Ashley thinking we knew nothing about what was in store for him, we suggested he try to get close to Richard as he made his entrance. Watching Ashley's face as he lined up to meet his idol was priceless. All too soon, Richard was whisked away, and we commiserated with Ashley that at least he got close.

As dinner was served, I was too excited to think about eating and there was no way I was drinking any alcohol. On the outside I looked calm, but on the inside, my stomach was doing back flips. I was thinking that perhaps this time I had bitten off more than I could chew.

Richard Branson appeared on stage and the crowd went wild. There was no acknowledgment of any dignitaries (only Richard could get away with something like that), and he went on to speak about Earth Hour.

Suddenly changing pace, he announced, "There's someone very special in the audience I'd like to say hi to."

I held my breath in anticipation.

"His name is Ashley Caldwell."

All eyes turned to Ash.

"Good onya mate. I'll be down to see you later. Keep up the good work."

As the cameras zoomed in, Ashley's image filled the huge screens that were dotted around the venue. Our son calmly acknowledged the applause with his cheeky grin and a very cool wave of his hand. How could Ashley remain so composed? If it was me, I would have been up on that table dancing with excitement!

Just to have had that moment could have been a highlight of his life, but there was more to come. After the charity auction, Ashley quietly said that he had to go to the toilet, and wouldn't it be funny if Richard came to see him when he wasn't there. Just at that moment, we were distracted by a commotion behind us and looked around to see Richard, Brett, the bodyguards, the film crew, and photographer all walking towards us as Richard sang out casually, "Ashley, where are you, mate?"

As they arrived, bodyguards surrounded our table so that it was only Richard with our family. Geoff was on the outside of the circle taking photos and the bodyguards weren't even going to let him in when he went to take his seat!

While Richard spoke to Ashley and signed some books for him, I thanked Brett for making Ashley's dream come true. Brett suggested I get in the photos, but I said, "Tonight is Ashley's night."

Next minute, though, Richard was calling out for Ashley's family to get in the photos. He then asked what we were doing the next day. We were bewildered and a little confused. Why on earth would he be asking us what we had planned?

To our absolute delight, Richard invited us to the V Music Festival at the Gold Coast the following day. We'd had such a memorable experience already – and now there was to be even more! It was totally surreal, and we were on cloud ninety-nine. We were due to fly home the next day but changed all our plans, hired a car instead, and drove to the Gold Coast where we had no idea what to expect.

We found ourselves at the venue with no tickets, just last night's personal invitation from Richard Branson. After some tough negotiating, ("Yeah right, that's what everyone says") we were soon wandering around inside with no idea where to go.

We came to the Virgin private marquee. Once again, the fact that Richard had invited us didn't go down well with the security staff when we tried again to enter without tickets. This time they weren't at all convinced, so we hung around outside Richard's private lounge. He eventually arrived at the marquee and began waving to everyone from his balcony.

The next moment was surreal.

Richard stopped as he recognised Ashley in the crowd and loudly asked why he wasn't inside the Virgin marquee? Geoff explained that we didn't have tickets. His photographer offered to come down and personally escort us in. Other people tried to get through the door with us, but the photographer told security that it was only for our family. Talk about feeling like royalty!

Sitting in the cosy private lounge with Richard Branson, I thought how right Ashley had been. Richard really is a super cool guy, is so down-to-earth, has a wonderful attitude and makes everyone feel incredibly special. He and his whole team went to so much effort to make Ashley, and our whole family, feel special and have such a memorable adventure. For a brief while, we were able to forget the horrific challenges we were facing with Ashley's battle with Leukaemia. Instead, we'd been truly spoilt and out of our comfort zone after being thrust into the limelight. Little did we know that it was not for the last time, either.

HOPE, GRIT AND GRATITUDE • 71

CHAPTER 9

A Star is Born... Reluctantly!

As 2009 was the Year of the Blood Donor, the Red Cross commissioned a film crew to produce a special documentary. They chose five families throughout Australia to tell their stories and highlight the vital role blood donors play in saving lives. Surprisingly, our family was chosen to be part of this documentary. Over the years of Ashley's treatment, I'd become good friends with Bruce Muller, the Community Relations Coordinator from the local Blood Bank, and our family had featured in several media stories to help raise awareness about the importance of donating blood.

One afternoon, the film crew arrived at our place, supposedly to just film Ashley on his motorbike. The next minute, however, they were setting up to interview both Ash and ME!

My heart raced. Hang on, I'm not prepared for this! I hadn't told anyone what we'd gone through and now I had to share it with others on camera? In fact, very rare words spilled out of me: "I don't know if I can do this!"

Some aspects of Ash's treatment were more challenging than others, and we were going through a particularly gruelling time. I was back in survival mode and felt as if I'd been running on empty for some time now. That afternoon, they also unexpectedly interviewed Geoff. Watching him, I saw and felt the heartache, rawness, and vulnerability of sharing our story with others. How was I going to relive our story and keep up my tough, strong façade and happy face?

"Here we go again," I thought. Nike... You know the rest!

Filming also took place at the Red Cross, and this had its challenges to say the least! Even though Stacey is needle phobic, she still bravely fronted up to give blood. She knew how important it was and naturally had seen what Ashley had been through.

This amazing young lady even said, "How could I say I was too scared of needles and deny someone the gift of life?"

Even so, attending the Blood Bank was a traumatic experience for her, and she privately struggled to keep her composure. Stacey once again showed her incredible strength and personal fortitude, and I was so proud of her.

The next filming session was water-skiing at the local Ross River Dam. Our family love water-skiing, and it's always an enjoyable social day as well. The film crew quickly became part of the family and the day turned into a fun adventure for everyone. All too soon our time was up, but the crew wanted to continue filming. After a quick phone call and sweet-talking the lovely booking ranger (who I'd also done some volunteer work with), we were allowed some extra time.

"What are you doing this afternoon?" one of the film crew asked, as we packed up.

I looked at him and asked cheekily, "Why? Are you stalking us? Next, you'll be moving in!"

At this suggestion, they did indeed follow us home for lunch and a great afternoon, with lots of laughter. The crew loved our place in the country. So much so, at about 6:00pm, I started to wonder whether they were going to stay the night!

"What are you doing tomorrow?" asked the director.

"Now I am worried," I replied. "You guys really are stalking us!"

As it was back to work for us the next day, the film crew arrived at our office and were in my face for the early part of the morning. Their flight was leaving at 11:30am and some of the camera equipment had to be returned on the way to the airport, so I kept an eye on the time. I ended up having to kick them out of the office because they were cutting it very fine to catch the plane.

It ended up being a fun and memorable experience, not only for us – the film crew enjoyed it as well. The documentary was a success and, when I eventually forced myself to watch it, I felt very privileged and honoured to have been part of something that included the amazing stories of the other families involved. I felt that ours was a very ordinary story of very ordinary people and still felt perplexed that we had been chosen.

I'm glad we overcame our fears to participate in this documentary and not only contribute to a greater cause but also with the hope that it inspires others to donate blood/plasma.

Many people say, "Oh no, I can't give blood, I'm scared of needles."

This makes me irate and frustrated beyond belief. If people could see how many injections and horrific procedures these sick kids must endure every single day, how could they complain about the opportunity to save lives? It can be a wonderful experience where you get to sit down and be looked after, read a magazine, be spoiled by the nurses and volunteers, have something to eat and come out feeling like an absolute legend because you have saved many lives!

Filming had been an amazing once-in-a-lifetime experience. Or so I thought. Being able to reveal my thoughts and feelings, let alone on camera, was extremely challenging for me. Little did I know what the future would have in store for me. But that was in the future, and we had more treatments and Ashley's High School Graduation to get through first!

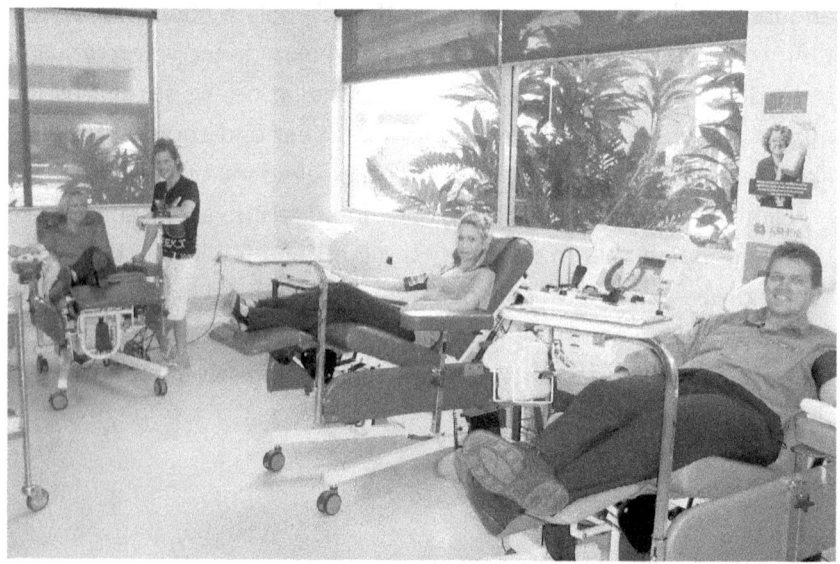

CHAPTER 10

A New Beginning

The fourth of March 2009 marked the end of the prescribed, very gruelling, three and a half-year treatment protocol for Ashley. Trying to live our best life amidst hospital visits, doctors, medication, blood tests, lumbar punctures, chemo, injections etc., handling all the things that were thrown at us, had become our new normal every day. We were really looking forward to returning to our previous normal life or 'LBL' as we referred to it (Life Before Leukaemia).

Our last trip to Brisbane had the nurses in tears. They were so excited and overjoyed to see that Ashley had completed his treatment so well. At the same time, we were definitely going to miss each other because we'd all formed such a special bond over the years. They'd become part of our family. It was the end of the journey.

Coming out of theatre for his last lumbar puncture, you should have seen the nurses! While he was still under anaesthetic, they painted his toenails and fingernails, putting little love hearts and messages on his arms to look like tattoos.

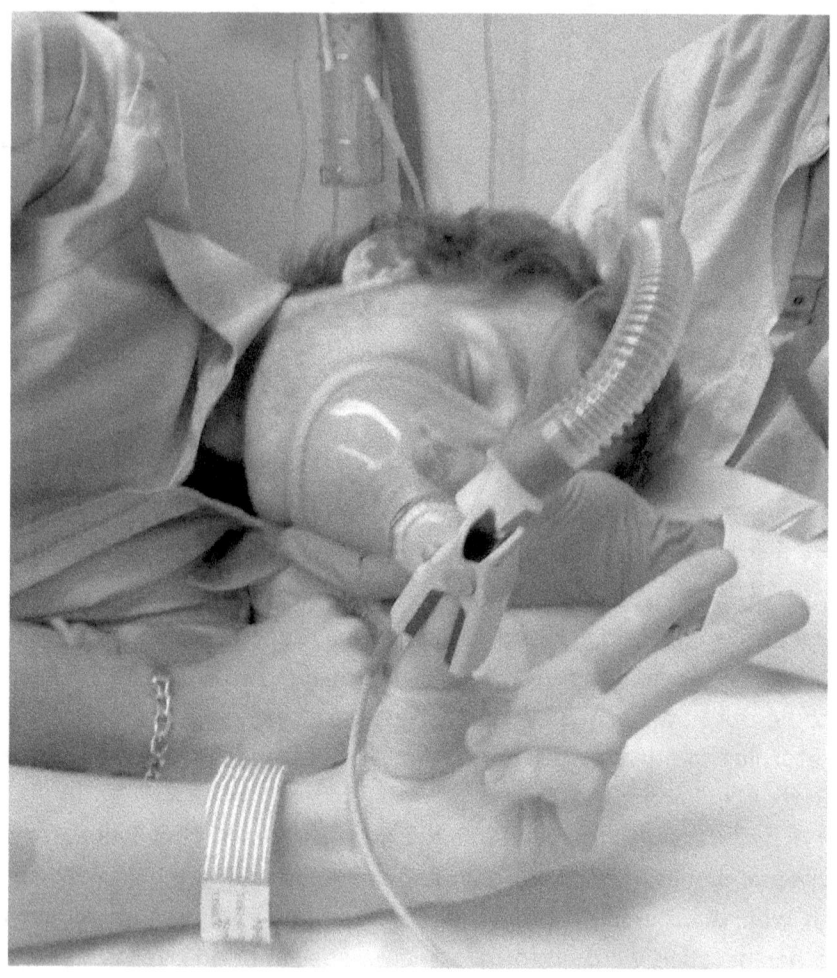

HOPE, GRIT AND GRATITUDE • 81

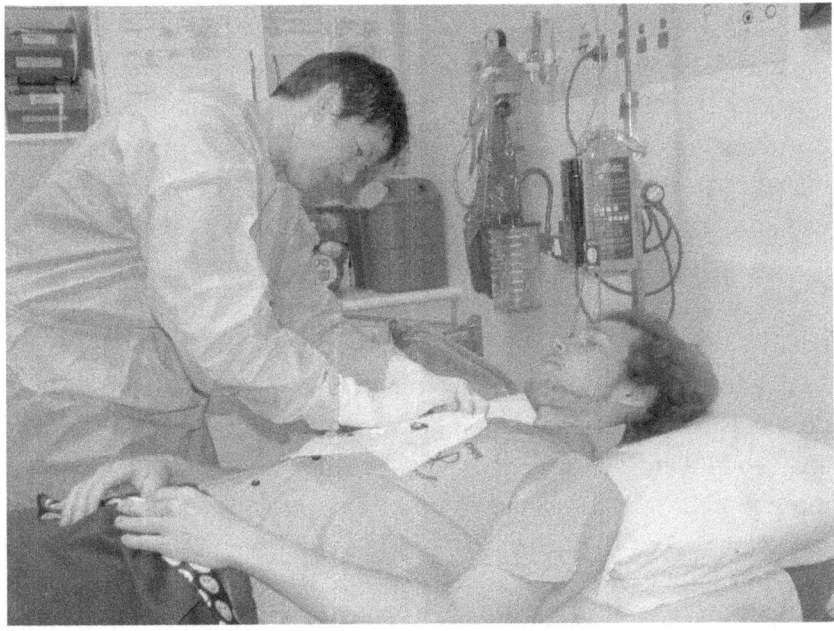

I felt a huge range of emotions and reactions. Topmost was sheer joy that Ash no longer had to endure horrific medication and medical procedures. I also felt relief that there would be no more medication alarms going off on my phone. No more waking up throughout the night to check Ashley's temperature for fevers. At the same time, I was so anxious that we no longer having the security of the medication to fight off the disease.

It felt amazing to be able to plan an event and not feel like we needed Plans B, C, D right down to Plan Z, in case we had to rush Ashley to hospital. Gone was the heartache of Ash not being able to do things and see friends when his immune system was dangerously low. Gone were the days of waking at 3:00am to fly to Brisbane for more lumbar punctures and painful treatments. It was a huge relief to put behind us the heartache and gut-wrenching sadness of being in that children's ward.

In line with my Mighty Mouse nickname, I thought our life would automatically return to 'LBL' when Ash's treatment ended. That I'd just bounce back into everything with my usual energy and enthusiasm. Surprisingly and frustratingly, it was not that easy.

I found it extremely challenging to transition back to what had been our normal way of life. The few months after the end of treatment seemed to be just as challenging as the previous three and a half years. I hadn't realised how much energy it required to get through the ordeal, and how much energy it took to remain upbeat, happy, and positive at the same time. I was utterly exhausted and just felt broken.

Living in the middle of the bush, I found myself desperately seeking the sanctuary of our natural surroundings. I felt like a wounded animal that needed to crawl away and lick its wounds. Here was Mighty Mouse, who could - and did - handle anything, sitting quietly beside our creek, watching the ducks and waterlilies. It was as though I had completely run out of fuel and needed to recharge my batteries (or probably more accurately, jump-start them).

It was during one of these solitary, reflective soul-searching moments when I had a phone call from a very dear friend of ours from Cairns. Knowing me so well, Wayne was shocked to hear the emptiness and lack of energy and enthusiasm that I'm usually brimming over with. He could tell I was searching for ways to regain my mojo once again.

It was at that moment he shared some of his brotherly advice.

"Leigh, you need to find a hobby."

"Are you kidding", I exclaimed. "I have a business, and I'm busy all the time, where am I going to find time for a hobby?!"

But those little words of wisdom were the beginning of my soul-searching journey to reclaim my life once again.

I dug out my crumpled, well-worn To-Do-list and smiled to myself thinking, 'I know exactly how this piece of paper feels!' Like me, it needed some attention, straightening and smoothing out the rough, fragile pieces to become whole once again. There was a very special project on the list that I'd put on pause during Ashely's illness, but I wasn't quite ready just yet...

Slowly, and without fully realising it, our whole family regained the confidence to start planning things again. We were able to do things together, such as water-skiing down the river or getting away for a weekend, without anything stopping us. We were ecstatic. Wow. This is what life was like before Ashley's ordeal!

Before we knew it, my family and I were almost back to 'LBL'.

The next momentous occasion for our family was Ashley's Graduation. I wanted it to be as memorable and special as Stacey's graduation. This was also a family celebration to mark the successful end to this chapter of our lives, so I asked Ashley how he would like to arrive at Graduation, if he could arrive any way he wanted. His reply was 'By tandem skydiving or by helicopter!'

Oh dear, why did I ask?!

Old Mighty Mouse went into action yet again. I made enquiries about a tandem skydiving entrance however, after investigating the venue, it was decided that there was not enough clear space to make a safe landing possible.

Plan B was arriving by helicopter. When I started investigating this option, I came across the most wonderful guy, Hylton, from Nautilus Aviation. Although I could tell Hylton was a little sceptical, he was open to the possibility and happy to work with me. I promised to get all the approvals required and get back to him.

My first meeting was with a representative from the venue who was rude and announced that if we were planning to land on the road, it was not on their premises so they would take no part in it. This made me even more determined than before, so I sought approvals from the council and police.

The brother of one of my very dear friends, who has sadly since passed away, was my next contact. Peter was in the police force. I explained my idea to him and how important it was to have Ashley arrive in a helicopter for his Graduation. For our family, it wasn't only the end of his schooling, it was also the end of three and a half very long, challenging years of treatment for Leukaemia. It was a celebration!

In my quest to make it happen, there were countless times when I was told this had never been done in Townsville before and that it just wasn't possible. But was this going to stop me? Heck no. I was going to make it happen!

Then finally, after months of preparation, strategic planning, and fine-tuning – with incredible attention to safety – Ashley's arrival at his Graduation was now only two days away.

The final meeting for 'Operation Touchdown' took place at the venue to go over plans once again for:

- where our volunteer police would be positioned to stop traffic and momentarily halt the other students
- whether there were any horses or other animals involved in other students' arrival plans that could be spooked by the noise of the helicopter, and if so, what was their arrival time?
- which area needed to be cordoned off so that no cars would be parked when the helicopter was to arrive
- the direction the helicopter needed to land so that Ashley would be facing the crowd, and
- where the additional pilot on the ground would be to escort Ashley and his partner safely away.

Everything was organised for the utmost safety of all, even to the point of being overcautious. However, I noticed a slight hesitation when Hylton was double checking some small trees that were in the path of the helicopter's arrival. When I quizzed him, he said that, because we were being overcautious with everything else, he'd be happier if the trees were trimmed.

You want it? You got it!

I had two options, I could come down at midnight and trim them myself or I could do it the correct way and contact the council. With my parents drumming into me about doing the right thing, you know which option I took.

When I explained the top-secret mission to the gentleman in charge of Parks and Gardens at the council, he agreed to meet me on site at 8:00am the following morning (the day before Graduation). I showed him the trees that only needed the slightest trim, and he said to leave it with him and that he would do the job himself. I was just amazed at how willing everyone was to help, and so thankful.

We also needed to cordon off a parking area for the helicopter to land. The morning of the ceremony, Ashley and I rocked up armed with safety tape and special stands to hold it in place. Our family business is a home building company, and our apprentices had made twenty-four stands out of leftover timber to do the job.

I said to Ash, 'I bet you had no idea you'd be doing this the day of your grad!'

Suddenly, I burst out laughing. Instead of the modest trim I had asked the council rep to do, he had completely lopped them off to make sure we were safe!

The afternoon began with countless photos of Ashley with the helicopter, which Hylton had meticulously shined. Our family then waited anxiously at the venue as we watched the other students arrive. The whole plan had been kept top-secret with only a handful of people knowing what was about to happen. My stomach was churning, and I wasn't going to let any disturbing thoughts ruin the moment.

Soon there was the distant whirling sound followed by a glimpse of the helicopter as Hylton teased everyone on the ground. I could hear the whispers in the crowd.

"Wouldn't that be the best, rocking up in a helicopter!"

"Yeah, but no way that could happen!"

The helicopter was soon forgotten, though, as Hylton flew off into the distance again.

As it returned, hovering along the creek, the sounds got louder. The helicopter came into sight! The crowd went wild, and there were cheers and loud applause as Hylton strategically and safely brought the helicopter closer.

Large as life and as cool as a cucumber, there was Ashley with headphones on and Tom Cruise aviator sunglasses, calmly waving from above.

"Oh my gosh, it's Ashley rocking up to grad in a helicopter! Good on him!"

Hylton expertly landed the helicopter in the exact spot for maximum impact with the crowd. The additional pilot on the ground safely escorted Ashley and his partner away from the helicopter as the cheers continued.

Already his phone was overloaded with texts congratulating him and saying how awesome it was to see him arrive in the helicopter. Long after the evening ended, emails and congratulatory messages continued.

After three and a half years of frequent absences from school, his fellow graduates and teachers understood the significance of what it meant for Ashley to graduate with his class, as a regular teenage lad, in remission and looking forward to his future.

Ashley's Graduation from school and his Leukaemia journey was incredible and unforgettable. We will cherish the memories of this special milestone for the rest of our lives. It was the perfect ending to that chapter of our lives.

CHAPTER 11

Serendipity

Our family had been super excited and really looking forward to a dream holiday of snow skiing in Canada when Ashley was diagnosed with Leukaemia. All the flights and accommodation were booked and paid for, our warm winter clothes and all the holiday gear had been eagerly gathered in the spare room and we were counting down the sleeps.

But we were now fighting for our son's life instead.

I remember sitting beside Ashley's bed in hospital, looking around my alien new environment as I arranged the cancellation of all our holiday plans. We were now going to Plan B.

So, when we had completed the challenging treatment journey, we decided to take that dream holiday off 'hold' and to celebrate life, cherish being together as a family and relish that sense of 'normal' we had been craving ever since the diagnosis.

Our Canada snow ski trip was everything we'd dreamed of and more. The beautiful scenery, large pine trees laden with glistening snow, it was all so picturesque. Having the adrenalin pumping through our veins as we came zapping down the ski runs, laughing and hugging each other at every chance was the best therapy ever and we all had the time of our lives.

On the way back home, we had to overnight in Los Angeles – our least favourite place. Stacey and my brother Bruce had earlier flights back the previous day as they had work commitments, but unfortunately flights weren't available for Geoff, Ash and I. Holed up in the motel, Geoff announced that we should go sightseeing to see if it might change our perception of the city.

Ashley and I looked at each other, raised our eyebrows, shook our heads, and said, 'I don't think that's possible.' But we soon found ourselves in the hotel foyer sifting through countless brochures for the various sightseeing tours available. Grabbing a handful, we returned to our room and laid them out on the bench. Only having the afternoon available, we didn't have many options, but thought a helicopter tour would show us the highlights of the city. It was weird, but sifting through the myriad of helicopter tour brochures, my gut instinct was to only go through one particular tour operator. The decision was made, and a tour representative soon collected us from our hotel.

Ushered into a little waiting room, we introduced ourselves, and well and truly being in holiday mode, we joked and showcased our Aussie humour. The owners explained that it was a family business, which prompted us to share that we too had a family business back in Australia. There was another guy waiting, looking very relaxed on the couch, and they introduced him as Harvey Mason Junior saying he was 'kind of a big deal'. Having just completed the documentary for the blood bank and being in a very cheeky mood, I shook his hand and joked that we too were 'kind of a big deal back in Oz!'

We continued to chat and joke until something happened that was totally out of left field. The company owners shared that they were shooting the pilot of a reality TV show and asked if we wanted to be part of it? We looked at each other with sheer amusement and agreed to participate, thinking it was all a joke. Next minute, a guy appeared with a huge camera perched on his shoulder and we soon found ourselves signing media release documents for the show. How bizarre! But we were going to enjoy the experience.

The cameraman captured our every move, following closely as we were escorted to the waiting helicopter. Luckily, he didn't join us on the tour so we could just relax and enjoy the trip. Getting back to earth, we gathered in the hangar for drinks and a catch up with the team. Chatting to Harvey, we explained that helicopters had a very special place in our hearts as that was how Ashley arrived at his school graduation. We went on to explain it wasn't to be pretentious, but that it signified the culmination and successful conclusion of everything he'd been through over the last few years with his treatment for Leukemia.

Harvey looked on with surprise as he explained that his own family were going through a similar experience as his daughter was receiving treatment for a brain tumour.

I spoke about having a positive attitude and how it helped our family get through the ordeal and gave him encouragement and hope that they too could get through this. Harvey seemed quite touched and asked if he could keep in touch with us as he handed over his business card. I'd helped countless other families through this challenge, so readily agreed, and stashed the card somewhere in my bag.

We were also introduced to some basketballer who made me look like a toddler when I stood beside him. Apparently, he was also 'kind of a big deal' so again we joked that we knew how he felt. Mucking around as group photos were taken, I said to make sure they got me in the picture seeing I looked so short beside the others.

It was soon time to say goodbye, head back to the motel, collect our luggage and make our way to the airport for the long journey home. Looking for something to pass time while we waited for our flight, we decided to Google this Harvey Mason Jr and see if it was all just a joke. I scrounged in my bag, and when I finally found his card, we looked up his website.

We were a bit disillusioned and thought it was misleading when his introduction page flashed names like Elton John, Justin Timberlake, Whitney Houston, Beyoncé, Michael Jackson and Chris Brown. However, reading further, our jaws dropped as we quickly discovered that Harvey Mason Jr was in fact, a 'really big deal'! He had not only penned and produced songs for industry legends like, Elton John, Michael Jackson, Aretha Franklin but also for today's superstars including Justin Bieber, Justin Timberlake and Chris Brown. Harvey had also been instrumental in producing memorable music for many of the biggest musical films – from Beyoncé and Jennifer Hudson in 'Dreamgirls', all three 'Pitch Perfect' movies and 'Shrek' just to name a few.

Oh no! Here we were joking, telling Harvey that we were also 'kind of a big deal'. We sat in stunned silence and struggled to process this information. But then again, we wouldn't have acted or treated him any differently had we known – that's just how we are.

Harvey and I kept in contact over the years as I shared little treasures to encourage his family to be positive and to reassure them that they will get through this. When you're going through such a journey, you're desperate to hear good news stories and positivity to give you hope and to be able to see a light at the end of that very long tunnel. It's important to be able to remember this when your child is experiencing so much trauma.

When Ashley's 21st birthday was fast approaching, I contacted Harvey to say that Ashley was interested in music and producing. We felt very privileged when he invited us to spend some relaxed time at his recording studio.

As Harvey worked his magic with the countless buttons in front of him, I watched the admiration, respect, excitement, and joy on Ashley's face. It made me reflect on my parent's little motto, 'With just a bit of effort, you can make a big difference in someone's life.' To think that just a few kind and caring words many years ago has blossomed into this incredible experience for our son after all the horror he had endured.

I feel extremely privileged to have crossed paths with another amazing, and very down-to-earth legend who we've had the pleasure of making a difference in each other's lives. Harvey is so busy and incredibly famous, and yet, he still makes time to keep in touch and we get to see the special, caring side of this extraordinary person.

Chapter 12

Where's That To-Do List?

Inspiration can strike at the most unexpected times.

During Ashely's illness, my brother, Bruce, joined us for dinner and my weekly ritual of watching Andrew Denton's 'Enough Rope'. We soon found ourselves reaching for the tissues as we learned all about the Sydney Merry Makers, a diverse and talented dance group. Most of The Merry Makers have an intellectual or physical disability and refuse to be defeated by the challenges life has dealt them. The program highlighted just how talented these people were as dancers and performers, while they lived with such varied challenges.

This episode really struck a particular chord with me as I as I'd spent about 15 years volunteering with people with differing abilities. Quietly dabbing the tears, I thought to myself, 'I know how amazing these people are because I only ever see their abilities not their disabilities. I'm lucky to be able to see through to their beautiful souls.' Those who can't communicate like you and I, often use their eyes to say what they want to tell you. Their sparkle, sadness, excitement, frustration, and joy can all be discovered in their eyes.

While moved by The Merry Makers dancers, I was frustrated by an angle of the episode that the reporter found it amazing that people with these physical and mental challenges could dance and perform. After many years working with people with similar challenges,

I knew they could. I'd seen people overcome severe physical disabilities and do amazing things when that person put their strength of will behind it.

As Bruce and I watched the interview, I announced, "I'm going to bring this to Townsville."

Having earned the nickname 'Nike' (because I 'Just Do It'), my brother had no doubt I would carry this out. You should have seen the look on his face as he was thinking, "Oh no, here we go!"

With Ashley's treatment taking up so much of my time and energy, I put my idea of creating a dance troupe like The Merry Makers on my To-Do list. When my friend Wayne had suggested a hobby to recharge myself, I really didn't have it in me. Then fate took a hand...

Towards the end of 2009, I again happened to see The Merry Makers on Channel 7's 'Sunday Night' program. The time was right, and I felt ready to take on the challenge of starting a group like The Merry Makers in Townsville. Checking their website, I discovered they were having their bi-annual concert in Sydney in a few weeks' time and was keen to go.

Running the idea past Geoff when we were enjoying our morning ritual of a cuppa on the patio surrounded by our skippies, I realised it wasn't his scene. We had been married 26 years at the time, and Geoff has always supported my ideas. With his encouragement, I rang my forever-friend, Joy McCarron, to see if she'd like to come to the concert with me. Unfortunately, Joy was going to be in Brisbane for work at that time.

Plan B! Geoff had the great idea that I should go to the concert by myself. It would give me the flexibility to speak to whoever was available and I wouldn't have to worry about anyone else.

I quickly zapped off an email to The Merry Makers introducing myself. I explained that I was inspired to start a similar dance group in Townsville, and that I was coming to the concert hoping to make some contact with them. After two weeks and a few emails resent, I still had no reply! That's OK, these days I was used to going to Plan C.

Mighty Mouse was on a mission. I knew in my heart that this was what I must do, and I had an idea. I decided to ring Merry Makers on the off chance that someone would be in the office on a Sunday. It was only days away from their concert. Three rings later and I was speaking with Janet MacFarlane, the wonderful coordinator for Merry Makers. She sounded relieved to be finally catching up with me as she'd been in hospital and hadn't had the chance to respond.

When I shared my plans to start a group inspired by The Merry Makers in Townsville and was coming to Sydney to experience one of their concerts, Janet invited me to join The Merry Makers and their families for their Christmas party weekend getaway as well. Instead of going to Sydney to see the concert, I was now going to help with their concert and spend five days with them. Plan C turned out to be far better than what I had imagined.

During the flight to Sydney many thoughts came to me.

"This is the craziest thing you've ever done!"

"You don't know anyone."

"You don't know what to expect and you don't even know where you will be staying or even if you have a bed!"

But remember, Mighty Mouse was on a mission. Most people would have checked into a motel first and then gone to the theatre, but not me! I rocked straight up to the Sydney Theatre Company dragging my suitcase.

Wow, this was a whole new world for me. I'd never had anything to do with theatres before, and here I was trying to navigate my way through a maze of rooms, props, busy people wearing headsets and racks of costumes. I felt like Alice in Wonderland. It was all so alien to me that I felt as if I was on another planet.

I was led to a kitchen where a dozen people were having lunch. Meeting Janet, I gave her an excited hug and was introduced to the rest of the team. Janet said later that she wondered who this excited girl was hugging her! Robyn Mackenzie, Janet's right-hand girl, immediately took me under her wing and welcomed me to the group.

The Merry Makers dancers all arrived at 1pm so I soon had the chance to meet everyone and tried desperately to remember all their names. When rehearsals began, I was the only one allowed to watch, as it was to be a surprise for the parents and relatives.

Lucinda (Janet's daughter and the chief choreographer) was still fine-tuning some of the steps to make sure everything flowed smoothly. There was a little tension in the air, which I could certainly understand.

I remember thinking, "Gosh, they're amazing to remember these changes so late in the piece. I'd be hopeless."

I was mesmerised watching Scotty Martin and Lucinda perform the most beautiful dance. As someone with down syndrome, Scotty didn't have a typical dancer's physique and yet moved so gracefully, and with such natural rhythm and passion. Dancing seemed to transform Scotty into a handsome, majestic prince who could take on the world.

Happy tears flowed down my cheeks, and I went into a kind of trance as I watched their graceful movements, not wanting the dance to ever end. I was glad to have the luxury of being the only one in the audience as I quietly wiped my tears and regained my composure. I felt so privileged to be able to bring this 'opportunity to shine' back to my hometown and my community.

In that moment, I knew that whatever challenges and obstacles were ahead for me, I would make this happen.

It was soon time for a break, and The Merry Makers spilled into the theatre and excitedly took their seats. When the drinks were distributed, I took a seat beside a petite young woman named Vanessa. Little Matilda in front of us turned to Vanessa to complain that the boy beside her was annoying her. Vanessa gently spoke to the young man and politely asked him to stop.

I was amazed at how skilfully she handled the situation. Turning to her, I complemented her on what she'd just done, and she went on to explain that she was a preschool teacher and dealt with these situations daily. I said that she must be a very good teacher as she was a natural with children. It was fascinating speaking with Vanessa, and I learned so much in such little time. We clicked immediately and I felt as if I'd known her all my life.

It was soon time to continue rehearsals, so we slowly moved everyone backstage. We looked like mother ducks rounding up their ducklings and shuffling them along protectively. I raced back to my seat to eagerly await the next dance. One by one, I recognised each dancer as they returned to the stage. Vanessa was encouraging little Matilda and the other younger dancers, getting them into position, and once again, doing an amazing job.

Suddenly and unexpectedly, I burst out crying (and remember, this doesn't happen often as I don't 'do' crying). Why was I so emotional? I saw the incredible effort and determination required for Vanessa to take every step. I'd had no idea that the talented and beautiful young woman I'd just connected with had cerebral palsy.

Watching her movements brought back memories when I moved in a similar way myself...

Chapter 13

Flashback

In early December 1992, Geoff and I were living in Mackay with our two very young children. Stacey was three and Ashley had just turned one. Upon waking one morning, the day looked like any other day - except I'd lost the use of my legs overnight.

It's not something many people know about, and given a choice, I'd rather not talk about it. But it gives an insight into why I'm so passionate about supporting people of all abilities.

That morning, Geoff had gone to work early and was coming home later for breakfast. When I went to get out of bed, my legs didn't do what my brain told them to do.

Hang on, what's happening? Don't be ridiculous. Surely, I can walk.

But when I tried again, I ended up collapsing on the floor. Mmmm, this didn't look good.

Maybe I should go for a shower and run the hot water on my legs? I was very lucky to have good upper strength from lots of water-skiing, and I managed to drag myself to the bathroom on my forearms.

It was clear this hadn't solved the problem. My legs were still pretty much useless.

I fumbled awkwardly to get dressed and pulled myself back into bed. By this time, Stacey had woken up and come into the room. We snuggled in bed until we heard Ashley wake.

How was I going to handle this? I didn't want to bother Geoff as I knew he would be home in the next hour or two. I told Stacey we were going to play a game and we were both going to crawl on the floor to Ashley's room to get him.

This was great fun for Stacey! For me things didn't look good at all.

I dragged myself up the side of Ashley's cot and managed to grasp him. It must have looked so funny: Ashley, Stacey, and me all crawling (or in my case, dragging) to the lounge. I realised I had to call Geoff. It was a phone call I was dreading, as I hate asking for help.

All I said was, "Geoff, can you come home now please? I'll need to go to the doctor."

When he realised what was happening, he was devastated. As my family was in Townsville five hours away, he organised for our neighbours to look after the kids and got me to the doctor immediately.

After examining me, the doctor talked about admitting me to the Mackay hospital. Now it was me who was devastated. "I can't go to hospital; I have two babies to look after!"

Realising I didn't have a choice, I told the doctor I would be going home first to organise the kids before I even thought of going to hospital.

By the time we got back in the car and Geoff had rung my parents to let them know what was happening, my mum was already on her way to the Townsville airport to fly down to Mackay. Apparently, Dad had rung our Mackay office and when he was told that Geoff needed to take me to the doctor, my parents realised it must be serious. I'm Mighty Mouse and for me to need someone to take me to the doctor meant it was a serious situation!

The doctors suspected Guillain-Barre - but I would need a lumbar puncture to confirm the diagnosis. Unfortunately, the specialist who was to do the lumbar puncture had hit his head in a bad fall before work and hadn't fully recovered. He was still dizzy and a little shaky – not desirable qualities in someone about to put a very large needle in your spine! Nevertheless, he was the only one who could perform the procedure.

As I lay there in the requested foetal position, thinking, "Breathe and relax."

The specialist apologised as he made several attempts to get the needle in the correct position in my spine.

"This is about as much fun as childbirth," I thought to myself.

Guillain-Barre is a virus that slowly paralyses the body. It starts at the lower limbs and works its way up the body until you can sometimes end up on a ventilator to breathe. The virus then slowly moves back down the body until, hopefully, after learning to walk, talk, eat etc, normal movement returns.

I'd planned to take the kids to Carols by Candlelight that evening to get into the Christmas spirit, but here I was in hospital. When the doctors delivered the verdict, I told them about my plans and asked if I could still go if my mum was with me. After receiving a very firm 'NO,' I continued. "Well, it looks like I have two options: you can let me go to Carols by Candlelight or I can check myself out of hospital and go anyway."

I wish I'd had a camera to take a photo of the nurses' faces. It was like, "You go, girl!" The doctor knew he was fighting a losing battle so he conceded that I could go if I went in a wheelchair.

Unfortunately, he was going to lose that battle as well.

"I'm really sorry," I said. "I can't go in a wheelchair. I've been helping people in wheelchairs for several years, and I know it would be too hard to get it up the big hill. It will be easier for me to go on crutches."

I caught a hint of a smile as the doctor shook his head and walked out. You should have seen the nurses! They were so excited; they were doing everything they could to get me to Carols by Candlelight. Looking like naughty schoolgirls planning mischief, they adjusted some dilapidated crutches for me. Talk about determination! The crutches had to be shortened because I'm 'vertically challenged' and you'll never guess what they used as a tool... a teaspoon! We were all laughing, and nobody would have guessed it was such a serious situation.

Carols by Candlelight was worth every bit of effort. It was very good therapy just being with my mum and family, listening to the beautiful singing. But when I rang the after-hours bell at the hospital, it was now me feeling like a naughty girl who had snuck out of boarding school! It was certainly a weird feeling.

The next day I learned that I would need a serious blood transfusion. I was to receive a product called gamma globulin, a class of blood plasma proteins that has antibodies to fight infections and disease. At the time, this procedure was found to help people recover from Guillain-Barre. I fully realised the seriousness of the situation from the way the specialist and two nurses were constantly monitoring me during the transfusion. Even though I was joking and laughing with them, I could see they were watching me like a hawk. With their expert attention, it all seemed to go well.

Adding to the dilemma, we were supposed to fly to Brisbane for a large reunion of Geoff's family. Everything was planned. Geoff wanted to cancel the trip, but I said if I was going to end up on a ventilator, it didn't matter if he tap-danced on the ceiling or sang me lullabies, it wasn't going to make much difference. I wanted him to go with Stacey so his family could at least catch up with them. Ashley was in good hands with my mum.

When Geoff and Stacey left, I really missed the two of them. Without the distraction, I worried about how I was going to look after our two littlies without the use of my legs. I also became aware that when I had visitors, I was the one cheering them up, not the other way around. This took energy I didn't have.

Luckily, the Gillian Barre didn't progress any further and I didn't have to go on a ventilator. When Geoff and Stacey returned, I was allowed out of hospital on the condition that I was to stay with my parents in Townsville and have help with the children. As it was just before Christmas, this was the plan anyway and it worked out fine.

During this time, I made a disturbing discovery. People were treating me differently. My parents had friends visiting and I noticed that one of them was speaking to me in a very loud voice.

"Surely not," I thought in disbelief as I lay on the floor. I'll just test her. Sure enough, she spoke to the others in a normal tone. "You've got to be kidding!"

I felt like saying, "Hello, I've only lost the use of my legs, not my hearing!"

Then there were others who would be deadly serious the whole time they were speaking with me. Once again, I'd think: "Hello, I've still got my sense of humour and I still love to laugh!"

Christmas came and went, and I was restless, wishing to go back to our house in Mackay. "You can't manage with no legs and two babies!" was the reaction.

But the old 'Just do it' determination was kicking back in, and I wanted to go home. Sure, it was far from easy. I would change Ashley's nappy on a mat on the floor and sit on a chair to do the ironing and cooking. I simply adjusted my way of life to overcome my disability – I'm talking about the loss of my legs, not my lack of cooking skills! I even did the grocery shopping, although it was rather like a military operation.

I'd manage to get the kids in the car and would park next to a trolley in the supermarket car park. Then I'd lean on the trolley while I got the kids out of the car and into it. I'll never forget one particularly challenging shopping trip, a lady stopped and kept staring at me wherever I went. She probably thought I was drunk the way I was shuffling along with near-useless legs.

I had learned to ignore this sort of behaviour; however, this really wasn't a good day! As if I didn't have enough to put up with without this blatant lack of empathy. I couldn't help myself, and said, "Why don't you take a @$*# photo, it will last longer."

This was extremely out-of-character for me, but the frustration I felt was enormous and threatened to engulf every bit of my being. It took every bit of effort and energy to simply get out of bed, let alone take care of my two young children. Anyone else would have sought help to look after the kids and manage the household duties, but being painfully independent, this was how I chose to manage. In those days, there was zero rehabilitation provided for this sort of diagnosis and no services to assist with the daily requirements. As always, I just got on with it, and did it.

After about five months, I wanted to get back into my aerobics. It was devastating standing at the back of a seniors' low impact class knowing I should be in the step and high impact class. It was even more disheartening to discover that I couldn't keep up with the senior members of that class! Seeing the looks on the gym instructors' faces when they saw how much my muscles had wasted, made me realise this was not one of my better ideas.

Mighty Mouse came to the rescue. I bought a few beginners aerobics videos so I could practice in the seclusion of my own home. I felt so pathetic as I struggled with the most basic moves. I wasn't giving up though. Every single day I would try again.

Eventually, I noticed I was having more good days than bad. I was almost able to complete one of the basic aerobic sessions. Finally, there was a light at the end of the tunnel, and it wasn't a train!

I believe that everything happens for a reason, and I always take something positive out of a bad situation. This period of my life gave me a better understanding of some of the difficulties people with disabilities face. I can demonstrate to everyone that no matter what the disability, these are amazing, wonderful human beings with all the same feelings as you and I.

They also want to be treated like the rest of us. I also hope that all parents can teach their children these important life lessons so we can break down the barriers for future generations to come.

Watching Vanessa dance at the Merry Maker's rehearsal, those feelings of frustration and the need for acceptance and validation came back to me.

Using sticks to help her walk, Vanessa had joined Merry Makers. Pushing herself through each movement, dancing, stretching, and using her sheer determination, she soon threw the sticks away. Every time I see or even think of her, she's my 'Beautiful Vanessa'. She has the most caring, generous, gentle, and cheeky personality; she's just amazing. Once again, I was glad to have the isolation and privacy of the empty audience, knowing nobody could see my raw emotion.

All too soon, it was time for the Merry Maker dancers to be loaded onto the bus to return home for a good night's sleep before the next day's big performance. After some finishing touches to the costumes, it was also time for us to go to our motel.

As one of the main organisers, Robyn ensured I was included in arrangements for dinner, and I already felt part of the Merry Maker family. Sitting around the table that night, I reflected how privileged I was to spend time with these amazing quiet achievers. Here was Robyn, who devoted hundreds of hours to ensuring the smooth running of Merry Makers – not only looking after all the costumes but also the fundraising, raffles, prizes etc. Seeing the endless work behind the scenes, I wondered if anyone saw the massive amount of work she did.

Then there was Bob, Robyn's wonderful and devoted husband. Like Robyn, Bob is generous, nurturing and has a heart of gold. Another behind-the-scenes person, he was often running errands, carrying out all sorts of obscure requests in the name of Merry Makers.

Looking around the table that night, I noticed Linda, who had also been working tirelessly preparing costumes for the concert. A gentle, warm-hearted member of the team, Linda kindly welcomed me into The Merry Makers family. Once again, I wondered if anyone realised just how much time and effort these quiet heroes devote to the smooth running of things because I certainly had no idea. I made a mental note to make sure our volunteers and helpers would always be thanked and recognised.

Lastly, seated at the table were Scott and his beautiful mum, Joy. Scotty wasted no time reminding me that he's a star and can even be seen on the internet! His whole face lit up when I told him how much I loved his solo dance with Lucinda that afternoon.

"Yes, Scotty, you are certainly a very special star."

His mum, Joy, is also a star - as are all the parents of these truly amazing people. Their unconditional love, patience, and devotion to their children, can certainly teach every one of us a lesson or two. How could we say we were having a bad day if the car broke down or we were late for work, when these parents face endless challenges every day? They too are our unsung heroes.

Our busy day was spent sorting, organising and arranging costumes; making sure the Merry Maker dancers were keeping their fluids up; and attending to their individual needs. There were fun times as shoes went missing, braids came undone, drink bottles disappeared and buttons needed a quick fix, but I was surprised at how composed and professional they were. I was the one jumping around excitedly, not them!

The dress rehearsal that afternoon was quite tense and there were some awkward and challenging moments, something I would later experience with my own group. This was certainly a very professional production, and I couldn't help questioning why I was thinking of taking this on.

Dragging myself away at the last minute, I swapped my daggy work clothes for something glamorous and took my balcony seat in the audience. The music began and The Merry Makers came to life during the concert.

It was difficult to tell they had any disabilities at all as they danced with such poise, grace, rhythm, and professionalism. Their sheer joy was contagious, and the audience of over 800 people responded accordingly. There were lots of happy tears and the applause was deafening.

As I watched, I kept thinking to myself, "I know every person on that stage has a disability, but more importantly, they all have amazing ability. I can't wait to bring this to our Townsville community."

After the show, The Merry Maker dancers were welcomed like royalty, and they loved every minute of it. Every hour of rehearsal was worth it for this memorable night. Their families finally convinced them it was time to go home even though they were still on cloud nine and didn't want the night to end.

Backstage, it looked as if a cyclone had swept through. Shirts and skirts were strewn everywhere, tap shoes were thrown about. Although our day had begun at 6:00am, we worked until 1:30am the next day, sorting out the aftermath. Returning to the motel at about 2:00am, we showered, caught some sleep and were all back at the theatre at 7:00am that same morning.

I'd never given a thought as to what goes into producing a show like this. When I'd been to a concert, I'd bought the ticket, turned up, watched the show and then gone home. I was totally naïve as to what was involved.

This was a complete eye-opener for me and had me thinking, 'Leigh, why the heck are you doing this?' This is probably the point where anyone else would think, "Great idea, but I think I'll take up golf instead!"

Inspired by the Merrymakers, I wanted to bring this same opportunity to our remarkable people with 'differing abilities' in Townsville. I was truly passionate about making it happen. This experience had brought back memories of my own frustration at being defined by what others thought I could or couldn't do, the struggles I went through to do what we'd consider normal or simple tasks, and how important it was to me to complete them by myself.

To make this happen, I had to just find a way forward - like using a trolley to prop myself up while shopping - and work out what worked for me and our Townsville community. Just like the steep learning curve to give Ashley his injections, I had to learn completely new skills and it would be worth it to see our dancers prove to others — and themselves — what they could do.

CHAPTER 14

Believe and You Can Achieve

Back home, I knew the time was right to work on my dream of creating a dance group for local people with special needs. Focusing on it completely, I took several months off work to get our new group started. Sourcing a venue, dance teachers, members and volunteers were the first things on my very long list.

I purchased books and DVDs about The Merry Makers and enthusiastically distributed them. I hoped they would give people an understanding of the kind of group I was talking about, but I kept coming up against brick walls.

People kept saying, "You'll never do it", "It can't be done" and, "You're crazy!"

I heard it so many times that I began questioning myself. Thank goodness I had my family's support and my unrelenting determination, and I kept going anyway.

Mighty Mouse took over. For the dancing style, I was keen to have Rock and Roll because it is such a happy genre of dancing, there are few steps to learn, and it is great to watch. Geoff and I had taken lessons when the kids were young, and it was so much fun. After explaining my idea to an enthusiastic member at the Rock and Roll club, she was very keen to help and said she would talk to other club members about it. Finally, something was easy!

For the venue, I had very specific criteria. I needed a timber floor, which is better on your joints, and good access and facilities for those with disabilities. Air conditioning would be preferable. It also had to be available on a Wednesday night. Ten pin bowling for the special needs group happened on a Tuesday night, and I would never interfere with that. Finding a suitable venue was not going to be easy.

Just when I was starting to think I'd never find a venue with all these requirements, I hit the jackpot. I met with the manager of a community venue to discuss our requirements and he was obliging, with the bonus that their venue was air-conditioned as well! Not only that, but they could also help with obtaining grants and insurance, and if we went under their umbrella, we wouldn't have to go through the red tape of registering our group. They would also provide independent annual audits. The more I heard, the more I was convinced that this was the home for our new dance group.

Along the way, I was very fortunate to have the support of some great people. Firstly, a very knowledgeable person, Melanie, had started a similar dance group called 'Dance Oolites' in Sydney. She was very generous with her time and advice, and it was great to be able to run things past her as they came up.

While my initial thoughts were that my group would use The Merry Makers' name, it became clear that for various reasons we would have to come up with our own name. Having put my heart and soul into this venture, I can now understand why every group needs to be a separate entity to protect the hard work, the blood, sweat and tears that have gone into it.

We wanted the name to reflect what the group was about so, after pages and pages of brainstorming, my hubby came up with the name 'Happy Feat'. The name reflects the fact that the group brings happiness to its members and audiences, and acknowledges that for our members, dancing is a feat.

Sometime after this, Geoff and I saw the 'Happy Feet' movie. We didn't know the story beforehand and were dumbfounded to discover that it was about an outcast penguin who gained acceptance through dance.

During the Easter break, I enthusiastically told a close friend, Lorraine, about my plans to start the group. When I mentioned that I was still sourcing dance teachers, she reminded me that her son's girlfriend, Rhi, taught a kids' dance class. When I mentioned her name to Ashley, he said that she would be wonderful for our group. I made an excited phone call to Rhi about helping teach our group and she jumped at the idea. We'd also gathered a few volunteers to help with the Rock and Roll dancing. Things were finally falling into place.

It was scary and exciting at the same time. I called all the volunteers together for a sausage sizzle to explain what the group was all about, what I was hoping to achieve, and what was expected of everyone. I also showed one or two dances from The Merry Makers DVD so that they had an idea of what could be achieved. I shared my absolute passion and determination, and just spoke from the heart. The night seemed to go well, and I was excited to have such a fantastic team of dedicated and caring volunteers.

There was so much to be done before our first night. I wanted to have individual name tags for all the dancers as well as the volunteers. Check! I needed to set up everything so that everyone could have supper. Check! I've been asked the question, 'Why have supper when Happy Feat only goes for two hours?' The answer is: it's not just supper, it's an opportunity for us to socialise, establish friendships and bond together as a group. Supper is a very important part of our Happy Feat family.

Then there was the mountain of paperwork! All dancers and volunteers needed to complete several forms, not to mention the paperwork for attendance registration and payments. Check! Rhi was prepared to do the warm-up and modern dance section. Check! The Rock and Roll team were ready. Check! The music and Merry Maker DVD were organised and ready to go. Check! The raffle prizes and raffle tickets were organised! Check!

I think we were as ready as we were ever going to be. With everything in place, the next step would be to see if we would have any interest from the community. Would there be much interest in learning to dance by people with enough challenges on their plate?

CHAPTER 15

A Dream Comes True

During a lifetime, it's not often we get to see our dreams come true but, at 7:00 pm on Wednesday 19th of May 2010, I watched my dream finally come true.

After getting the venue, teachers, and volunteers ready to go, I contacted the local disability services providers to spread the word about our new dance group. As everything was happening through mostly trial and error, and we only had our 'learner's plates', I thought I'd probably start with about five to eight dancers. Was I in for a surprise! The demand was so great that twenty-five dancers with special needs came along to our first night!

Casting eager eyes around the hall, I saw the excited and enthusiastic faces of our new Happy Feat group as they greeted each other. It was hard to tell who was more excited, the dancers or the eager volunteers and parents!

After welcoming everyone, I wanted to share the big picture of Happy Feat and show them what could be achieved. Our overhead projector came alive with the vision of The Merry Makers, expertly dancing to 'Love Is in The Air.'

Everyone watched mesmerised and as they took it in, discovering the possibilities of Happy Feat, the looks on their faces told me everything I need to know. This was definitely the right thing to do. There were big smiles, hands shaking excitedly, and bodies moving closer to the screen to capture even more. Yes, here was my dream coming true, and here were all these other special people sharing that dream with me.

Happy Feat had begun.

Bursting with energy, the Happy Feat dancers lined the dance floor on their individual spots, eager to begin the warm-up. To help our 'Happy Featers' differentiate between left and right, each one was given a red band to wear on their right wrist and a blue one on their left. To help with their feet, red and blue tape adorned their shoes as well. (This was probably more for me as I'm hopeless when it comes to left and right!)

Hands and feet seemed to be going everywhere but the smiles on their faces said it all. At one point, one of the mothers let out an excited whoop! Her gorgeous four-year-old daughter had just walked backwards! This was a wonderful feat for someone with down syndrome and we all shared her excitement.

At Happy Feat, we've learned there are no limits.

Following the warm-up came the Rock and Roll session. Even though at times it looked like complete chaos, the laughter and noise filling the room showed that they were having a ball anyway. A few times I stood at the front of the room and just marvelled at our dancers' ability shining through. It was hard to believe this was only the first session of Happy Feat!

After twenty minutes, we coaxed them into having a drink and some supper even though some wanted to keep dancing. Then came the start of another important ritual of the night. The raffle tickets!

Each week, I buy a little gift for the raffle prize and every 'Happy Feater' is given several free tickets upon arrival. Ceremoniously lining up their tickets, they wait in the hope of having the winning ticket. Funnily enough, they never show disappointment or sadness if they don't win. This is another wonderful thing we could all learn from our Happy Feat group!

Next was the jazz ballet session with Rhi. They certainly got into the swing of it and seemed to really enjoy themselves. Things went a bit haywire when we tried to move left hands and right feet at the same time. Perhaps it was a little too soon for this concept, though possibly more so for the volunteers! It was all part of the process and didn't seem to faze anyone.

All too soon, 9:00pm arrived and it was time to go home. I absolutely loved seeing the huge smiles, contented looks and excited chatter as I checked them off at the door.

We'd done it!

What a night!

Happy Feat had begun with gusto and was already a success.

My wonderful brother, Bruce, had already swept and cleaned up everything, so I was also able to go home shortly afterwards. Driving home that night, I just felt so emotional.

I walked in the door to find my wonderful hubby unpacking the dishwasher and cleaning up the kitchen. Geoff put his arms out and said, "Do you want a glass of wine?"

You know by now that I don't usually 'do crying' but I just fell into his arms and burst out crying with joy and happiness at the realisation that tonight, after so much hard work and uncertainty, my dream had come true.

I had amazing feedback in the following days. Comments included:

"I had the most incredible time last night I was so overwhelmed with emotion myself that I went home and cried."

"Tonight, I met the most beautiful people I have ever met. I have never experienced something as amazing as tonight. I cannot wait for next week. I think what you are doing is a great thing that will be making people happy. Not only the dancers but also the helpers looked like they were having the time of their lives. I have always got time to do whatever needs to be done for these special people."

And from one of the mums: "I loved tonight and cannot stop telling everyone how wonderful Happy Feat is. We had so much fun ourselves and it's a great family night. There are terrific role models for our children, and I can't wait 'til next week. I was a bit sore the next day so it's also a workout for me!"

Another volunteer wrote: "I went home and said to my husband that joining Happy Feat was absolutely the best decision I've ever made in my entire life!"

Word got out and soon I not only had a waiting list for the dancers, unbelievably, I also had a waiting list for the volunteers. Can you believe it? What group has a waiting list for volunteers?

I was approached to do newspaper, magazine, and other media - but everything had been strategically planned. Promotion wasn't in the plan until later down the track when our Happy Feat team were ready for it. We already had enough dancers and volunteers to work with for the first six-week term, and we didn't need any more at this stage.

As we were all new to this, I wanted everyone to get some experience so we could progress from our L-plates to our P-plates! I also wanted to establish a routine for Happy Feat and there was a considerable amount of trial and error involved – certainly lots of error!

It made me feel truly blessed to receive daily phone calls and comments expressing how much this program was desperately needed in Townsville. It was validating after so much hard work, while doing my best to ignore discouraging comments from those who didn't believe I could do it. This support and enthusiasm from the new Happy Feat family and local community reinforced my commitment to make a positive difference in these peoples' lives.

CHAPTER 16

Watching Flowers Bloom

In those early days of Happy Feat, I think the best way to describe how I was coping was like watching a duck in a pond. Above water, everything appeared to be serene and composed but underneath, I was paddling like crazy! When I began Happy Feat, I had no idea of the complexities and challenges of running a group of this nature. There were times when I felt completely out of my depth as I'd had no training whatsoever. It was all trial and error and certainly learning on the job. These were unchartered waters and this little duck had to quickly work out how to get to the other side – but the rewards made it so worthwhile.

There were so many astounding moments where I wondered, 'How did that just happen?' and, quite simply, I didn't have an answer. By giving our Happy Featers the confidence and belief in themselves, they now achieved things that even surprised their families.

Alice, one of our dancers, was celebrating her 30th birthday. She came to me with a special request: "Could you get everyone to form a circle while I dance in the middle?"

This wasn't in the program, but it was going to be added. We gathered the circle and held hands (a first time for Happy Feat) and I led Alice into the middle. I wasn't sure how it would all go but I just followed my gut instinct and trusted all would be well. What I saw in front of my eyes, was astonishing.

Alice danced solo in the middle of the circle and became an absolute superstar! We clapped and cheered as little four-and-a-half feet tall Alice became 10 feet tall and bulletproof. She called me into the circle to dance with her and we quickly gathered the others to join us. Well, we all became 10-foot-tall and bulletproof that night.

The free-spirited dancing went so well that we decided to make it part of the regular program and to this day it is known as our 'Moment to Shine' time. Would the dancers have any trouble playing up to the audience? No way!

Each day I was hearing mothers commenting on how their Happy Feat children were just blossoming in front of their eyes. Others around them also mentioned the transformations: how the dancers had become more outgoing, seemed to be more confident, showed their sense of humour and became more socially interactive. This was music to my ears.

I know they have these wonderful gifts, but for some reason, whether it's because society places labels and limits on them, or whether it's because that is what society expects, these characteristics are often suppressed. At Happy Feat we emphasise that there are no limits and no labels. It's an environment where everyone can be themselves, achieve incredible results and really shine.

Sadly, this wasn't happening as quickly for all our members. Each week, Theresa would hide behind her mum, and refused to speak or dance with anyone else no matter how hard we all tried. The first time I met her was at a local tavern where a group met every week to listen to music and dance. Theresa was sitting very quietly with her mum but even then, I knew there was something special about her.

Although I hadn't seen her dance, I could sense she had a grace and presence that was truly unique. There was something in her eyes that I can't explain but it had been my mission ever since, to bring that special something out for everyone to see. Several volunteers were frustrated with her lack of progress and appealed to me to give up the losing battle. That wasn't in my nature.

In a last-ditch effort to overcome Theresa's barriers and get out of her shell, I took her and her mum along to the theatre to see the ballet, Swan Lake. It was priceless to see the look on her face as her arms moved gracefully to the music. This began the very slow process of forming a bond with Theresa and gaining her trust so that when I told her how amazing she was, hopefully one day she would believe it herself. Until then, I had to be patient.

Dean also blossomed by dancing with Happy Feat. His support worker was absolutely stunned as she'd never seen Dean so happy and confident in the 12 months that she'd known him. He was rap dancing and doing the 'worm' at that stage. She said he was always so quiet; she didn't know he had it in him.

Yes, that's what Happy Feat is all about, and the magic continued.

I had to laugh when I caught up with Aidan's mum to see how he enjoyed his first week. He was so keen that he wanted to practice his dance steps as soon as he got home. It was already 9:30pm so his mum suggested a shower instead. A long time later she checked in on Aiden and discovered him practising his dance steps... in the shower!

A wonderful, generous person had offered to make special outfits for each of our Happy Feat dancers. Our girls were to get a beautiful bright Rock and Roll skirt each and our guys were to get their own Rock and Roll vest with plenty of bling. After hours and hours of sewing, the whole wardrobe was finished, individually wrapped and ready to present.

Our Happy Feat dancers could hardly contain their excitement as they eagerly waited for their name to be called. I knew this was going to be a special event, but I wasn't prepared for just how momentous, heart-warming and emotionally overwhelming this experience was going to be. For most, it was as if they'd never received a present in their life before let alone received something so special to call their own. And now they really looked like a team.

Later, when I tried to describe it to Geoff, I said, "When they put on their special outfit, it seemed to transform them into movie stars. It was like watching a chrysalis morph into a magnificent butterfly!"

Then I saw them dance like I've never seen them dance before!

We finished the night by practising our dance for 'Grease.' As I looked around, I asked myself, 'Is this really only the second night we've done the dance to Grease?' They danced in time, enthusiastically and absolutely loving it. They could already impress an audience with their skilful dance moves. They certainly impressed me!

You never know when a transformation will come to fruition, and one magical night started with a very special moment when Jackie, Jemma's mum, came up to me all excited. She couldn't wait to tell me something important. Jemma had never worn a skirt in her life, but while they were shopping through the week, she had spotted a skirt in the shop window. When her daughter tried the skirt on and it fitted, Jackie bought it thinking it would sit in the cupboard and never get worn.

As Jemma had also never wanted to choose her clothes, Jackie went into her bedroom to put clothes out for her to wear to Happy Feat. She couldn't believe her eyes when she saw, all laid out on the bed, Jemma's brand-new skirt, a white top and her shoes...all prepared for Happy Feat! Jemma had chosen and prepared her own clothes for the first time. Special moments like these make your heart sing.

Continuing my mission to draw Theresa out of her shell, I had spoken with her mum to discuss my plan to overcome her reticence to join in. I suggested that perhaps her mum might like to have a rest and send Theresa along with her support worker.

Well, to our delight, Theresa arrived at Happy Feat with her support worker. She was a totally different person! When it came time for the progressive dance, I told Theresa's social worker how it went and showed them where they could join the circle. (I happened to be right beside her and had strategically placed everyone). There's a lot of very quick thinking involved with Happy Feat. To our amazement,

Theresa moved on from dancing with her social worker, to dancing with the person next to her, then the next, and the next.

"What's the big deal?" you may ask. This was a very big deal, a momentous feat for Theresa. After all these months, she was finally coming out of her shell and showing everyone how truly amazing she was.

Before we knew it, the last night of Term One had arrived, and I came up with the crazy idea of having a low-key break-up celebration.

The atmosphere at any regular night of Happy Feat was absolutely intoxicating. That night you could multiply that by one hundred as people filled the room for our last night of Term One. With the opportunity to invite their family and friends along to this special night, our Happy Featers were excited to share their 'Happy Feat fix'. So much for trying to keep our group secret until we'd gained experience and could at least fake that we knew what we were doing!

The night began by welcoming everyone and thanking our guests for coming along to Happy Feat. I shared my emotional experience at the very first night of Happy Feat – the moment when I looked around the room and realised that my dream had come true and was now shared by others. After sharing some magic moments of the first term and acknowledging our wonderful team of volunteers, the fun began.

An energetic warm-up was followed by our modern dancing session. When the music started, it unleashed our stars of 'So You Think You Can Dance!' There wasn't a doubt in my mind that our precious Happy Feat dancers would be able to perform anywhere, anytime. Having the extra audience seemed to boost their dancing skills tenfold. Our all-time favourite was a big hit as our John Travolta's and Olivia's rocked to 'Grease' and played up to the crowd.

Just when we thought the night couldn't possibly get any better, well, it did! Our 'Moment to Shine' session began, and truly lived up to its name. We all gathered in a circle and one by one, our amazing dancers came out into the middle and danced their hearts out as if they were the only person in the world. It was their moment in the spotlight, and they glowed.

After all this dancing, it was time for supper and, as always, it was a great social time for everyone. We started with our birthday celebrations and gave a very interesting version of Happy Birthday.

There was no way we could have forgotten about drawing the raffle as we had many reminders. It was a very important part of the night, and everyone's tickets were ceremoniously lined up while eager faces awaited the ticket draw. Two of our Happy Feat dancers were the lucky winners and couldn't contain their excitement as they gathered their prizes. Priceless!

The Hokey Pokey always gets the group going again after supper - and when it's followed by our Rock and Roll session, the atmosphere once again becomes electric.

As it was the last night of our first term, I had prepared individual certificates for our Happy Feat dancers and volunteers. Seeing their own photos on each certificate was very popular.

All too soon it was time to go home, although nobody wanted to go. As we farewelled our Happy Featers, I handed them our next newsletter as well as another little surprise. Bruce and my dad had organised to have countless photos printed. These were a big hit, and everyone took them home to treasure.

People weren't so much walking out the door but drifting along on cloud nine. The wonderful comments, excited chatter and infectious laughter all proved that Happy Feat was already a huge success.

Before I even got out the door, I received text messages such as: "That was awesome. You should be so proud. I loved every minute of it. Thank you for letting me come."

"Wow! How magical was tonight? It was hard to keep a dry eye. Congratulations. You are a champ."

At 10:30pm, another special text message came through: "Sorry it's late but I just had to tell you that Mum said it was the best night she has ever had out in Townsville! We all loved it. Don't know what that says about us, but it says a lot about you. Thank you."

There was also a lovely email: "Congratulations on the first very successful term of Happy Feat. It would not have happened without your efforts. Our Happy Feater would very much like to continue to participate next term and he is already counting down the days on his calendar. For him, Happy Feat is the high point of his week. On his behalf, thanks to you and all the wonderful volunteers for your efforts in making Happy Feat as successful as it is."

In just one term, Happy Feat had come so far. It was fun, exhilarating - and already making a difference in everyone's life. Our dancers were becoming more confident as individuals and coming together as a group. They were growing and achieving things thought impossible before. All of this was new to me too. I had already learned so much with a steep learning curve, but our next steps would push me further, harder, and give a me a deeper understanding of their world.

A Glimpse Behind Closed Doors

Happy Feat brought unexpected opportunities to our dancers, which brought both joyous and heartbreaking glimpses into their lives. Here is a little insight into how the very first term of Happy Feat evolved.

Oh, what a night! It was the first round of the Queensland & New South Wales State of Origin, which is a very serious event here in North Queensland. As we had some die-hard footy fans among the Happy Featers, I didn't think we'd have many people. Wrong!

I kept thinking during the week that if not many turned up, it would be a great opportunity for us to practice and get more experience. Well, that theory went out the door - we had a fantastic turn up.

During the week, I'd come up with our very own 'Happy Feat Chant', so we began the night with this. I'd watched sporting movies where pre-game they pumped everyone up by gathering in a circle and chanting. That was exactly what I wanted for our team, and they loved it.

'We are Happy Feat; we love to dance.
We can do anything given a chance.
We laugh, we dance, we have lots of fun.
We are Happy Feat, we're number one!'

Everyone was pumped and raring to start as the warm-up jazz ballet session with Rhi began. It was a great opportunity for me to join in the dancing as I had been too busy running around last week. Red arm up, blue foot forward… Wow! It certainly makes you think!

I looked around and saw the determined looks, the concentration on their faces and the effort everyone was putting in. I thought how good this must be for the group. They were getting the best work out possible and because they were having so much fun, they didn't even realise it.

In the Rock and Roll session, everyone was linking steps with more fluid movement and loving the music. Grooving to the song 'Greased Lightning' was a hit. Their expressions were priceless, so thrilled to be dancing to their favourite movie. The dance floor was flooded with John Travoltas and Olivia Newton Johns.

As I looked around the room, I kept marvelling at our fantastic volunteers and helpers. I knew for certain that many had given up their beloved State of Origin just to be here for Happy Feat tonight. I was just so grateful for their amazing dedication, and their caring and generous natures. The evening would have been impossible without them.

One of our wonderful volunteers, Kevin, owned a Crash Repair business and started a whole new adventure for our Happy Featers. He had two V8 Supercar racing cars in his workshop for the weekend and called me wondering if our Happy Feat dancers would like to see them and maybe have their photos taken. I didn't get home from work until 6:30pm that night so it was late when I proceeded to ring our twenty-five dancers to offer them this wonderful opportunity.

At 11:30am the next day, the Happy Feat team and their families were all lined up excitedly waiting to get their photos taken. I'm not a V8 Supercars fan so I was amazed to see just how excited everyone was to be near these cars, let alone sitting in them and posing as though driving the beasts! The families were having just as much fun as our dancers were. It was such a special experience.

Then, if that wasn't enough excitement, our Happy Featers were personally invited to meet Shane van Gisbergen, a racing driver, and spend some time with him. It was such a surreal moment. I wanted to pinch myself to see if it was really happening. Happy Feat had only been operating for a couple of weeks at this stage, and for me, this signified we were already breaking down some barriers and our members were being included in the community...big time!

One of the dances I really wanted the group to perform was 'Don't Worry, Be Happy'. This dance would highlight the wonderful personalities, amazing characters, and great sense of humour of the dancers. Not being a dance teacher... heck, or even a dancer, I decided to have a go anyway.

When I was introducing the dance, I announced that we wanted to show everyone how at Happy Feat, that no matter the challenge, 'Don't worry, Be happy'. Other people complain if they sleep through the alarm and are late for work, and here are these Happy Feat members facing the tremendous challenges, and yet they are happy and vibrant. I said that in this dance we wanted to have heaps of fun and show some attitude.

Well, I got what I asked for! They were wiggling those hips and to my amazement, even singing the words.

During the dance, as I watched my beautiful Happy Feat team, I brimmed with pride and joy. It made me think of the words to Ashley's and my special Bon Jovi song: 'Welcome, you gotta believe that right here right now, you're exactly where you're supposed to be.'

There are certainly many surprises with Happy Feat, and you never know what to expect. One of our dancers greeted me excitedly with the news that her cranky cat had to be put down that afternoon. Hang on, why was Samantha happy about this news? I was perplexed so when I asked how she felt about it, her beautiful blue eyes lit up as she happily told me about getting a new kitten. I laughed, shook my head, gave her a big hug, and shared her excitement. These amazing people teach me so much about life, loving and living.

Then there are nights that challenge you to the core.

The night began with our Happy Feat Chant and the energy in the room nearly lifted the roof off -with one exception. Jane seemed very quiet, sad, and was standing on the side with Jasmin, one of our volunteers.

I gave her a hug and asked if she'd like to join in and learn the new dance. Jasmin gave me a private look and said that Jane had had a big day. She later shared with me that Jane had self-harmed that day and had spent several hours in hospital. She got out of hospital just to come to Happy Feat.

I'm a very strong person but this news shattered me.

The old Mighty Mouse attitude quickly returned with a plan of action. It had to; I had so many people relying on me. I told Jasmin that we had to reassure Jane how very special she is and how much everyone at Happy Feat cares about her. Wonderful Jasmin had already been telling her how much she was loved by everyone but there are times when that can be hard to believe.

I went on a mission to coax Jane to laugh and have a good time, all the while making sure she didn't know what I was up to. She loves it when I act the fool, muck things up and be a total dag, and I subtly made sure she'd be able to see me. Together with Jasmin's motherly instincts, caring nature, and down-to-earth humour, we soon had Jane laughing and happy again.

The one song that had her dancing her heart out was 'Don't Worry, Be Happy.' I felt myself tear up as I saw Jane not only dancing enthusiastically but singing the words at the top of her voice.

Raffle time often gave simple yet classic lessons in life. The first lucky ticket we drew that night was Samantha's, but she announced that as she had already won two raffles in the past and would like a redraw to give someone else a go. The second lucky ticket was Damien's, but he also announced that he had won before and would like to give someone else the chance to win. Can't they teach us all a lesson in life?

Andrew, another of our Happy Feat dancers, is a terrific organiser. Asking him to help makes him feel important, so I gave him the mission of getting everyone ready to do the progressive jive. My hubby thought to introduce this idea as it gets everyone used to dancing with different people and increases their comfort zone. The dancers with Asperger's and autism can feel challenged by social interactions, but they have so much fun with this dance they don't realise the hidden benefits.

Sometimes it's easier to give up - but that's not necessarily the right choice to make. You quickly forget all the challenges, setbacks and hurdles when you reach the finish line, with your hands in the air and feeling triumphant.

Sometimes, these victories are short lived.

Happy Feat has given me the opportunity to fight for our member's rights and there have been times when I've had to fight for their lives.

I've really struggled whether to ever share this following story, however if we keep doing the same thing and sweeping these critical issues under the carpet, we'll keep getting the same results. It was a situation I was unexpectedly faced with, and it rocked me to the core. It even made me question whether I could continue running Happy Feat.

I noticed one of our very devoted Happy Feat dancers, Abagail (not her real name), hadn't been coming along each week and decided to pay her a visit. I had taken along some tambourines and my Abba CD to get her dancing and cheering her up.

I couldn't believe her condition.

This normally happy, smiling girl had lost so much weight, was now so weak she could hardly walk and looked dreadful. Abagail had been screaming out and crying each night, lost her appetite, wouldn't eat, and didn't want to come out of her room.

I was horrified.

I managed to get her out sitting on the patio where I could speak with her without the other residents milling around. I can't divulge what came out of that conversation, but we put a plan of action in place and now it was time to work on getting her eating again.

I knew from looking after Ashley during his treatment that there were critical times when immediate action was required. If this special lady didn't start eating and drinking immediately, she would end up in hospital.

She had seen my Abba CD on the table and said she would like to have it. Then it clicked...she absolutely loved receiving the different gifts, photos, certificates etc at Happy Feat so I decided to try a bit of 'bribery and corruption.' I told her if she started eating and drinking every day, I would get her a copy of the Abba CD.

When I enquired what was for dinner and heard it was sausages and vegies, she objected and said she wasn't hungry. (I couldn't blame her). I asked her if there was anything she'd like to eat; I would get it for her. Well, McDonalds won the vote along with a milkshake.

Forty minutes later I arrived back with the goodies and quietly sneaked them out to the patio. She still wasn't really interested but was drinking the milkshake which was a start. I reminded her about the Abba CD and said I would be checking on her.

On the slow walk out to my car that late afternoon, I thought about how naïve I had been in the beginning to think that Happy Feat was only about dance moves and music...it couldn't be further from the truth!

It was 6.30pm and I was desperate for some time-out to gather my thoughts and work out the best plan to help Abagail. Even though it was late and getting dark, I decided to still walk up Castle Hill. Geoff and Ashley were on their big motorbike rally, so I didn't have to get home and cook dinner.

As I walked up the road that night, I admired the full moon rising over the ocean; it was lovely and cool, the city lights were twinkling, and it was the best therapy ever!

That Wednesday night as our Happy Feat dancers arrived, there were even more cheers than usual. I soon discovered that Abagail had arrived, although she had to be supported by two others because she was so weak. She received a very warm welcome and everyone made a fuss of having her back at Happy Feat.

This triumph was only short lived however and sadly she continued to deteriorate rapidly.

Two weeks later, I decided to 'drop in' (unannounced) to visit Abagail. I was shocked by what I saw. I'm a very strong person, but what I witnessed that afternoon, will haunt me for the rest of my life.

After the visit, I returned to my car. It wasn't long before I burst out crying and just sat there sobbing my heart out, shaking from head to toe.

When I finally gained some composure, I began driving home. It was now after 7pm and I still had to get home and cook dinner. I didn't get very far when I had an idea of someone who might be able to help me fight for Abagail's life. I pulled the car over and made the phone call.

I'm normally bright and bubbly on the phone, but not tonight. The first question I was asked was "Leigh, are you alright?"

"No, I'm not. I know this isn't a good time of night, but could I come to your place to speak with you please. I don't want anyone else to see me like this, so could you come down to the car to talk to me."

It wasn't long before we were both sitting in the car as I sobbed my heart out and shared the horror I had just witnessed at Abagail's place. I had certainly chosen the right person to confide in as, sadly, he was familiar with these horrific situations. Over the next hour, we planned a course of action, and I finally drove home feeling like I'd been hit by a bus and totally drained of all emotion.

Knowing in my heart that I needed to inform her family, (who lived out of town), I made the unenviable phone call. Her family members were elderly and had health issues, so they asked if I could be their voice and fight for Abagail's life.

At 2am the next morning, I set about my mission to save Abagail's life, and sent an email to the head of the National Disability Abuse & Neglect Department.

The following months weighed me down as I secretly fought this heart-wrenching battle; wading through the red tape, and slowly seeing critical rules and regulations implemented.

Sadly though, I saw Abagail continue to slip away, and she was eventually lost to early dementia.

This situation felt like an earthquake; it shook my foundations, and I had crumbled. I really battled with my thoughts and emotions. Feeling like a complete failure, I could easily have walked away from Happy Feat forever. But, if I had given up after that devastating and traumatic experience, every one of my Happy Featers would have missed out on so much happiness and memorable experiences in their lives.

It was time to put my big-girl pants on once again.

I still struggle with the knowledge that I wasn't in time to save Abagail's life but speaking out and fighting for my Happy Feater resulted in critical changes being enforced that will hopefully save other lives in the future.

Chapter 18

A Great Excuse to Shine.

How can one crazy idea to hold a Happy Feat Graduation make a difference in so many lives?

It all began when I heard one of our dancers' dreams to get married and wear a beautiful white gown. It hit me that the families of our Happy Feat dancers may not get the opportunity to see their sons and daughters graduate from school, get married, or even go to a formal ball. Why shouldn't they have these opportunities that others take for granted? The seed was planted, and I could feel an idea emerging.

That's it! Let's have our very own Happy Feat Graduation where our dancers could dress up like they'd never dressed up before and, together with their families, get caught up in all the excitement.

"What would they be graduating from?" you may ask. Who cares?! It was a fantastic excuse to let them have the experience of a lifetime.

One of our team members at Grady Homes (our family business) happened to read about the Graduation in the Happy Feat newsletter. She enthusiastically chased up friends to gather formal dresses that were sitting in wardrobes, not being worn. One by one, stunning dresses appeared in our lunchroom and transformed it into a scene from backstage at a fashion show. It also doubled as the fitting room where our Happy Feeters had the opportunity to try on the dresses and have them free of charge if they suited.

The first formal dress model was Samantha. When she floated out in a dazzling black gown, the look on her dad's face as he fought back tears was priceless. He saw his little girl become a beautiful young woman before his eyes. It was like watching a butterfly emerge from a chrysalis. Seeing Samantha's parents' reaction confirmed that hosting our 'Graduation' was the right thing to do.

The next model was Jemma. I had spoken to her mum to make sure Jemma had a dress for the Graduation and Jackie assured me that she was 'all sorted'. But later that day, I noticed a dreamy pink gown hanging up and immediately pictured Jemma floating around in it. At 6:30pm, I rang Jackie and convinced her that Jemma just had to try on this dress. The look on Jemma's face as she paraded in the gorgeous gown was worth more than any Lotto win, and it immediately became her fairy-tale dress.

Another of our other Happy Feat dancers didn't have her own transport, so I decided to take some dresses to her home to see if any of them were suitable. Her eyes were huge as she saw the wonderful gowns.

"Are these really for me? I've never worn such beautiful dresses. Which one will I try on first?" she asked excitedly.

I had to catch my breath as she appeared in a magnificent shimmering gown. She looked like a royal princess. It happened to belong to the generous and thoughtful girl at work who had gathered the dresses. How fitting that this Happy Feat dancer should be the one to wear this special dress. "Do you have any good shoes?" I asked.

"I only own one pair of shoes, these black thongs," she replied. Her answer brought up many emotions for me and I had to fight back tears as I adjusted the hem.

When she was trying on the other dresses, I asked her mum what their plans were for Christmas. Quietly, she admitted that she could only afford one present each for her two daughters, but that was OK. She excitedly showed me the two small packages under their tiny

Christmas tree. When I asked whether they were having a special Christmas lunch, she admitted that if Centrelink mucked up their payment again, they would have to make do for another week with the food they had. But that was OK, they had some potatoes as well as some mixed vegies in the freezer.

I struggled to keep my happy face and stop the river of tears that were threatening.

"Pull yourself together," I said to myself. "You have to be strong!"

This is the unfortunate reality of the challenges faced by many families living with a member who has special needs. Creating a community that is inclusive is essential to helping identify the help they need and deserve.

Thanks to an anonymous donation, the next day I was able to deliver a Christmas hamper to the family and tell the mum she could give some Christmas treats to her girls. She could hardly believe me. I don't know if anyone had ever done anything like that for her family before. They were stunned as they sorted through the huge hamper.

After Christmas, preparations were in full swing for the Graduation in January.

Marion, one of our wonderful dancer's mums, called in a bit of a panic. When I'd previously checked with Marion to make sure her daughter had a grad dress, I was assured that everything was organised. However, the dress still didn't fit after several alterations.

When Allana and Marion were on a shopping mission for another dress, they ran into a Happy Feater and her mum who told them that I may still have some dresses available. I only had one donated dress left at that stage, a lovely blue one, and thought it would look wonderful on Allana. I loaded it into the car together with Stacey's grad dress (I don't know why I hadn't even thought of it earlier) and off I went to meet them.

In the beautiful blue dress, Allana simply took my breath away. Her face lit up and the dress fitted her perfectly.

Marion had tears flowing down her face. "I've never seen Allana in such a special dress. Allana and I are usually the ones watching her sister get dressed up."

Now it was all about Allana. How can you describe moments like these?

Next mission was Fiona, our gorgeous 'fashion princess'. She always looked beautiful and wore outfits that were perfectly coordinated. If a friend was wearing something that didn't quite match, Fiona would march her back into the house to get changed!

When Fiona saw our daughter's dress, she was over the moon. Her mum, her support worker, and I were so excited to help her into the exquisite dress. It looked as if it had been made for Fiona - she looked like a royal princess. Mother and daughter had tears pouring down their faces and Fiona was shaking with excitement. I fought back my own tears, and we hugged each other, sharing the joy.

It wasn't to end there. I answered a call from Jemma's mum, Jackie, who told me about a wonderful thing that happened when she took Jemma to her dressmaker. Jackie proudly explained to the dressmaker that Jemma's special dress was for the Graduation and told her all about Happy Feat. Before they left, the dressmaker asked if we needed any other dresses and disappeared out the back. When she reappeared, she had three brand new dresses in her arms, two of which were worth over $600 (they still had the price tags on). She handed them to Jackie and said that she would like to donate them to Happy Feat!

The whole Graduation journey was profoundly moving. I'm a very generous person and it's usually me who's doing the giving, so it was quite overwhelming to be on the receiving end of all this generosity.

Graduation day arrived. The red carpet was literally rolled out and our hall was transformed into a scene from a Hollywood Movie (well, almost!). Our Happy Feat dancers began arriving, looking utterly splendid in their dresses and suits, and each was met with a huge round of applause.

What's that? It looks like a limousine! Yes, two of our dancers and their folks arrived in a shiny stretch limo, something they had only ever dreamed of. They felt like movie stars as they emerged to claps and cheers. Being true stars, they waved graciously and acknowledged the waiting crowd. Just when they thought it couldn't get any more exciting, our special guest arrived. The Happy Feat dancers absolutely idolised our local radio and media star, Steve 'Pricey' Price, and when he walked in the door, another loud cheer went up.

There were so many magical moments throughout the night. Some parents saw their sons and daughters achieve things that even they didn't think were possible. There wasn't a dry eye in the room when one proud father walked his daughter down the red carpet as she wore her dream 'wedding dress'.

When the local newspaper ran a story about the Graduation, featuring two of our dancers, it didn't take them long to adjust to their newfound fame! One Happy Feater rang the other to make sure he'd seen the article in the paper, only to be told he'd been receiving phone calls all morning. In fact, he informed her that he'd better get off the phone in case he had more calls coming though!

Despite my earlier reluctance to introduce any media coverage, fearing our Happy Featers weren't ready, this moment certainly proved they were well and truly ready - and would love every minute of it. The newspaper feature had shone a spotlight on our dance group and pushed us to the next stage – whether we were ready or not!

CHAPTER 19

Preparing for More Than a Concert.

The success of our Graduation and the following media attention led to more wonderful opportunities for Happy Feat. One of our first big events was when we were invited to perform at the Premier's Queensland Disaster Appeal Concert at the Townsville Civic Theatre! This event was to raise funds for the unprecedented natural disasters that devastated so much of our southern state in the summer of 2010–11.

There was a lot of work to do and decisions to be made. Costumes would have to be made for the new members, and it was also a great opportunity to source our Happy Feat shirts with funds we'd received through a grant. I was certainly burning the candle at both ends. Life was already very busy as I was working full-time in our business again, but our wonderful group deserved to have this opportunity.

I was so lucky that Anne Sanker, another of our valuable volunteers, was able to help with the 'Happy Feat Shirt Project'. Even though she had her own successful interior design business, Anne volunteered to chase up the shirt supplier, organise for samples sent up and get everyone fitted. After many phone calls and emails, the order was finally placed with the assurance that the shirts would arrive the Wednesday before the concert.

Little did we know what was around the corner that would challenge all our plans! On the 30th of January, just 12 days before the concert, we began hearing about a category 5 cyclone that was making a direct path to North Queensland! Category 5 cyclones are classed as the strongest tropical cyclones, with damaging winds up to 280 kilometres per hour! Naturally, there was a great deal of discussion and anxious waiting. By Tuesday, the first day of February, we knew it was inevitable that Townsville was going to be greatly affected.

At our family business, we decided to close the offices on the second and third of February until the cyclone had crossed the coast. All hands were on deck to clean up our building sites. We secured all the outside furniture at our display homes and elevated as much office equipment as possible in case the predicted tidal surge was forthcoming. The council sent out warnings for different areas to be evacuated, showing the situation to be very serious indeed.

Importantly, it meant I had to cancel Happy Feat for the very first time – with our first major event just days away. Having a dangerous cyclone on the doorstep still didn't stop phone calls from some of our dancers asking, "Why can't we still have Happy Feat?"

At home, we carried out every possible preparation and all that was left was to bunker down and wait it out. On Wednesday, the second of February, the wind grew stronger, and our concern grew for our family of Tawney Frogmouth owls. Together with their parents, the latest brood, two very cute fluffy babies, were having difficulty hanging onto their branch.

Later in the day, we decided to rescue the chicks. Geoff braved the unfavourable conditions, placed the ladder precariously under their branch, climbed up and gently placed the babies in a special wildlife cage. To minimise the stress on the parent owls, we placed the cage just inside the garage doorway and left the door open so they could see and hear each other. However, as conditions deteriorated, we had to place the babies in a safer part of the house, hoping that the parents would return safely after the cyclone.

During our preparations that afternoon I was packing the esky (so the fridges could stay closed) when a bottle fell from the top shelf and landed right on my toe! I saw stars and knew from the pain that my toe was broken. There wasn't much I could do in the middle of a cyclone, so I ignored it and got on with the cyclone prep.

Our power went out at about 8:00pm that night. We were left listening to the radio in the dark and glued to the laptop, watching the radar as the cyclone kept tracking closer and closer. We had set up our walk-in-robe in case we needed to hide in the safest place in the house.

At about 11:00pm, we decided that everyone would be safe sleeping in their own bedrooms, so we all headed to bed. At midnight, we checked the radar and radio reports to discover that the eye of Cyclone Yasi was going to cross the coast between Cardwell and Innisfail, some 200km away. We had escaped the worst of it.

Even so, we woke the next morning to an unfamiliar landscape. Looking out of the window, we discovered that we were surrounded by water; the trees were stripped bare, and the ground was littered with fallen trees and broken branches. It was surreal. There was total devastation everywhere. The wind was still gale force, but our home was standing. How lucky we were, and how fortunate to have only been on the edge of the cyclone.

"What on earth had happened to those towns further north?" we wondered.

Fortunately, we had a generator, so we had some power to keep up to date with the progress of the cyclone. It was still too windy to put the baby owls back outside and there was no sign of the parents. I must admit, I was a bit anxious about whether we'd done the right thing, but Plan B was that I knew some wonderful wildlife carers.

Later that afternoon Geoff grabbed the ladder again and tied the wildlife cage up to the same branch the owls had been raised on.

That way they were safe but could still call out to their parents. What a great idea!

At about 4:00am the next morning, I heard the adult owls. I shook Geoff awake, telling him it was important for the parents to feed their chicks before it got light as they would be very hungry. I had a little giggle as I watched him trek over to the shed - in the dark - to grab the ladder once again. Up he climbed and returned the bubbies to their branch. Mum already had food hanging from her beak ready to feed them. It was a wonderful ending to a very challenging couple of days.

Our clean-up had begun, and we raked up the leaves and debris from the house yard. It was amazing to see fallen branches not lying flat but impaled and sticking out of the ground. They would have been dangerous missiles during the cyclone. I can't remember how many wheelbarrow loads we carted away, and that was just the house yard. The real clean-up began the next day when Stacey and I attacked the area outside the yard while Geoff and Ashley went to check the office.

My toe was very swollen, bruised, and throbbed with pain. This meant I worked barefoot, as there was no chance of getting a shoe on. It wasn't until late Saturday afternoon that I remembered I had a concert coming up and had better do something about my toe! I joined the 'walking wounded' at the hospital, where x-rays showed I'd broken the toe in two places. Oops, how was I going to wear a shoe for the concert?

It was back to work on the Monday, even though we still didn't have power at home after five days. The most challenging part was sleeping in the sweltering heat with no fan and no air conditioning. But when I found myself thinking about how difficult it was, I would quickly remind myself how lucky we were to even have a house.

As the days rolled on, it became evident that people were suffering from what I called 'Post Yasi Stress.' It's hard to explain, but there was an atmosphere of disbelief and shock. People were very unsettled. Working at reception and answering the phones, I heard story after story of people's dramatic and stressful experiences and tried to reassure them that things would work out. With my nature, I wanted to help them all, so it was quite a challenging time.

By the Tuesday following the cyclone, as we still had no power at home, we were debating whether to stay overnight at my brother's place closer to town, just for the chance to get a decent night's sleep. We'd visited him for a family dinner and the thought of sleeping over in an air-conditioned room was very enticing. In the end, though, we decided to go home, only to discover that our power was back on. I surprised myself by my reaction; I couldn't stop laughing. I was so thrilled to have power again. I must have been delirious from lack of sleep.

Life had been slowly getting back to normal and missing a night of Happy Feat the previous week meant we only had one more Happy Feat night to practice before the concert at the Townsville Civic Theatre.

I was feeling the pressure of this bizarre situation. My broken toe was still throbbing and painful and the lack of sleep wasn't helping me think clearly. Spending my nights organising this event and not climbing into bed until 3:00am was creating more than fifty shades of charcoal under my eyes. For the first time, I struggled to hide the strain.

I emailed our Happy Feat team to update them about the concert and to let them know I needed their cooperation as it was a very stressful time for me, and I was feeling fragile. Quite a few of the families relied heavily on me for guidance, motivation, and counselling and I needed them to know I didn't have anything left in the tank; I was on survival mode myself.

The final weekly Happy Feat night was crazy busy and had a weird, undertone of excitement and anxiety. We decided to rehearse our dance 'What a Wonderful World' a couple of times during the night. As I danced with the new members, I again marvelled at how amazing these people were. With only limited preparation, they were actually doing the moves, trying their hearts out and having heaps of fun.

It was time to distribute our brand-new Happy Feat shirts and our members were thrilled to receive them. Most waited patiently for me to hand them out, but some got anxious as they feared missing out. One Happy Feater reacted by throwing a tantrum. I sat with her and explained that it wasn't a good choice of behaviour and was unacceptable.

As this was happening regularly, I explained that if the tantrums kept up, she wouldn't be allowed to come to Happy Feat for a couple of weeks. I also let her know how sad I would be if she missed out on all the fun. In part, I was concerned that others would see the bad behaviour and think it was an acceptable way to react.

When you're on top of things, you can handle anything. At this point, however, I was running on empty and just felt out of my depth with how to best deal with this situation. So, I rang one of the wonderful mums for some advice. We had an in-depth conversation about acceptable behaviour, during which she said "Leigh, you don't know what it's like to live with a child who has special needs or a disability."

It's a statement I've heard many times and each time, it brings up a range of emotions and can be quite frustrating for me. While I couldn't completely understand of course, I do in fact have a great deal of empathy and awareness of how it feels to want to protect your child, especially when they're in a vulnerable condition.

No parent knows what it's like for the next parent, and many of us will go through times where we have ongoing daily challenges with our children. Even so, I don't accept it as an excuse for not being the best I can be and ensuring that my child is being the best they can be.

I believe you should always take something positive out of a challenging situation and I've been fortunate to have learned many valuable lessons from Ashley's diagnosis and some of his challenging outbursts and behaviour resulting from his treatment. One of the treasures I've taken from this journey is a greater understanding of having a child with a degree of 'special needs.'

The fact that I have kept this private until now, makes it understandable for other mums to make assumptions about me and underestimate my capacity to comprehend some of their challenges. Going through the treatment, even in the darkest of times, we said how fortunate we were that hopefully, we'd only have to go through these trials for a quantifiable time, not a lifetime, whereas these families don't have that opportunity.

I learned many skills and had many character-building experiences resulting from the three and half years of Ashley's treatments. Three and a half years of being constantly on call, the late nights, constantly monitoring Ashley and his environment, tracking treatments and medication, coping with his frustration with his limitations and side effects from his medication, pushing myself to do things that my instinct was to run screaming from – like giving injections. These moments gave me what I needed to make Happy Feat the success it was. The surprise bonus must be specialising in the art of rapidly 'going to Plan B!' With Happy Feat, there's loads of quick thinking, needing to be flexible, and if you end up at Plan Z, you can always start at the beginning of the alphabet again.

Like during Ashley's treatment, when I thought my energy was at its lowest ebb before the concert, I found a source of strength inside of me to push through. We had a show to put on with a group of excited superstars-to-be!

CHAPTER 20

Another Star is Born... In Fact, Lots of Them!

Rehearsal day for the Premier's Queensland Disaster Appeal Concert had finally arrived. We all met at the theatre at 5:00pm and, as usual, the Happy Featers streamed in early as they were all incredibly eager and ready to get started.

Our team was fortunate to be allocated a huge brand-new air-conditioned dressing room where we could all wait in comfort. Initially we were to gather in the green room, but as this area can sometimes be a stressful place, I requested an alternative location. I wanted everyone to be excited but not anxious.

With experience now from performing in different locations, I've learned that our Happy Feat team has some very specific requirements. I will only approve performances if the parents or support workers can stay, if there is space for approximately forty dancers on stage, and if we can have somewhere to meet and wait as a group. This can mean room for 80 – 90 people, so it's not always easy!

We gathered for the rehearsal and the atmosphere in our room was electric! Everyone was in costume and raring to go, so I ran through with them what would be happening. I've found that the more information I can provide before a performance, the more settled the group is. I also explained that there would be quite a bit of waiting to do, but now that they were stars, this was what they had to do.

We gathered to rehearse our dance numbers, starting with our Happy Feat Chant. We usually have the words to follow, so we had fun pretending to turn the pages as we shouted the chant. A technical issue with the music didn't seem to perturb them as we carried on practicing the dance for 'What a Wonderful World'.

The backstage staff soon advised that time was approaching for us to go on stage. To keep in our places, we did another dance while we were waiting. Oops - we were told it would be another 15 minutes. I reminded our team again about being 'stars' and waiting!

After this quick chance to go to the bathroom or have a drink one last time, the stage staff once again advised us to prepare. We lined up ready to go. This time, we were to quietly move out of the hall into the dark, cavernous, and cluttered backstage. To keep everyone together, we had them hold hands as they went. It was so exciting!

We could hear the previous act singing so I lip-synced and clowned around to keep everyone from getting nervous. The dancers had fun telling me to behave, which kept us occupied until it was time to go.

As we went through the huge heavy stage door, one of the dancers objected to squeezing through the door which meant they could no longer hold hands. This caused quite a commotion when trying to line up on stage, as we were no longer in the correct order.

The teachers and I had deliberately put one of our dancers in the second row because she tended to get in the front row and look at everyone else instead of dancing. Well, this little reshuffle became her opportunity to slink into the front row, blatantly ignoring her instruction. We had spent considerable time and effort planning the positions of each dancer, so to us, this behaviour was unacceptable and would be dealt with later. Everyone else found their places, got into position, and were ready to impress.

The music began. Our Happy Featers danced beautifully, completing their first on-stage dress rehearsal with the utmost professionalism. I was so proud.

Moving offstage and returning to our room, the whole team was buzzing with excitement and there was much chatter. The mums and support workers had been allowed to sit in the theatre to watch, and they joined us teary eyed and enormously proud. Everyone was so thrilled with their performance, especially with the disrupted dance practice in the previous weeks thanks to the cyclone.

Happy Feat were also dancing in the finale, so we waited for our second stage call. To keep the energy up, we gathered to practice some more dances even though technical difficulties continued with our music.

The Happy Feater who had chosen to ignore the rules certainly knew she had done the wrong thing. As soon as she was called aside, her head went down, and she kept saying "Sorry!"

I explained that I was disappointed she'd chosen this sort of behaviour once again. We would have to think long and hard about what action was required, as it was happening repeatedly.

At 8:00pm, we were notified that we could go home and that we would be advised as to what would happen with the final curtain call.

Our other Happy Feat dancers had all conducted themselves so well through the long evening. No one complained about the waiting, they just enjoyed themselves and the new experience, just living in the moment.

The next day, the 11th of February 2011, was performance day. I was experiencing a whole range of feelings, so excited to think that it was not even eight months since our first night of Happy Feat - and here we were performing on-stage at the Townsville Civic Theatre. At the same time, I was also a little anxious about the unknowns. How would our Happy Featers react? Was everything done that needed to be done? Had I thought of everything? Happy Feat didn't come with an instruction manual!

In the morning, the first thing I had to do was make a call to the Happy Feat dancer who had chosen to disobey directions; the same member we'd had continuous behavioural issues with.

I really didn't want her to miss out on this experience, but it was hard to know what else to do. Even if I put her in the back row, I couldn't trust that she wouldn't just move to the front, making it difficult for the other dancers.

As with parenting, sometimes you must make tough calls. This was one of those moments. I spoke to this Happy Feater at length about how important it was to follow the rules. She certainly knew and understood. I asked her to imagine what Happy Feat would be like if all our dancers didn't do as they were asked. She understood it wouldn't be a very happy Happy Feat. There were consequences for disobeying, and because she kept choosing this behaviour, the decision had been made that she would not be performing at the Civic Theatre. We were both upset about her missing out, but a line had to be drawn.

At work that morning, we were shifting furniture at our display home, and I couldn't help feeling miserable. My nature is to care for everyone and here I was hurting someone's feelings. I felt shattered instead of looking forward to tonight's performance.

My spirits were revived later that day, however, when I rushed over to help one of my beautiful work associates. Karen had volunteered to do the girls' hair and makeup and had set up a mini salon for our dancers in the side of her shop: mirrors, brushes, hair products, the works! You name it, Karen had it!

I find people truly fascinating, and their hidden talents never cease to amaze me. I'd known Karen for some time and had no idea she was also a fully qualified hairdresser. Not only that, but she had also given up her Friday afternoon to make our Happy Feat dancers feel even more special for the concert. Seeing their faces was priceless as they looked in the mirror after their makeovers. It was great to see these wonderful individuals enjoy opportunities they wouldn't normally experience.

As expected, that night everyone arrived at the Civic Theatre early. While our original cohort of Happy Feat dancers were very excited, our new dancers were feeling a little nervous. This was perfectly understandable, as they'd only been dancing with Happy Feet for about three weeks and here they were, about to perform on stage in front of an audience!

I let them know that Happy Feat wasn't about getting all the dance moves perfect, it was about having fun and giving it a go. It didn't matter that they'd only been doing the dance for a few weeks, they were now part of Happy Feat and would be given the same experiences as the others.

It was our mission to keep the energy up and distract them from what was ahead, so we gathered for our Happy Feat Chant and a little practice doing what we love best: dancing! The excitement rose another ten levels when we lined up, joined hands, and prepared for our final call. Here it was – SHOWTIME!

Quietly weaving our way through the dark corridors of backstage was another new experience for the group. Once again, I acted the fool, keeping their spirits up as we made our way onto the stage.

After ensuring everyone was in their correct position, I hid behind one of our very tall dancers who was in the second back row. I wanted to make sure the back row could see and follow my dance moves, but as I looked around to check our dancers, I was astounded at their professional manner! They all stood so tall, proud, and still. It made my heart swell with pride. We hadn't even thought to tell them to stand like that.

Watching the huge dark curtain rise, everything seemed to move in slow motion - just like you see on TV. The music began, and they danced like they'd never danced before! Towards the end of the dance, I watched the faces of those new members, and saw the complete concentration as they put their heart and soul into it.

I felt myself losing it. I told myself, "Leigh, you can't start blubbering on stage in the middle of a dance. Pull yourself together!"

The auditorium was dark, and we couldn't see anything beyond the stage lights. Our world had been reduced to this one magical moment. One of our beautiful dancers, who is famous for swirling her skirt, was showing her style as the curtain came down on our first on-stage performance.

Looking around, I saw our amazing dance teacher, Rhi, turn towards me with tears streaming down her face. A quick glance over to our other volunteer and I saw that she too had tears tumbling down. Well, that was the end of me too. We were a fine bunch, all crying with pride and joy.

We led our team back to our dressing room. The noise of their excitement threatened to lift the roof! There were loads of hugs, slaps on the back, and high fives. We did it all! After about 15 minutes, I was jolted back to reality when I remembered that I had to take a handful of dancers out to the foyer to join their parents in the audience.

As I led the group down the backstage corridor, I was stopped by a young lad walking towards me. He smiled and said, "Your Happy Feat group is an absolute inspiration."

I stopped in my tracks. I thought perhaps I hadn't heard correctly. I apologised and asked him to repeat himself. Sure enough, that's exactly what he said. I was floored but quickly remembered to thank him. Wow, I certainly hadn't expected that!

Getting to the foyer meant sneaking through the green room. I quietly opened the door, not wanting to disturb anyone and we proceeded to tiptoe through. When they saw us, however, a loud cheer went up! Everyone exclaimed how much they enjoyed our performance. Double wow! I couldn't believe the reaction we were getting but the dancers who were with me loved every minute of it. Reaching the parents in the foyer, we were again met by cheers as they said how wonderful it was. One of the parents mentioned a standing ovation and I giggled. But when it was mentioned again, I looked at her questioningly.

She said, "Happy Feat got a standing ovation. Didn't you see it?"

I looked at the other parents for verification. They were all nodding their heads, saying that Happy Feat certainly received a standing ovation. The impact of this news literally dropped me to my knees. I broke down crying with joy. I believed with all my heart that my Happy Feat team was talented and amazing - and now everyone was finally realising it too. Words cannot describe that moment.

I couldn't wait to get back and share the news. It was priceless to watch their faces as they received the recognition and adulation for all their hard work. For the majority, this was probably the first time in their lives! It turned out that of the thirty-two acts performing at the concert that night, Happy Feat were the only ones to receive a standing ovation.

Whether we were ready or not, Happy Feat was out there, and people loved it. We'd come so far already. From being unsure how starting a dance troupe for people with disabilities in Townsville would go, the trials to get started, and learning on our feet literally - to our beautiful Graduation Ball, now dancing on stage in front of a packed theatre and receiving a standing ovation - you just had to wonder where on earth could Happy Feat go from there. What new opportunities, experiences and life lessons did the future have in store for us now?

CHAPTER 21

Million Dollar Memo

After all the late nights and stress of both the concert and the cyclone, it was time to recharge our batteries. My brother, hubby, and I were able to escape for a well-earnt holiday, arriving back in Townsville the following Tuesday afternoon. At dance practice the next night, I felt refreshed and ready to go again. Little did I know I would need every ounce of energy for this next evolution of Happy Feat, and the mind-blowing opportunities that would come our way.

It began with an innocent remark during dance practice. One of my Happy Featers asked where I had been on holidays. I told her, but it wasn't until the next dance that she said, "Leigh, next time you go, I'd love to come with you!"

I stopped dancing and looked at her beautiful innocent face thinking, "If I won the Lotto, I'd love to take the lot of you!"

The next morning, as Geoff and I still had a couple of days of leave left, we happened to have the television on, catching up on news. Well, it was a case of being in the right place at the right time!

Queensland Tourism was launching their promotion called 'Million Dollar Memo' where they were inviting companies from all over the world to submit a video with the possibility of winning $1 million dollars' worth of holidays. The videos would be on the Queensland Tourism website and would be voted on by viewers from all over the world. My ears pricked at the prize, thinking of my wistful Happy Feater and the rest of the team.

I desperately tried to put it out of my mind as I'd only just got back from holidays. One part of me was saying, "Just have a few easy, uneventful weeks." The other side was saying "Wow! There are so many possibilities for our group. Imagine being able to give them another opportunity they've never had in their lives."

Several days passed and I could feel an idea brewing for the Million Dollar Memo. Having several hours of mowing to do on our property, I armed myself with a notebook, pen, my mobile phone and the house phone and set off for the shed.

I had texted one of the volunteers: "I have an amazing idea that's even bigger than the Graduation. Text me when you finish work."

Before setting off for the mowing, I researched the Million Dollar Memo promotion. Companies and organisations were invited to produce a 60 second video showing why you enjoy working with your company or organisation, and why Queensland is the ultimate holiday destination. When I first heard of the promotion, I thought it was only for businesses, but my excitement grew when I read the following paragraph:

'Companies must meet the following eligibility criteria. For the purposes of the competition, a 'company' is defined broadly to include any organisation, company, business, or workplace.'

But what sealed the idea was reading the following words:

'Whether it's awe-inspiring adventure, relaxation on tropical islands and beaches, up-close encounters with some of the great wonders of the natural world or simple enjoyment of the laid-back Queensland lifestyle, we'll tailor the experiences to suit the wishes of the winning company.'

When you're dealing with special needs and disabilities, you certainly need to 'tailor' everything, so these words were very enticing. The fact that the prize didn't have compulsory bungee jumping or trekking up some mountain meant that our special needs could be catered for.

My wonderful hubby was working in the shed and watched curiously as I approached. He grinned and said, "All I'm going to ask is why you are taking the house phone on the mower as well as everything else?"

"I'm waiting for one of our volunteers to text when she finishes work," I said. "Then I want to discuss something that might take a while."

He smiled and shook his head. I think he realised some significant idea was brewing and was scared to ask! Despite the fact he thought it was too wet to mow and that I'd probably get bogged, he saw that I was on a mission and mowing was where great ideas transpired!

Several hours passed and a plan of attack gradually formed as I transformed our overgrown yard. Oops, I got carried away with my thoughts – and the front wheel of the mower caught on a very soft ant hill. I wasn't bogged, it was just that the wheel kept slipping!

I frantically tried to keep the mower going, but the wheel slipped even more. Not bogged, just slipping! Not one for admitting defeat, I desperately tried to lift the front of the heavy ride-on-mower without success. After exhausting all ideas as well as my energy, the expected text finally came through.

"Oh no, what are you up to now!" was the question she asked.

I excitedly told her about the Million Dollar Memo promotion. But how was I going to organise it? I had no idea - but would 'Just Do It', as always, and find a way.

I would need help – as I needed help with the situation I was in at the time. I dreaded admitting to Geoff that I needed his assistance with the mower. Oh well, I would get out of it somehow. I sheepishly walked into the shed.

"It's like this: it's not bogged; the wheel is just slipping a bit!"

He grinned and shook his head. "You're a dag, hon!"

I linked my arm through his as we walked back to the mower and said, "Let's skip, it's really fun to skip!"

Once again, he grinned and shook his head. "Yep, you're a dag!"

It didn't take long to get me back mowing again with a new plan soon developing in my mind. I didn't want to do a dodgy job of the filming. I wanted to make sure my team was shown the respect they truly deserved. This meant I'd somehow have to get a professional videographer to do the job properly.

Time was ticking. Other companies had already submitted their entries and voting had already started. I decided that I would rather forgo votes in the short-term, to have a professional and high-quality submission which would hopefully attract more votes later. Parking the mower, I picked up the mobile and organised a meeting with a videography team for 8:00am the next day.

I drove into town the next morning with no idea where the meeting – and in fact, where the whole Million Dollar Memo adventure – would take Happy Feat. I just knew it was going to be exciting for everyone.

As a wildlife carer for many years, my strategy for Happy Feat was like looking after and raising a young bird. Initially it needs intensive and delicate nurturing as you work out what works best for the fledgling. Then, as it became stronger and more confident, it gradually spreads its wings to taste what it's like to fly.

For Happy Feat, they brought down the house with at their performance at the Premier's Queensland Disaster Appeal Concert in front of several hundred people. They were ready to fly. The Million Dollar Memo was the next step, but it was a HUGE ONE - an opportunity for them to perform in front of people all over the world, and just eight months after our very first Happy Feat gathering!

At the end of 2010, I had spoken to several families to let them know I felt ready to formally launch Happy Feat in 2011, wanting to make sure they were also ready for it. Now that our Happy Feat members were stronger and more experienced, I was going to hold them up in the palm of my hand and if they were ready, let them fly out into the big wide world.

The families' reaction was, "Bring it on! We've waited our whole lives for something like this."

With that in mind, I sat at the table with the videographers Blake and Peter, enjoying watching them get caught up in my excitement and passion for Happy Feat and this new project. I grinned and felt proud as Blake tried to explain to Peter what Happy Feat was like.

"It's the most amazing experience, and you just can't stop smiling. In fact, I don't know how to put this properly but when you watch Leigh and the group having so much fun, it's hard to tell she's not one of them!"

As the meeting progressed, we all got caught up in this adventure's potential. We loved Peter's suggestion of using the song, 'Walking on Sunshine' as our theme song. Ideas were coming thick and fast, and it was soon decided that filming would begin on Wednesday – only two days away!

After the meeting, I ran to my car (in the rain), making calls while I headed back to work. How was I going to organise 30 dancers to be at The Strand at 8:00am on Wednesday ready to start filming? There was so much to organise!

The dancers needed to be contacted individually; a bus organised to take us to the different locations for filming; permission from the various organisations our dancers worked for; carers to accompany us; and Blake and Peter had said something about organising a Lollipop Lady to be in the filming! By lunchtime, Stacey saw how busy I was and offered to cover reception so I could get everything organised from home. What a lifesaver...and a wonderful, thoughtful daughter!

But just when everything was coming together nicely, I had a text message come through that afternoon: a severe weather warning for Tuesday and possibly Wednesday!

For a moment, I thought, "Why can't anything just be easy?"

Thinking on my feet, I immediately cancelled the pity party - and went to Plan B! After a quick call to Blake, our plan of attack was to wait until the 5:00am report the next morning and then make the call.

There wasn't much sleep to be had that night. I was probably the first person to view the 5:00am report which was still advising a severe weather warning for Tuesday and possibly extending to Wednesday. Not convinced, I rang the Bureau of Meteorology only to be told that Wednesday was looking the same. It just wasn't meant to be - we would have to postpone filming for another day. Time was ticking, the other entries were gaining votes, and ours hadn't even started!

Beginning a new ring-around, tentative arrangements were quickly made to do the filming the following Wednesday, a whole week away! We had Happy Feat as usual that week and it was quite a weird night. I don't know if it was because our dancers had been excited to do the filming that day and to have it postponed felt like an anticlimax. Either way, it was an unusual night of Happy Feat.

You would think getting 30+ dancers with special needs organised for something like this would be challenging, but it wasn't nearly as challenging as getting a Lollipop Lady for our filming! It meant numerous phone calls and emails back and forth to Department of Transport and Main Roads, trying to cut through all the red tape. They were keen to help us, but it took so much organising! They wanted to know what we had in mind for the filming, and I had no idea! We just had to make sure we didn't depict a road crossing in an unsafe manner. I assured them I wouldn't dream of putting my teams' safety at risk by letting them on the road. In the end, they gave me a Lollipop Lady's mobile number. I was to ring and let her know when and where we wanted her to meet us.

Days went by, and still it rained. I checked the forecast constantly and crossed my fingers that Wednesday would be sunny. Disappointingly, Monday afternoon's prediction was 'rain and showers for Wednesday'.

After a week of anxiety, I'd had enough. I needed to get all the tension out of my system and chose to power walk along Townsville's The Strand. Hopefully I could come up with an alternative arrangement if it was raining on Wednesday.

I finished work right on 5:00pm and headed off in the rain. On the drive to the ocean, I rang Blake and said, "You know what, we're going ahead with the filming whether it's raining or not."

While we were speaking, I saw the most spectacular rainbow across the sky.

"Blake, everything is going to be OK in the morning, I've just seen an amazing rainbow and that's my sign to say it will all be OK."

Arriving at The Strand that afternoon, I changed into my daggy walking shoes, put my headphones on, and off I went at a cracking pace. The first song to play on the radio was an introduction to Alicia Keys' song, 'Everything is gonna be alright.'

I couldn't believe my ears. It was as though she was singing directly to me. I instantly had a feeling of peace and calm and set about keeping an eye out for different ideas for our filming.

I soon came across the C Bar, a beautiful little café with a deck directly overlooking the ocean. A covered deck! Bingo! Perhaps we could film there. At least we'd stay dry.

With no hesitation I approached the waiter and told him of my plan, mentioning that we were doing a promotion for Queensland Tourism to get his attention. He enthusiastically gave me the manager's contact details and said to give him a ring. Within minutes, I was pitching my idea to the manager who was keen to help us out - not only with the filming, but in the future as well. He told me to email him my plans and said he would get back to me with the details.

That night we were to have dinner with my family, so I couldn't email him until I got home much later. I tried not to look at my watch during dinner. Family time is extremely important to me, but time was ticking, and I needed to email him as soon as possible. At 9:00pm, I hugged everyone, said good night, and zoomed home to prepare and send the email. By 10:30pm, I still hadn't had a reply, so I logged off for the night.

Being an early riser, I checked my emails at an ungodly hour of the morning. Sure enough, there was a reply from the manager of the C Bar.

Still half asleep, I misread the first line as, "I am more than willing to support your organisation but not on this occasion." As I kept reading, I thought, "Hang on, it sounds like he's keen to help us with the filming!"

Re-reading the line, I realised it said, "I am more than willing to support your organisation, and not just on this occasion."

The email went on to say that we could have 60% of the C Bar decking (which meant he was willing to forgo clientele for Happy Feat). I had to giggle when I read, "However, I do ask that you respect the business as a commercial entity and please consider those patrons who may not be as excited or as passionate as you are about your activities on the day."

Mmm, maybe I was a little too enthusiastic about Happy Feat, but that's just the way I am!

It looked like we had Plan F in case it was raining on Wednesday! I quickly set about emailing and contacting everyone with yet another change of plans. Over the weeks, I was regularly blown away by the support I was given. Everyone I spoke to seemed to get caught up in the excitement and wanted to do everything they could to help. Sometimes it felt quite surreal.

That Wednesday morning, I woke at 2:30am and was too excited to get back to sleep. After getting up and doing some computer work, I went back to bed at about 4:00am hoping to get a little more sleep... wrong! My mind was racing with thoughts of what the day would bring. My priority was for everyone to really enjoy themselves without any stress. By 5:00am, Geoff whispered, "Are you a bit excited? Do you want to see all the stars?"

"Stars? What stars?" I thought. "Oh! That means it must be a clear sky!"

As we lay snuggling, we looked out the window to the most beautiful view I'd seen in a long time. The sky was clear and twinkled with thousands of brilliant stars. What an amazing sight. If I wasn't excited before, I was well and truly excited now.

"Let's get up and have our morning cuppa while watching the sun rise!"

That was something we hadn't been able to do for many weeks and yes, it was a beautiful morning for our filming. The rainbow and the Alicia Keys were right.

I couldn't wait to get to The Strand to catch up with everyone. It was the most beautiful weather, a stunning North Queensland day. We all met just outside the C Bar, where the team had already moved tables and chairs from the deck.

Usually when you are filming, there are run sheets, scripts, and a plan at the very least, and we had none of that! It was all going to be capturing spur of the moment material. We didn't even know where we wanted to film but had a bus on standby ready to take us wherever we needed to go. After some discussion, Blake and Peter decided to start the filming with everyone down on the beach just beside the C Bar.

Excited, we quickly gathered on the sand, cranked up the music and began our warm-up dance. What better place to dance than on a beach overlooking spectacular Magnetic Island, with the ocean glistening in the sunshine? It was unbelievable. After so many anxious weeks waiting for good weather, it was finally happening!

Then we gathered in the little outdoor Amphitheatre, deciding to film the boys dancing on stage, with the girls cheering and having a good time. The view to the stage was amazing. Not only could you see huge tropical palm trees, but also Castle Hill in the background - a perfect way to highlight key elements of our stunning piece of paradise.

The boys had their moment in the spotlight, and now it was the girls' turn. They were filmed dancing along the footpath along The Strand, while I held the beat box on my shoulder with the music pumping. The song 'Walking on Sunshine' got us all rocking!

I felt so much adrenaline pumping through my body that when the filming was complete, I lay flat out on the grass. This had the

Happy Featers in fits of laughter, drawing in people stopping to share the fun and happiness.

For the next part of the adventure, we jumped in the bus, making our way to the top of Castle Hill. We discovered that one of the mums was terrified of heights and had never been to the top of Castle Hill in all the years she'd lived in Townsville. Sitting beside her, I talked with her all the way, trying to take her mind off the view outside. I'm not sure it worked but it was worth a try.

There is an impressive lookout at the very top of Castle Hill where there's a huge deck overlooking the ocean and Magnetic Island. Our Happy Feat team gathered and danced on the lookout with this magnificent backdrop. Not one of them mentioned a fear of heights; when the music and cameras started, nothing else mattered. They were true professionals.

Blake and Peter were absolutely enthralled, caught up in the fun and magic of Happy Feat. By midday, they had captured so much great footage they said they had everything they needed. As they say in the film world, "That's a wrap!" Everyone was having so much fun that nobody wanted it to end. After the long wait for a clear sky, we'd had an amazing morning and certainly another memorable experience for the whole group.

But there was loads more excitement to come! Though I may have sacrificed some early votes in my commitment to making a quality video of Happy Feat, I believe that everything happens for a reason. Taking care to create a professional production with our team of filmmakers, led to an undreamed-of opportunity and a connection that lead to adventures none of us could have imagined.

Chapter 22

New Legends at the Cowboys Stadium

During my first meeting with Blake and Peter about the Million Dollar Memo promotion, Peter had enthusiastically recommended that Happy Feat should make contact the North Queensland Cowboys team, our national rugby league champions. True to his word, he organised for one of their members to contact me.

At work a short time later, I received a call from Lisa, a representative of the Cowboys. She invited me to do a brief interview in centre stadium at the next Cowboys' home game which would show our Million Dollar Memo video on the big screens all around the stadium! After thanking her for this amazing chance to promote our film, I explained that as Happy Feat was about our dancers, it would be fantastic to have them with me during the interview. The crowd would absolutely love our Happy Feat team! They wouldn't need a mascot to excite the crowd, our Happy Feat dancers would do that naturally.

"Gee, that sounds so good!" was Lisa's response.

Being quick to promote the idea, I said, "That's because it would be awesome!"

"Let me make a few calls and see what I can organise," she said. "How many people did you want to have with you?"

"Well, there are about 35 dancers in our group, so it would be fantastic to have them all" I said, not missing a beat.

I heard a sharp intake of breath. I could imagine the complexity of trying to organise and get security clearance for 35 extra people onto the stadium, never mind the requirements for our people with special needs and varying disabilities. It was a big call, but I would do anything for our group.

"So that we can keep them safe, it would also be great to have their carers with them in case any situations arise." I knew this was brazen of me, but our Happy Feat team consists of both our dancers and their carers. This makes it very tricky when we are asked to perform anywhere as we are dealing with so many people - but that's Happy Feat.

If Lisa wasn't worried about organising an extra 35 people, she certainly was about organising an extra 80! The entry tickets weren't the issue, it was organising security to 'The Tunnel', as well as planning the security to enter centre stadium. This was well and truly a big call. But like I said – that's Happy Feat.

The next day, I received the call saying that we could have whatever we'd like. Lisa would have eighty security tickets available the following day and arranged a time to meet and run through arrangements.

Wow, how fantastic was that?! Ask and you shall receive...well, sometimes!

During my meeting with Lisa at the Cowboys, it didn't take long for her to get caught up in my enthusiasm and passion for Happy Feat! We ran through the procedure, made the necessary arrangements, and I met others from the Cowboys.

Becoming quite serious, I said to them, "I have a very important question."

They all looked concerned and leaned in as I asked the question, "Have you voted for Happy Feat in the Million Dollar Memo promotion yet?"

They all laughed and to my surprise, they had already voted that morning.

Geoff and Ashley had gone to Cairns to look at a second-hand motorbike that weekend, so it was my first weekend home alone. Usually if I have that opportunity, I quickly organise for my 'forever friends' Joy and Katie to come over for a girly weekend. Being so busy with the Cowboys and the Million Dollar Memo arrangements, I was happy to have some recharge time-out at home. Most of Saturday was spent on the phone and computer until the most bizarre thing happened.

I heard a low rumble and thought, "What the heck is coming down our dirt road?"

As the noise grew louder, I got up and looked out our lounge window. Nothing looked out of the ordinary, but what was that noise?

Suddenly, every piece of glassware in our wall unit rattled and shook.

"Oh, my goodness, we've just had an earthquake!" I went outside in a daze to see if I could work out what was going on. I don't know why, but I looked at my watch and saw it was 3:33pm. I decided I must be imagining things; I really needed to get more sleep and wouldn't tell anyone about this weird experience!

Still feeling foggy, I wandered back inside. My mobile rang.

"Mum, did you just feel that?" Stacey asked in disbelief.

"Oh, my goodness, we have had an earthquake!" I said, snapping back to reality. "I thought I must have imagined it! Did you hear the noise?"

I was going to ring the Bureau of Meteorology, but Stace was ten steps ahead. She rang the Cairns Bureau thinking the Townsville office would be busy and quickly rang back to say we'd had a 5.2 magnitude earthquake near Bowen, 200kms away. It wasn't long before I started to get heaps of text messages. Everyone was in shock.

I had to pull myself together. It was only a couple of hours until the Cowboys event and I needed to be 'on my game' (pardon the pun!).

Imagine thirty five very excited Happy Feat dancers plus fifty just-as-excited parents and volunteers, all waiting to get their special Cowboys security bands on! The anticipation, excitement and eagerness were radiating through the group as we were led through security and into The Tunnel. Even though I wasn't a huge footy follower, I'd heard about the famous 'tunnel', and to think – here we were with our whole Happy Feat team!

That tunnel was bursting with so much joy and happiness that everyone around got caught up in the excitement. We had the Young Guns (junior Cowboys in the making) giving our Happy Feat team high fives, and one member even joined them in the change room! All the mascots joined us for countless photos with our team, and huge cheers erupted as the Cowboys came through.

Lisa, the wonderful lady in charge of arrangements, said she'd never had so much fun or ever felt that much joy in the tunnel before! We could have gone home after the tunnel experience and still had an awesome night. But wait, there's more!

When it was time for our dancers to go out on the field, I asked Lisa if it was OK for the parents to peek out from the tunnel entrance so they could see. Lisa was so caught up in all the Happy Feat hype that she exclaimed, "Heck no, let them go out onto the field as well!" Luckily, I'd printed and laminated eighty sheets with "Vote Happy Feat", so we all had a banner to wave.

I get a bit choked up just thinking about how I felt, leading my incredible team out into the middle of the Cowboys stadium. It hadn't even been 12 months since we had our first night of Happy Feat, and here we were in front of over 20,000 people.

Minty, a local radio star and announcer at the Cowboys, asked the questions. Earlier he'd joined us in the tunnel to meet our team and shared that he was the biggest fan of Happy Feat and that he'd loved our video. He was so genuine and passionate about it that I was quite surprised, coming from someone I'd never met before.

Our team gathered and waved their signs while Minty interviewed me about our group. Then onto the big screens beamed our Million Dollar Memo entry around the stadium. If I didn't get choked up before, I certainly was now. Watching our dancers' faces as they saw themselves on the big screen...what can I say? We already had our million dollars' worth. Then we heard the crowd roar when the video finished – there was another million dollars!

The interview went well, and I radiated the passion and excitement that comes naturally when talking or even thinking about our group. The crowd cheered as we walked back into the tunnel. The joy and excitement threatened to shake the cement walls!

I discovered a week later that one of the dancers was so excited about shaking hands with her heroes that she didn't want to wash her hand!

Our Happy Feat entry for the Million Dollar Memo gathered over 5000 votes in record time and even though it didn't win, it gave our Happy Feat team such a multitude of phenomenal experiences to cherish for the rest of their lives...and that's priceless.

Our Million Dollar Memo adventure started an ongoing relationship with the Cowboys which meant our Happy Featers had the privilege of being associated with their heroes on several occasions.

For instance, Happy Feat were invited to join the Cowboys for their annual Christmas party at the Billabong Sanctuary, a local wildlife park. I boldly asked if it would be possible for Happy Feat to do a dance or two. Most of our team are very passionate Cowboys fans, and you should have heard the Happy Feat gang cheer and yell when I shared the news with them. Some started counting the sleeps immediately!

The venue was a half hour outside Townsville, a bus was organised to take those members who had trouble with transport. When the big day finally arrived, everyone was as excited as you could get.

The noise level was tremendous! The dancers eagerly posed for photos with the Cowboys - and some of our Happy Feat girls even quizzed the Cowboys to find out if they were married or had girlfriends! They were certainly not the shy butterflies they used to be.

We made our way around the wildlife park looking at the cassowaries, crocodiles, and dingoes. Some of our team hadn't been to Billabong Sanctuary before, so to be there with the Cowboys was a double treat.

It was an extremely hot and humid December day in the tropics. I was busy making sure they all had hats, sunscreen, and plenty to drink. Getting a visible check on everyone, I noticed that Ally (one of our biggest Cowboys fans) looked flushed, and when I asked her if she was OK, I found myself grabbing her before she collapsed to the ground.

It's amazing how things appear when you need them. In an instant and out of nowhere appeared an umbrella, water bottle, and face cloth to cool Ally down and get her rehydrated.

I looked up to see several Cowboys players gathered around, looking very concerned. When it was time to take Ally back to the restaurant, I decided to commandeer the help of some burly Cowboys. Well, you should have seen her face as her biggest idols came to her rescue. I joked that she was the only girl who had been rescued by the Cowboys that day!

After lunch, it was time for Happy Feat to perform a few dances, and we surprised everyone with a Happy Feat rendition of the Cowboys' theme song. The boys were singing along, and you should have seen our dancers' faces when several Cowboys players even joined in the dance!

The following year, our Happy Featers had the privilege of dancing at the North Queensland Toyota Cowboys' home game, wowing the whole crowd once again. How many people get the opportunity to be centre stadium at their football team's home game, let alone perform there, doing what they love?

As our Happy Featers walked onto the field, they were thrilled to pass the Young Guns, who had just finished a game. There were handshakes all round and pats on the backs – they were having a great time! The fact that our Happy Featers were only scheduled to perform from 6:58 to 7:01pm just wasn't important to them.

Lining up in our places, one dancer, Josephine, was set with the wheelchair close by, just in case, and the others were beaming with excitement as they waved to the crowd, savouring the moment. When I checked on one of our newer members to see how he was coping, he said he was a little nervous. I replied, "At Happy Feat we don't get nervous, we get excited!"

He then grinned and said, "I'm perfect and getting better every day!"

How priceless is that?! One of the biggest thrills for me on the Happy Feat adventure has been seeing our members gain confidence and become proud of who they are, sometimes for the first time in their lives.

The music began and so did the magic of Happy Feat. Our team danced their hearts out, having their own little party doing what they love best: dancing and performing. All too soon our time was up, and as the Happy Featers left the field, they waved, twirled, and encouraged the crowd.

It was another wonderful and memorable experience for our Happy Featers to cherish. The team at North Queensland Toyota Cowboys have been extremely generous in the time and opportunities they've extended to our Happy Featers. We received wonderful feedback, not only from the staff, but also social media comments from the crowd raving about the performance. One cheeky fan commented, "They were amazing. Please thank them all on behalf of all the Cowboys for a fantastic performance." Fiona Pelling - Community Relations Manager, North Qld Toyota Cowboys.

CHAPTER 23

Meeting The Wiggles

A lot of folks have goals they'd like to achieve one day, a 'Bucket List'. I prefer to put things on my 'To-Do' list. For me, goals seem more like dreams - but if something gets added to my To-Do list, it is going to get done. Like getting a helicopter to take our son to his Graduation dance. Like creating a dance troupe for people with disabilities when I had less than zero dancing skills. You do your best and make it happen, even if sometimes it takes Plans B – Z.

One item on that list was arranging for one of our younger dancers to meet her favourite group, The Wiggles. The very first time I spoke to Pauline, Hannah's amazing mum, she told me what an avid Wiggles fan Hannah was, and how she'd been dancing to their music since she was about four years old. When I heard this, I immediately decided that if The Wiggles ever came to Townsville, Hannah would have to meet them. It went straight onto the 'To-Do list'!

Fourteen months later, I happened to be reading the local paper when an advert for an upcoming Wiggles Concert grabbed my attention. Immediately, I started researching how I could contact The Wiggles, and quickly sent off an email.

The next day, I received a call from Sue from The Wiggles asking how many people I'd like to take along to meet the famous group. When I informed her that I had over thirty Happy Feat members, she burst out laughing. I couldn't possibly take that many. Plan B! I said I'd be very grateful for any members I could take along, and she generously gave me ten tickets. A dilemma. How do I only choose only ten out of thirty? Whatever the answer, I knew this was too rare an opportunity to pass up.

Giving it some thought, I realised that there were only about five younger members who'd really be interested, which left me with another five tickets I wasn't going to pass up. I mulled it over for several days, confident I would come up with a new plan.

When I rang Pauline with the exciting news, I felt like Father Christmas! At first, she couldn't believe it, but when it started to sink in that I wasn't kidding, she was ecstatic. She decided that as the concert was still months away, she would buy their tickets to the concert but not mention anything to Hannah about meeting The Wiggles until it was closer to the time. It must have been very difficult to keep it a secret from Hannah. These incredible parents deal with so many challenges every day, keeping their sense of humour and positive attitude.

The next Happy Feat member I'd chosen to meet The Wiggles was Sophie. Her mum Wendy was over the moon at the news as Sophie was also a keen Wiggles fan and had her iPod full of their music. I continued ringing the younger members of Happy Feat but what was I going to do with the remaining tickets?

Two days later, huffing and puffing my way up a Castle Hill track, it came to me like the light bulb you see in cartoons. I would get in contact with friends from the children's oncology ward and invite some of their patients.

When Ashley was going through his treatment, I always tried to have something for him to look forward to encouraging him through the horrific periods. With something nice in mind, he would keep fighting and not give up. When I rang the ward the next day, I explained I had five tickets available to meet The Wiggles and could they let me know which kids would like to come along? The girls in oncology were all super excited and couldn't wait to tell the families!

I contacted Sue to let her know that I was taking five young Happy Feat members as well as five children from the oncology ward.

It wasn't long before I heard back from the oncology ward with the question, 'Are they able to bring their siblings?' This question tugged at my heartstrings as I know this is one of the hardest things the parents of a sick child must endure: worrying about their other children, making sure they're okay, and not missing out.

I contacted Sue at The Wiggles again, explained that I knew how hard it was for the siblings of a child going through treatment and wouldn't it be fantastic if they could also feel special for a change. And wouldn't it also be great if the parents could be there to share the excitement and take photos! I could picture Sue throwing her hands in the air as she replied, "Just let me know how many tickets you need!"

A couple of weeks down the track, I had another light bulb moment. Why don't I contact Peter, the wonderful guy who filmed and produced our Million Dollar Memo entry? I could see if he'd like to bring his children along and capture The Wiggles meeting on film! I excitedly rang to ask him, and once again he jumped at the opportunity to be involved with Happy Feat.

It wasn't long before I received the list of kids, mums and dads who were attending from the hospital, and when I added them to my Happy Feat team, there were rather more than the original ten tickets I had received. I now had forty-two meeting The Wiggles! This was going to take some sweet-talking, but I was on a mission.

When I contacted The Wiggles, there was a voice message to say that Sue no longer worked in that department, instead Christine would be looking after it. Oops, this was going to make things a bit more challenging! Speaking with Christine, I explained the situation and sent her my previous emails, casually letting her know the number of people attending. The response was not over-enthusiastic but once again, if it's on my To-Do list, that's not going to stop me.

Hannah's mum made me laugh as usual as she shared 'Hannah's moments.' After Hannah heard the exciting news, she'd been coming into her mum's bedside at 5:30am each morning and physically opening Pauline's eyes so they could go and mark the remaining sleeps off the calendar. Hannah even got in trouble one morning because she'd marked off an extra week of sleeps, so she wouldn't have as long to wait!

Another precious moment was when Hannah worked out the DVD player all by herself and could now watch the 'extras' on The Wiggles DVD. She proudly gathered her family to show them footage of The Wiggles meeting their fans and excitedly said, 'Me!' How clever is that?!

Finally, there was just one more sleep 'til the big day and I needed to check my action plan for the event. Our special nametags were prepared; attendance list printed; the emails to and from The Wiggles printed; Peter was coming along to film; my brother, Bruce, was coming to take photographs; everybody had the final details; I'd notified the local TV news stations, and text messages and phone call had been made to get everyone excited. When the big day arrived, I woke up excited for the kids and families who were to meet The Wiggles. I knew how much it meant for Hannah and Sophie, and I couldn't wait to see their beautiful faces as they got to meet their idols.

Getting ready that morning, I had another light bulb moment and wondered if The Wiggles could say a hello to one of the young girls who was too sick to attend the concert and had to return to hospital in Brisbane. Nicola was a huge Wiggles fan and had her whole room decked out with Wiggles stuff. I really felt for her and her family. I remembered the many times when special events had been planned but Ashley was too sick to attend. I rang one of the girls from the hospital. I wanted to check on Nicola to see if she was all right and run my idea about getting The Wiggles to say hello by her parents. Yes, the idea was a goer!

Bruce and I were there to greet the families as they arrived, and I was glad to have the nametags. When an official gave me fourteen security bands to meet The Wiggles, I quickly told her I had approval for forty-two of my group to meet with them. Luckily, I had printed the emails and gave her a copy.

Time was moving on. People were arriving early for the concert, and we still hadn't met The Wiggles! Apparently, they were running behind. Eventually we were ushered into a small room where we waited to meet them. We were told that each family could only have one photo and they wouldn't have time to sign autographs. That was a bit disappointing, but we were grateful to have had such an amazing opportunity.

The look on Sophie and Hannah's faces as The Wiggles entered the room was priceless! They lit up and their hands began to shake excitedly. The Wiggles gathered behind some seats and began speaking with everyone seated. I quickly zoned in on Hannah to make sure she didn't miss out. Oh no, I could see her getting overwhelmed with it all and silently prayed that she wouldn't lose this chance.

Just as suddenly, I could see her expression change as she regained her composure, moving over to the chairs.

"Thank you," I whispered as she moved forward. I told The Wiggles that Hannah was probably their biggest fan and they all gathered around Hannah, cameras clicking away. I wished the clock would stop so Hannah could have had more time with them. It is fantastic to have the photos and video to remember it by.

I told The Wiggles that Nicola was also a huge fan but had been too ill to attend and asked if they would say hello into Peter's camera. The Blue Wiggle, Anthony, said that he hoped Nicola was feeling better soon, then said they'd try to 'Wake up Jeff' for her.

Everyone in the room chorused, "Wake up Jeff!" and so we had an extra precious moment. My heart ached for Nicola and her family with what they were going through and hoped this moment would bring some joy to them when they got the chance to watch it.

I made sure every family got to speak and have a photo with The Wiggles, but as they were leaving, I noticed that one family hadn't been up. The mum said that it was OK, but I stopped The Wiggles and asked if they could get a photo with this family, knowing how busy they were that day. All too soon the families went off to the concert and I drove home with a super-sized smile, knowing how much that meeting meant to everyone.

Hoping to send The Wiggles video to Nicola, I contacted the hospital. I thought it would provide a ray of sunshine but was told it was a very grave situation. It wasn't a good time to get in touch.

Sadly, some months later, I learned that little Nicola had lost her battle and felt devastated for her parents and family. Should I try to contact them, or would this just add to their grief? After some time, I received this email from Nicola's father out of the blue:

> 'Hi, just over a year ago The Wiggles came to Townsville and we were in fact due to meet with them with our beautiful daughter 'Princess Nicola' but we rather unexpectedly ended up with a diagnosis of cancer for her, were rushed to Brisbane to begin treatment, and we didn't get to see them. I heard a rumour on the grape vine after we got back from Brisbane that The Wiggles had in fact recorded a video for her while they were here, and that it was Happy Feat that had recorded the video. It's been a pretty wild ride this last year and Nicola lost her battle at the end of October. I was thinking about it earlier and thought of the video we'd heard about as we never actually saw it. I was hoping that you might remember something about it, and if it was in fact recorded, that you might still have a copy you could forward to us. Either way I'd love to hear back from you and look forward to your reply. Thanks, Michael.'

Immediately I contacted our videographer and explained the situation. He was quick to help and soon produced a DVD to send to Nicola's family who were extremely grateful to have 'one more memory about our special little girl.'

My wonderful parents taught me long ago, 'with only just a bit of effort you can make a difference in people's lives.' Ashley's illness had taught me to think on my feet, to make contingency plans in case the first try failed, and to never give up. Happy Feat brought all these lessons together in the best way possible and opened up so many amazing and precious moments that wouldn't have happened any other way.

CHAPTER 24

Sharpening the Saw

Another lesson that Ashley's illness and having Guillain-Barre syndrome had taught me, was the importance of looking after myself - though sometimes life gets in the way. Connecting with the bush surrounding our home, the peaceful creek, and our furry and feathered family, kept me grounded and helped me recharge both during and after those hellish years of his treatment. The personal and professional growth I was experiencing juggling both a business, family and Happy Feat meant that, at times, I needed to 'reconnect' once more. In June 2011, I had the opportunity to experience a 'recharge' like no other.

Back in September 2010, I had seen a preview of a television special about swimming with the minke whales. At the time, I said to Geoff, "There's no way I could watch that show because I'd be too jealous!"

The Universe had other ideas. Preview after preview of the minke story had me hooked, so when the program came on that night, there I was - glued to the television!

Tears streamed down my face watching the most beautiful whales swimming comfortably among the snorkellers – wild animals at one with human beings. The program went on to say that this graceful species of whale had only been recently discovered, and they were found to be very curious and playful at a certain time of the year.

Seeing this story, I knew that swimming with these whales had to go on my To-Do list. It had to happen. The dwarf minke whale expedition takes place during a six-week period every year, in June and July. John and Linda Rumney, from Eye-to-Eye Marine Encounters, together with their dedicated team of researchers and crew, have been organising swims with minke whales for many years. With the happy tears flowing, I felt an instant connection with these mesmerising creatures. The story went on to show an elderly mother enjoying this experience as a birthday gift from her family. I wasn't elderly, but I did have a birthday soon...

My birthday was at the end of the month. I immediately began hinting (actually, not even hinting, just outright stating!) how that would be the BEST birthday present I could ever receive in my whole life. There was no reaction.

OK, I'll say it again - even louder this time! Perhaps if I put pictures of minke whales up around the house, they will get the hint.

Days passed and these fascinating creatures continued to fill my thoughts – the look in their eyes, how peaceful they were interacting with the humans. After a week, I still couldn't stop thinking about my incredible minke whales (notice the 'my!'). Jumping on the computer, I started some serious research and couldn't believe what I found. Surely, we'd have to travel to the other side of the world to have an experience like this, not just a five-hour trip to Port Douglas! I couldn't print the information fast enough.

As Geoff and I had our morning cuppa with the skippies, I just happened to mention that I'd discovered all about the minke whales and how this amazing adventure took place right on our doorstep.

When Geoff asked more about it, I just happened to have all the information at hand.

"We should do it!" he announced. "It would be an experience of a lifetime."

I raced to the door, telling him to enjoy his cuppa while I booked our tickets. And that's exactly what I did.

A couple of mornings later, Geoff asked if I had invited my brother Bruce to come. Bruce has always gone on holidays with our family. Sometimes we don't even ask; we just book his tickets. However, this time, I hadn't invited him.

"Don't be ridiculous," I said. "Bruce doesn't even swim and he sure as heck doesn't snorkel. Why would he want to come?" Geoff looked unconvinced and said we should at least ask if he'd like to come.

When I mentioned it to Bruce, his reaction was surprising. "Hell yes!" was his instant reply.

I sent a quick email to Eye-to-Eye Marine Encounters to add yet another ticket for us. We had a mere nine-and-a-half months to count the sleeps until our adventure of a lifetime. Oh, my goodness, how was I going to handle the wait. I was so excited already!

With everything on my plate, our adventure came around quicker than I thought. Before I knew it, we were soon boarding the Elizabeth Ell to begin our journey. After motoring all night, the next morning we were up bright and early to have breakfast, and a snorkel on the Great Barrier Reef. The weather was quite lousy with strong winds and rough seas, which made the snorkelling challenging. The beautiful reef made it all worthwhile.

The next day dawned with similar lousy weather, but I was on a mission. When the welcome shout of "Minke whales!" went out, I was suited up and in the water before the rest of the gang could even blink. After waiting so long for this holiday, I was finally in the water waiting for my first minke whale encounter.

My heart was pounding so loudly that I'm sure others could hear it, and my stomach was doing back flips. Holding onto the rope line, I bobbed up and down in what felt like huge waves. I wasn't scared, I was excited! Making sure I didn't make any sudden movements that might scare them away, I scanned around me for the sight of a whale.

What was that in the distance? A faint white colour gliding through the water...oh my goodness, I had seen my first minke whale - even though it was only in the distance. All too soon, the cry went out to say the encounter was over and we must return to the boat. It had been my first taste of swimming with the minke whales, and I was totally addicted.

On day four, we awoke with serious intent to find those elusive minke whales. As I sat with two other passengers, June nearly jumped on the table and shouted, "MINKE WHALE!"

She had spotted our first minke for the day not far from us. Excitement quickly travelled through the boat, and once again I was suited up and in the water in no time! Trying to quietly float, holding onto the line, I can't even begin to describe my feelings of excitement.

Silently, and ever so gracefully, a minke whale passed by, and looked directly into my soul! That immediate connection was such an emotional moment that tears began to flow (yes, into my mask). You can't imagine how it feels to look into the eye of most inquisitive and amazing ocean creature, one that's five to six metres long and weighs up to five tonnes!

I felt totally safe, peaceful, and completely at one with Mother Nature. As the whales disappeared into the distance, we reluctantly returned to the boat, recalling our excitement over a delicious, cooked breakfast. Preparing to move to another part of the reef, another very welcome shout went out, "MINKE WHALE!"

Yes, you guessed it. I was suited up and first in the water with John Rumney. This time, I was totally relaxed and more familiar with scanning for the minke whales. It was priceless to share this experience with someone who was so passionate about minke whales, like John. It was contagious - I was becoming more so with every sighting. I felt the most amazing connection with the whales. For several hours, they paraded past us, playing, showing off, and gazing at us as though they were trying to communicate some mysterious message.

At no time did we swim to the animals or try to touch them in any way. They approached us as they pleased. As they grew more confident, they sometimes passed very close by – right beside me, and underneath me. What an incredible feeling!

One unforgettable passing, the minke seemed to stop right in front of me, sharing a 'minke moment' with me. It was so powerful that once again, it brought tears to my eyes, and I became quite emotional. This experience was indescribable. I'd become completely hooked on these magnificent animals, and thoroughly enjoyed my time with them.

The next morning when the now familiar cry, "MINKE WHALE!" went out, I found myself suiting up at 7:15am. How soon we forget about winter cold when there are minke whales! My adrenaline and emotions were in overload.

For seven hours, the whales stayed close by the boat. Time stood still as we moved through the water with these magical creatures, many times they looked us right in the eye with that magical connection. It was truly a life changing experience having these incredible animals wanting to be with you, showing off. They made every person feel as though they were the only person on earth. During my own eye-to-eye encounter with one of the minkes, I thought how special it would be to have that ability, to make every person you meet feel as though they are the only person on this earth."

We had the most extraordinary and indescribable moment with one of the minke whales. It had become very comfortable and familiar with myself and Vicki, who was swimming next to me on the rope. The whale hovered in front of each of us for quite some time, giving us that soul-piercing concentration. We were totally mesmerised and captivated.

Finally, the whale swam away from us. Vicki and I put our heads above water, took our snorkels out, and yelled with excitement. We hugged and high fived each other in the water. "Can you explain what just happened there?!" I gasped. Before she could answer, the whale emerged from the water not far from where we were and erupted into the air as if to say, "Where did you go? Why aren't you still looking at me?"

We couldn't believe our eyes. The people on the boat also witnessed this incredible display of inquisitiveness, connection, and playfulness. When I finally dragged myself out of the water with the biggest grin, everyone asked what it was like. I was totally speechless. I fell into Geoff's arms and just sobbed with the overwhelming euphoria of it all. When I looked up, I saw the understanding joy on John Rumney's face. I gave him the biggest bear hug, thanking him from the bottom of my heart for giving me an adventure of a lifetime.

After quickly devouring the lunch plate waiting for me, I was back in the water. Later that afternoon, Geoff swam up to me several times. I thought he was just telling me he was returning to the boat - I was still on a 'Minke Whale Mission' so I was staying! By this time, the minke whales had disappeared - but there was always the hope they would return.

At last, I lifted my head out of the water and realised I was the only one left. Everyone else had returned to the boat. The crew sang out to get my attention, saying that a shark had scared the minke whales away - that's why everyone was on board!

Hang on, did they just say 'SHARK'?! That's why Geoff had repeatedly tried to get my attention - to warn me about the shark!

I swam the fastest I'd ever swum in my life and nearly kissed the deck when I was safely back on board.

The minke whale expedition was a trip of a lifetime, one I'll remember and cherish for the rest of my life. Whether you have a bucket list or a To-Do list like me, book a trip to see the minke whales now! But be warned, you too will become mesmerised, captivated, and totally addicted!

Life can throw many curve balls your way, and sometimes you will feel like you have no stretch in yourself left to deal with them. I find that connecting with nature – be it with whales in the ocean or the birds in your backyard, can help you find that space to breathe, resettle your burdens, and power on.

CHAPTER 25

Making a Difference

It had been a while since our family had been water-skiing, so we decided to have an afternoon at the river. I had great intentions of warming up first, getting my muscles prepared for the ski and taking it easy. I had a Happy Feat performance that night, I had to take it easy - but as soon as I strapped that ski on, I became 10 feet tall and bulletproof. Skiing my heart out and putting up my hand for a final ski after the others had had enough, probably wasn't the smartest idea before I had before a performance, but gee it was fun!

One of our dancers, Arlia, lived nearby so I decided to call in to see if she'd like a lift to the performance. Transportation was an issue for her as her family didn't have a car. Arlia was excited to see me. She thought that she was going to miss the performance because nobody had been available to pick her up. She quickly grabbed some things and came racing out to jump in the car.

After checking to make sure she had her performance shoes, socks and hairbrush, Arlia admitted she didn't have a brush. I made a mental note to buy some more little necessities for her. Her sister stealing her gear was an ongoing issue.

It was too far for me to go back home to get ready so we went to my brother's house. As I was blow-drying my hair, Arlia and I chatted. She couldn't believe how quiet the house was, even with the hairdryer roaring. At her home, there was constant yelling and turmoil. Arlia wasn't used to being surrounded by peace and quiet. I did her hair and asked if she'd like my hairdresser to cut and style it sometime. She said she would have to check with her mum, and we left it at that.

That night, the Happy Feat performance at the Endeavour Birthday event was a roaring success. Everyone enjoyed watching our stars dancing their hearts out. Most of the team had purchased tickets to stay on at the disco after the performance, but Arlia and I left not long after. In our rush to get to the performance, we had missed out on dinner, so we dropped into McDonalds. I ordered and collected Arlia's dinner, then returned to order a frappe for myself. When I turned around, Arlia had set herself up at one of the tables and was tucking into her food.

After such a huge day of water-skiing then performing, all I wanted was to get home. I suggested to Arlia that she eat her meal in the car - and then I saw the worry on her face. Realising her dilemma, I said, "You want to finish it now because your sister will take it when you get home?"

She didn't need to answer, her face told the story. So, we sat there while she enjoyed her dinner in peace before she had to return to the noise and disturbance at home.

That Friday night, our Happy Feat volunteers were helping at a community teen Halloween disco. When my brother Bruce and I rocked up, we saw Arlia out the front looking lost and upset. Her sister, on the other hand, was quick to be in our face showing off her elaborate costume. I asked Arlia why she was upset. She admitted she didn't have anything to wear and was feeling out of it.

My heart sank as I explained that it didn't matter what she was wearing, that she should go inside and show them what an amazing dancer she was. Sometimes I wished I could snap my fingers and make everything right for her.

Later that night, one of our Happy Feat volunteers commented that Arlia didn't have any money for a drink or food. Unfortunately,

Bruce and I hadn't taken any money to the function, but we wanted to help her out. I approached Arlia's sister, asking what had happened to the money left after she'd paid the admission. She didn't realise I'd seen how much money she had handed over, so I knew how much change she should have. She tried to give me some lame excuse like she'd lost the money. I must admit I was really frustrated with her.

A generous Happy Feat volunteer made sure Arlia had a drink and we all included her, so she didn't feel so lonely. After what she'd been through, I told Arlia I would be taking her to the hairdresser and would pick her up Wednesday afternoon.

On Wednesday, Arlia bounded out to the car to inform me she wouldn't be coming to Happy Feat as she was receiving an award at school that night. I was so excited for her and asked what time she had to be ready. If we had time, I could still take her to the hairdresser -and might even get her hair done nicely for the presentation. We made a mad dash and my hairdresser washed, cut, and curled her hair so she felt like a star.

I also took the opportunity to teach her about the importance of washing her hair and keeping it clean. I'd bought her a brush, scrunchies, face cleanser and some toiletries the week before. I'd been doing this for years, replacing what Arlia's sister had stolen.

When I dropped her home, her sister came bounding down the stairs. When she saw Arlia's styled hair, she went screaming back up the stairs and threw a huge tantrum. Poor Arlia just stood there looking heartbroken. Giving her a big hug, I reminded her, "Tonight is your special night. Don't let anyone or anything spoil it!"

I drove away with a very heavy heart. I kept thinking people really have no idea what heartache and effort goes on behind the scenes at Happy Feat.

But the heartache and frustration didn't stop there for Arlia.

One night at Happy Feat, I was shocked and upset by a dramatic change in Arlia's face which looked as if she'd had a stroke. I quietly took her aside and discovered that she had been diagnosed with bell's palsy, a temporary condition of sudden weakness or paralysis in the muscles of one side of the face.

Poor kid! She had a dreadful home life, suffered continuous bullying and had so many challenges – and here she was, with another challenge to face! Because she had no proper parental support, I'd become her surrogate mum and mentor over the past six years. I quickly went into 'mum' mode.

Reassuring her that the condition does get better, I asked Arlia several questions, trying to get a better sense of the situation. It turned out that she was having to tape her eye shut at night because it wouldn't close. While she'd been given a script for medication, she hadn't got it filled because she was 'waiting for her pay'.

At that point, it took all my being to hold back tears of frustration, feeling them well up inside. As Arlia's mentor and tower of strength though, I felt I had to put on a brave front. Giving her another hug, I promised I would get the script filled and drop it around to her.

The next day, things came unstuck at the chemist. When I was asked if the patient had any allergies, I didn't have any Happy Feat paperwork in front of me. At that point, I knew I had to reveal my secret mission.

The ladies behind the counter were wonderful. As mums themselves, they also really felt for this young Happy Feater and we soon found a solution. While I was waiting for the script, I gathered the usual toothpaste, toothbrush, deodorant, and moisturiser etc., to also take to Arlia. I couldn't help welling up with tears when one of the chemist attendants came up with several useful items that she'd gathered for me to give to Arlia as well. So often, you hear of all the traumatic things that happen in the world: shootings, killings, and violence. It's heart-warming to know there are also very special, caring people out there with beautiful souls.

As the shop assistant was helping me choose a good face cream for Arlia, I let slip that she had to hide everything I bought for her because her sister kept stealing it. I said it more to myself, out of sheer frustration. The young woman helping me stopped in her tracks, then said she'd be right back.

Once again, she appeared bearing gifts: a waterproof bath bag for Arlia to store her gear and hide it easily! I was already feeling quite emotional and was overwhelmed by this lady's generosity. I found myself fighting back tears once again. Such goodness certainly restores your faith in humanity. Thanking her again, I told her she could go home today knowing she had truly made a difference in someone's life.

When I arrived at Arlia's place, I was confronted by their vicious dog. Having been bitten by this dog on several occasions already, I was terrified and physically shaking. Surprisingly, Arlia's mother came out to the fence and opened the gate to let me in. I wasn't going anywhere until I knew that horrid dog was secured behind the other fence.

I went to the front patio, and when Arlia came out, she proudly showed me their new puppy. I couldn't believe it! This family now had two dogs to look after, and Arlia couldn't even get the medication she desperately needed. I wanted to scream with frustration!

Unfortunately, Arlia's sister and her boyfriend were there. They knew that I looked after Arlia and brought her goodies, and they gathered around like vultures, waiting to see what I'd brought. I took Arlia out to the front gate instead, away from the predators, oops, I mean 'others', - and away from the horrible dog that was standing up at the fence on its hind legs, still barking incessantly.

Making sure that Arlia understood how to take the steroid medication, I stressed how important it was that she take it first thing in the morning with her breakfast. Because the medication can cause sleeplessness and an upset tummy, I hoped to get the message through that she really needed to take it as early as possible in the day, and to take it with food. The eye drops could be administered every two hours, so to make it easier for her, I suggested she put them in at 2:00pm, 4:00pm, 6:00pm, and so on. I'd also bought special adhesive tape for her eye that would be easier to manage each night.

When I gave Arlia the bag with the other goodies, to my great surprise, the item she was most excited about was the deodorant. I stood there like a stunned mullet! Hearing the vicious barking dog didn't improve the situation. To think that these two dogs were fed and looked after while Arlia couldn't even get her medication and basic necessities made my blood boil and my heart shatter all at the same time.

My role in Happy Feat was expanding so much further than organisation and administration. These were my people, and while I loved watching them shine on stage, I wanted to see them happier at home too. The frustration I felt at Arlia's situation made me more determined to fight for a better life for our more vulnerable dancers. After all, Happy Feat was about helping them achieve and step forward. Performing was a great way to show the community what they could do and that amazing connection between the dancers and the audience was proof of that.

The private battles I could and would fight for a better life for my Happy Featers. Unfortunately, life was pushing me into in a more public role than I was comfortable with. As with the documentary for the Blood Bank, for the good of others, I had to get used to something I found *really* uncomfortable.

CHAPTER 26

Dodging a Bullet

It all started with a bizarre phone call while I was at work. A gentleman rang to say I'd won the John Simpson 'Standing for Something' award and asked to meet me to give me the letter.

"Seriously?" I thought. "Why would I receive an award? And what on earth was the John Simpson award anyway?"

I informed him that I work full-time as well as my Happy Feat commitments and asked if he could just post the letter. He asked if it was possible to drop into work to give it to me personally. I was a little perplexed and wondered why he would go to all the trouble.

Meeting the gentleman at work, he asked if it was possible to present me with the award at their national conference that was to be held in Townsville at the end of October. Feeling a little bewildered about the whole thing, I enquired if he could just post it or give it to me at Happy Feat one night. Although he was keen to come along to Happy Feat, he said it certainly wasn't going to be an option for the presentation of the award.

After looking up the award on the internet, I discovered that the Standing for Something Award is given to 'an individual whose service is exemplary in bettering the life of the community'. Learning about other extraordinary recipients of this award still left me feeling totally discombobulated and uneasy. I couldn't believe this had happened to me – and I felt nervous about the presentation. That sounded huge and something I wasn't ready for!

Surprisingly, the gentleman and another member of his organisation came along to Happy Feat that week. They stood by themselves, watching. Naturally, Happy Feat was having one of those nights where anything and everything was happening, and not all of it was good!

I had one of our 'challenging' members rolling around on the stage holding his knee and seeking attention. As I knew he was perfectly fine, I talked him into joining in the dancing (secretly getting one of the volunteers to keep an eye on him, just in case). The music wasn't working properly, and we had several other character-building issues. I remember telling our audience of two, "Some days are diamonds and other days... just aren't!"

As they knew Theresa and her family, I was hoping they would notice how much she had come out of her shell and was blossoming at Happy Feat. But, like I said, it was one of those nights. Theresa refused to come into the middle of the Moment to Shine circle and recoiled from the other members. Just when I was beginning to think the night was a total disaster, Theresa quietly walked out into the middle of the circle unprompted and proceeded to dance her heart out. I walked over to our two special visitors and excitedly shared, "That's why I do what I do!"

They looked on in amazement as Theresa twirled and relished all the attention. Seeing the look on Theresa's face made it all worthwhile. She knew she should give someone else a turn in the middle of the circle but was enjoying herself so much that she didn't want it to end.

Was this the same young woman who, just twelve months ago, was so introverted she wouldn't leave her mother's side? I fought back tears of pride as I watched her reluctantly let someone else have their own 'Moment to Shine'.

It wasn't long before I received the formal email requesting that I receive this award at the national conference. What was all the fuss about? I'm not into awards and it's certainly not why I do everything for Happy Feat. I thought that if I ignored it, it might just go away.

Several days later, though, another email arrived, followed by a phone call. I thought that by explaining how uncomfortable I felt about awards they would forget about having a special presentation. Wrong! Perhaps I'd try another tactic. I suggested bringing along my Happy Feat team to be with me and maybe even do a performance. Maybe this would put them off doing the presentation. They said they'd check and get back to me.

In the meantime, I realised we had another performance booked in, so I contacted the 'Standing for Something' people and advised that perhaps I could go, receive the award, and then leave them to their conference. Happy Feat wouldn't be performing as we already had another performance booked in for October and that was more than enough.

A couple of days later, Mary (who had nominated me for the award) rang to say that she thought Happy Feat really should be there to help me celebrate the award and perform. It was an ideal opportunity to show their achievements and increase their exposure in the community. Chuckling, I said that at 80 years young, she was a remarkable saleswoman. I would see what I could do to arrange for our Happy Featers to come and join in the event. Looks as if Plan D would be needed!

The award night soon arrived, and I turned up at the venue armed with tambourines, music, and no idea what to expect. As I was greeted and shown to the room, I was blown away by the trouble they had gone to. I looked around, discovering multiple laminated photos of our Happy Feat team, a huge poster outlining my life story, and programs for distribution with my photo on the cover!

I felt totally overwhelmed. I wanted to run out to my car and drive off into the night. I felt uncomfortable enough at the thought of an award presentation, and now I wanted the earth to open and swallow me. How was I going to get through the night?

The ceremony turned out to be very enjoyable, but all too soon I was called up to receive the award and give a speech. Like most people, I struggle with public speaking and being in the spotlight alone. But this was about Happy Feat. I just spoke from the heart.

My speech seemed to be well received and I returned to my seat with an enormous sigh of relief. With the presentation over, trays of delicious homemade goodies were offered around. Someone had obviously gone to a lot of trouble with the food. The Deputy Mayor at the time introduced himself and said he didn't want to rush me, but he had another appointment at 6:30 that night and didn't want to leave until he had seen our Happy Feat team perform!

Quickly gathering our team, the dancers wowed the audience with their ability, joy, and love of life. Making the speech and being the focus of attention for a night made my heart leap out of my chest with nerves. It was worth it to see our team treated like royalty afterwards - and even more wonderful to see them fully accepted, interacting with other members of the community.

Later that night, Geoff, Mum, Dad, Bruce, and I went out for dinner. Bruce must have been asked to do a speech at the event but was very relieved when he didn't have to present it. He had prepared a speech (written on the back of a Kodak brochure) so Geoff said we'd still love to hear it and suggested that Bruce give the speech while we waited for dinner.

So, in a very unusual setting, my brother delivered a heartwarming, moving speech – certainly something you don't hear every day! As always, we laughed, enjoyed our special family time and I was extremely relieved the award ceremony was over!

Chapter 27

Reliving the Horror

Alarm bells rang when Ashley called to find out which doctors' surgery he should visit as he was feeling unwell. I was able to get him an appointment with my doctor, so I dropped off the Medicare card to him. It only took one look to see how sick he was; his eyes were bloodshot, and he had a temperature. Nevertheless, he insisted on driving himself to the doctors.

A short time later he rang back to say he'd just vomited and, although he'd had a red Gatorade earlier, what he brought up looked more like blood. I reassured him it was most likely the Gatorade mixed with his stomach juices. I told him he shouldn't be driving and was on my way to pick him up.

We were early for his appointment, and it wasn't long before we were in the doctor's office. We went through the usual things, but when the doctor asked if Ash had suffered from migraine headaches before, Ashley replied, "Only when I've had lumbar punctures." The doctor quickly snapped to attention as Ashley shared his years of treatment for Acute Lymphoblastic Leukaemia. After a physical examination the doctor said he'd like to check something with his supervisor.

Oh no, what's going on?!

The supervisor joined us, and the two doctors examined Ashley as he lay on the bed.

Struggling with my emotions, I relived the horror of the day Ashley was first diagnosed. I could easily have lost it there and then, as I fought back a flood of tears. Fear and anxiety threatened to engulf me as I sat listening to the doctors conferring with each other. It was decided that urgent blood tests were needed. Anxiously, I asked when we would get the results. The supervising doctor instructed the younger doctor to make sure the results were sent to his mobile phone, and he said they would be back before sundown. This was a serious situation, and the doctors were clearly concerned.

As I drove Ash to get his blood test, we got caught up in peak hour, so I dropped him off at the pathology lab and left to find a park. We'd done this many times in the past and had certainly lost count of how many blood tests he'd had. By the time I got inside, Ashley was already having his bloods taken. The three girls in reception were laughing and commented on how they'd been giving Ashley heaps about his funky and different hair style.

I smiled sweetly at them and debated whether to hold my tongue or not. I was struggling with my emotions that afternoon and had instinctively gone into survival mode. I'm a very private person and rarely talked about Ashley's journey, but I did decide to tell the girls that Ash was used to banter. After losing his hair during chemotherapy, he was grateful for having any hair at all. Well, you could have heard a pin drop. What followed was a very awkward silence.

I don't usually do that, but sometimes it's good for people to have a reality check. A lot of people are so quick to judge. They would have seen a lad with a funky hairstyle and thought he was some hooligan, but it couldn't be further from the truth. Like I say to my kids: don't judge!

Ashley soon returned to the waiting room, thanked the girls, and wished them a great afternoon. I would have preferred to take him home so I could keep an eye on him, but he was happy to go back to his place and just sleep. Although I went back to work that afternoon, I had to fight hard to concentrate and keep my 'happy welcoming voice' when answering the phone. I felt like a caged animal, but if I could wear my happy face for three and a half years, I could certainly put it on again for one afternoon.

At 5:30pm, I rang the doctor's surgery to see if they'd received Ashley's blood test results. After some time, the receptionist said they hadn't come back but should be there the next day. I explained that the supervisor had marked them urgent and organised for the results to be sent directly to his phone. This certainly wasn't the normal procedure so I asked if she could check with the doctor. It transpired that the young doctor had gone home for the day, however the supervisor had rung him, told him to follow up the results and get in touch with us. It was wonderful to get such service, but it also showed how seriously they were treating the situation.

The clock ticked, and as the surgery closed at 6:00pm, I rang Ash to see if he'd heard anything. Still nothing! When I called back and got the after-hours message at the surgery, I dreaded the long anxious night ahead as we waited for the results.

Geoff had been in meetings all afternoon. He didn't even know Ash was sick, let alone know how the situation had unfolded. I was on the phone filling him in when I heard the other call come through. Quickly, I hung up on my poor husband to take the call.

It was Ashley! The results we were concerned about, Neutrophils, white cell count, and liver function, were all fine. They would rush the other results through, and we'd have them by 5:00pm the next day. Yeehaa!!! Tears of joy, relief, and happiness flowed down my cheeks. In those few hours, I had been to hell and back reliving the anguish of those years of treatment.

I packed up at work and went to the chemist to get Ash some paracetamol, cold and flu drugs, and tissues. As I dropped them off, I hugged him with all my might and didn't want to let go. It felt so good to hold him in my arms and know that he was OK.

After I shared a brief version of Ashley's latest drama with one of the Happy Feat mums, which was very rare for me, she sent me a beautiful card with an inspirational quote by Helen Keller: 'The best and most beautiful things in the world cannot be seen or touched but are felt in the heart.'

She then wrote:

> 'Leigh, there is a great deal I don't know about living with a child with a life-threatening illness. But I do know the struggles and difficulties of life with a disabled child. I think the place where our two hearts meet is called courage.'

CHAPTER 28

Celebrating Two Years of Wow

If Ashley's illness had taken me back in time for an afternoon, then Happy Feat's second birthday would be a night to celebrate how far we'd come. I'd decided to have a huge celebration, making another excuse for our wonderful group to have special memories to cherish.

My objectives were to create an excuse for our Happy Feat members to dress up and feel special; to give our members an opportunity to be included and accepted in the community; and to give the public the opportunity to experience the magic of Happy Feat.

My first thought was to celebrate by having a Happy Feat Ball, even though I'd only ever been to one ball in my life. But how on earth was I going to organise something I knew nothing about. True, it's never stopped me in the past, and it was certainly not about to stop me now. Like with many things, I let the ideas brew in the back of my mind until the solutions came to the fore.

"That's it!" I thought, sometime later. "I'll ring Sharon, the very talented, super-efficient organiser of several successful Ronald McDonald House Charity Balls." I was sure she would be able to offer great advice. After a long phone call, Sharon generously offered to help with our Happy Feat Ball.

After tentatively booking a venue recommended by an associate, I couldn't help feeling disappointed. It just wasn't what I had in mind for this event. On returning to work, I decided I should ring my contact, Margaret, at the Mercure Inn. Maybe this venue would be available for the Saturday night of our birthday? As if! With its beautiful pool and tropical gardens, the Mercure Inn was highly sought after for weddings. It was sure to be fully booked. But, if nothing else, I've learned to go with my gut instinct, so proceeded to make the call anyway.

When I rang, Margaret was on another call, so I left a message for her to give me a tingle. Just before I hung up, I asked the representative if the venue happened to be available on the 19th of May. Time ticked by as she checked the date and I thought to myself, "Leigh, you're wasting your time. There's no way it will be available."

The voice came back on the line, "Ahhh, yes. Well, I can't believe it, but the ballroom is available for Saturday the 19th of May."

Wow, that gut instinct never ceases to amaze me!

Without hesitation, I booked the room for our Happy Feat Ball and waited for Margaret's call. This venue was exactly what I had envisaged for our special birthday event, and it looked as if it was actually going to happen!

To my surprise, when Margaret called, she hadn't heard of Happy Feat! Proudly and excitedly, I explained what Happy Feat was all about – and what I had in mind for our birthday celebrations. Margaret got caught up in the excitement and offered to approach her boss about providing the venue free of charge! I suggested that if she could do that, I would send through some information on Happy Feat so that she had something in writing to help our case. You know the old saying that a picture tells a thousand words – well, that's certainly true when it comes to Happy Feat!

It wasn't long before I received an excited call from Margaret. Happy Feat not only had the ballroom available for the 19th of May, but it was also going to be offered free of charge! Our Happy Feat motto is just so true: 'Believe and you can achieve'.

Soon we had our first meeting of the 'Birthday Ball Committee' and plans got underway. There was much discussion on what to call the event. As my hubby had mentioned, calling it a 'Ball' would conjure up images and expectations for those attending. We agreed to call it the '2012 Happy Feat Birthday Gala.'

There was so much to organise, including raffle prizes, a live band, birthday cake, commemorative gifts for our members, supper and drinks, ticket design and sales, an MC for the night, a PowerPoint presentation of our achievements, formalwear, a run sheet, a band, and Gala programs for distribution.

I must admit, there were times when I asked myself, "Why am I doing this?"

My very special friends, Joy and Katie, were certainly baffled as to why I put myself through the added stress and pressure of organising a gala event when there was already enough in my life.

So many times, when the three of us would get together for our girly catch up, my mind would be a thousand miles away thinking of everything that needed to be done. My constant distraction made them concerned that I was burning myself out. Maybe I was, but I knew it would be worth it in the end. I knew we would make it the most wonderful event for our Happy Feat team.

A volunteer's summary of the night: -

> 'To see our Happy Featers enjoying themselves and being the stars was incredible. Also, seeing them all interacting socially, going up to buy drinks, interacting with the live band—wow—what a bunch! Huge credit to you for making our Happy Feat a family with your warmth, compassion and dedication. You congratulate everyone around you, however this time around I think you should be giving yourself a huge pat on the back as it was a huge success and probably one of the best functions I have been to. The atmosphere was... I don't even have the words to express it. It warmed your heart and filled your soul with love. So be very proud, Leigh, of what you have achieved and mark this one down as a huge milestone for Happy Feat.'

CHAPTER 29

Another Magical Night Full of Surprises

I focused on wearing my happy face for the big Happy Feat night ahead. After spending a challenging 24 hours helping a friend with her very sick hubby, I had this weird feeling of peace and calm. It was as though I knew everything possible had been done for my friends and that they would be fine while I went to Happy Feat. I was certainly looking forward to some well-earned fun and laughter.

It turned out to be a night where the magic just kept happening.

Firstly, one of our new members arrived looking gorgeous. Zoe had only been with us a couple of weeks, a young girl with down syndrome. She was well spoken and had lovely manners. I commented on how pretty she looked with the diamante bow in her hair, and lovely outfit.

Noticing one of our young male Happy Featers looking interested, I brought Justin into the conversation as well. As he was right in my face, I smiled and asked him about the four wiry hairs on his chin. He puffed his chest out, looked directly at Zoe, and with an unusually deep voice said, "It's my beard!"

It was so special to witness the relationship that blossomed between them, and for them to have an opportunity most take for granted. Later, Justin's mum shared a story that made me smile from the inside out. The morning after their first meeting, Justin had gone to his mum and said, "We have to go shopping today."

When his mum asked why, Justin answered "I have to buy some jewellery for Zoe."

She replied, "Justin, I've been married 25 years and I'm only just getting jewellery now. Zoe can wait!"

That night, our Happy Feat team continued the special rehearsals for their next special performance - the opening of the annual Townsville V8s Supercar racing event. To be included in a flash mob with 400 school students was a huge coup for Happy Feat; it showed we were being recognised by, and included in, the community.

After the special rehearsal, I got on stage holding five glossy magazines opened to a particular page.

"You know how I'm always saying how incredible and fantastic you all are?" I began. "Well, because you're so amazing, there's a story about Happy Feat in this glossy magazine!" An excited cheer erupted throughout the hall. Holding up the cover of the magazine and showing everyone, I went on to say, "You've all seen these magazines in supermarkets, well, our Happy Feat team are featured in Family Circle, which is sold all around Australia not just in Townsville!"

Another loud cheer erupted, and I quickly declared it supper time. I said I would hand the magazines around so they could see themselves and realise what stars they'd become. It was such a magical moment. I was surprised at how excited they were to see the article – even those with limited communication skills made it clear that they wanted to see the story.

After supper they were all keen to get back onto the dance floor – all except Justin, that is, who was sitting with his arm proudly wrapped around Zoe.

"Come on Justin, it's time to dance." I coaxed.

"But I'm on a date," he said, smiling from ear to ear.

"Well, it's got to be a dancing date, then. Get on the floor, you two!" I said, grinning, while my heart did a backflip. The music began and we ramped up the energy in the room once again. And just when I thought the night couldn't get any better, another beautiful moment transpired.

Anthony had been in a serious accident ten years previously and had lost the use of his left arm. While dancing, he proudly showed how much the movement in his arm had improved since coming to Happy Feat. I stopped dancing and watched him dance in awe, and the more I watched, the more he performed. By the time the song finished I felt very emotional, looked him in the eye and gave him a heartfelt high five. As I turned to sort out the music, he stopped me, then reached out and high fived me...with his left hand!

What a powerful and emotional moment.

I looked at his proud face and said, "Anthony, that's exactly why I do what I do with Happy Feat."

CHAPTER 30

Hang on, is That in My Job Description?

Given how effortless and fun our dancing looks on stage, people could be forgiven for thinking that having a group like Happy Feat is just about putting some music on and having a dance. But oh, it's so much more than that. Here's a sneak peek into one of my Saturdays.

One of my missions was to find some of our members reliable and consistent transport to and from Happy Feat each Wednesday night. Some have elderly parents who don't have licences or don't drive at night, some reside in shared houses and simply don't have transport. This was before the National Disability Insurance Scheme (NDIS) was introduced. When I drop multiple members home, it means I don't get home 'til very late. Working full-time and already devoting so much time to Happy Feat motivated me to find a solution fast.

It's funny how people come into your life when you need them. Earlier in the week, I had contacted a community transport organisation that had approached me after one of our performances. They were thrilled and very eager to help so we exchanged numbers and agreed to meet soon. All I needed was a bus driver. Amazingly, only 10 minutes before meeting with the transport people, I discovered that the new volunteer I had invited to join Happy Feat had a bus licence!

At the same time, I was approached by a gentleman who was very keen to meet and tell me how much he thought of Happy Feat. He'd posted our Million Dollar Memo entry on Facebook and was appealing to everyone to vote. I wanted to ask who he was, but my gut instinct told me not to go there. He eagerly gave me his business card and said to contact him if Happy Feat ever needed anything. I soon found out he was a local councillor. Little did I know I would be contacting him so soon to help with the bus project costs!

On Saturday morning, I had arranged a meeting with the community transport people but I had several phone calls to make before then. I wanted to make sure that parents would still come along, even if their children came on the bus. Part of the Happy Feat magic is seeing the parents get together, socialise, and have some fun - and I would have hated to see this fall by the wayside.

The bus list was complete, the paperwork prepared, and I was ready for the meeting. A 23-seater bus was organised to be picked up Wednesday afternoon and dropped back either that night or Thursday morning. As the community transport group was a non-profit organisation, we negotiated that I would seek a grant to cover the fuel expenses. Two hours later, we reached an agreement and there were hugs all round.

It was on to the next challenge.

One of the dancers had been getting a little too amorous with her partner who she kept inviting to Happy Feat. I also needed to speak with her about her attitude and how she was treating the volunteers. We arranged to meet, and we had a heart-to-heart. I started by asking if she enjoyed coming to Happy Feat.

Her eyes lit up and she answered with a very enthusiastic "Absolutely!"

I explained that we'd noticed that some nights she was very moody and didn't even acknowledge myself or the volunteer team. Giving it to her plainly, I said that our volunteers were the most wonderful people who had given up their precious time so people like her could have fun and have an awesome night. How dare she treat anybody like that? It's unacceptable. She didn't seem to appreciate how some of those helpers had been so caring and amazing with her. In fact, one of the volunteers would go out of her way to drop her home, despite living nearly a half an hour out of town.

As far as the constant moodiness went, we were over it. Some Happy Featers and volunteers had gone through traumatic experiences yet made sure that they brought happiness and positivity to dance practice. We expected no less of her. Being moody and cranky brought everybody down. 'We're all happy at Happy Feat.' I also brought up the feedback about her making out with her boyfriend at Happy Feat. This too would not be tolerated.

I wanted to end with something positive, so I told her about having the bus to collect her and drop her home each week free of charge. She seemed to accept it all so I left hoping we would see some improvement in her behaviour.

Next on my list was a biggie. Over the past several months, we'd watched another dancer regress and become very introverted. She was just not herself. It started at about the same time she went into a shared home, so I had been keeping a close eye on her. One Wednesday night she looked devastated, and I knew I needed to have a little chat with her.

Holding both hands, I asked what was worrying her. She wouldn't say. Gently, I asked if anyone at Happy Feat was making her sad.

"No," she said.

Was it someone at the share house?

She had tears in her eyes - and said nothing. I went on to ask about whether the different people at the home were upsetting her. There was a particular person I knew that was also in the home (not a member of Happy Feat) and who was someone her mum had concerns about. When I mentioned them, once again she teared up and was visibly upset.

Seeing her like this tore me apart. I looked her in the eyes and told her I would make some phone calls to stop this happening. I promised that I would help her, that she wouldn't have to put up with it for much longer.

Dancing started again after supper, and I noticed this young lady smiling like I hadn't seen for months. What a difference a single conversation, and a bit of hope, can have.

Back to that hectic Saturday - I met with this girl's wonderful parents. For some time now they'd been concerned about their daughter, keeping in touch with me to get some feedback. They loved her and hadn't wanted her to leave home but sadly, due to their circumstances, they had no choice. She'd had to move into the shared home.

As I sat in front of them, it broke my heart to tell them what I had discovered the previous Wednesday night. But I reassured them that when I make a promise, I keep it. I offered to go with them to meet with the manager of the organisation. Together, we could stop their daughter being harassed and bullied.

That afternoon I drove away with a very heavy heart. How many other families are going through something like this with nobody to help them and nobody to stand up and fight for them?

I wasn't home for long before I was back in the car, heading into town for pizza and a movie with one of my Happy Feat dancers. She was a very intelligent and switched-on lady but sadly, due to living with her elderly parents, also very lonely and a bit isolated. Watching a chick-flick, eating chocolate, and catching up on what's been happening, we discussed ways for her to find friends to do this with regularly. Sadly, it's something many of us take for granted.

I got home that night and thought about what a diverse day I'd had: a meeting to arrange transport for our members, being a (cranky) mother to one of our dancers, a counsellor and advocate for another. Finally, the day ended with me just being one friend on the couch with another.

Running a group like Happy Feat had developed my skills and talents in ways I would never have imagined - and given me new ones! Multitasking and wearing different hats, like I had that Saturday certainly highlighted the need to be flexible and able to deal with challenges. Confronting my discomfort and stepping forward into the limelight as I had for the 'Standing for Something' national conference. Conceiving of and organising our Graduation, and Gala. It was all leading to some of my biggest challenges yet. Time to go big or go home.

CHAPTER 31

Performing with Guy Sebastian - A Crazy Idea!

When I first came up with the idea of getting in touch with Guy Sebastian to tell him we had danced to one of his songs, I thought, "Don't be ridiculous!"

Remembering our Happy Feat motto, "Believe and You can Achieve", I sent Guy a video of our Happy Featers dancing to his song 'Don't Worry Be Happy'. Only a short time later, Guy replied saying how much he loved the clip!

It was sometime later, I heard that Guy was holding a concert in Townsville at the end of May 2013. Immediately I investigated the possibilities of Happy Feat performing the dance for Guy in person!

I didn't get a reply to my email this time, so I decided to get in touch again (or would you call it stalking) as a little reminder. Still, I heard nothing. I got in touch with a wonderful friend who runs an agency for speakers and entertainers. It was this contact who had put me in touch with Guy so I could send the video. I explained that the concert was only a short time away and asked for her help in getting the message through to Guy's manager.

With only days to go until the concert, I was getting desperate. Yes, you guessed it, I sent yet another email. It wasn't really stalking, was it? I was just keeping in touch!

While scoffing lunch at my desk very late one afternoon, my mobile phone sprang to life. Big decision time: do I keep pigging out on this totally boring salad or do I take the call? Little did I know that phone call was going to change the lives of many, many people.

"Hello, this is Dan Redgrave, Guy Sebastian's tour manager. I wanted to talk to you about your Happy Feat group performing with Guy at his concert on Friday night."

After a brief silence I replied casually, "Oh yeah, sure!"

"Seriously, Leigh. This is Dan, Guy Sebastian's tour manager, and I really do want to talk about Happy Feat performing with Guy."

"Sure, Dan! We'll party with him all night! So, which of my smarty pants friends is taking the mickey out of me?" I asked.

There was chuckling on the other end of the phone. "No, honestly! It's Dan, Guy Sebastian's tour manager."

"Oh sure, Dan, and I'm Angelina Jolie. Would you like to come over for dinner with Brad and my ten kids?"

The chuckling on the other end erupted into a huge belly laugh. "No, Leigh, this really is Dan, Guy's tour manager."

It finally dawned on me that this was for real. Red faced and feeling very silly, I whispered, "So, you really are Guy's tour manager, aren't you?"

"Yes!! And Guy wants your Happy Feat group to perform on stage with him at his concert on Friday night."

There was an awkward pause. I sat in stunned silence.

After a while, I murmured, "Certainly, Dan. Just give me a moment."

Covering the phone, I danced around the office laughing, and squealing with excitement! Our staff must have thought, "Oh no, what's she up to now?"

Uncovering the phone again, I continued in my best official voice.

"OK, Dan, I'm ready. Now how can we make this happen?"

That was the end of getting any work out of me for the afternoon.

I called each Happy Feat family personally.

"I have very exciting news for you. Are you sitting down? OK, now close your eyes. Picture your son/daughter dancing on stage at the Townsville Entertainment Centre this Friday night performing with... Guy Sebastian!"

There were a lot of excited squeals and whoops of joy.

That night I sent truckloads of emails, made endless lists, and gathered details to forward to our Happy Feat families. Luckily, Geoff was away on a motorbike rally, so I didn't feel guilty about the long hours I put in to making it happen. After work on Tuesday, I stayed at the office to finish a range of tasks, leaving after 11:00pm to yet more work waiting at home. There certainly wasn't much beauty sleep that week. I got three or four hours a night if I was lucky.

At Wednesday night's Happy Feat, we practiced the dance and prepared for the concert, though nothing much went to plan. Imagine trying to contain thirty extremely excited Happy Featers in the very limited space they'd be performing in during the concert! You need space for enthusiastic Rock and Roll moves.

Between juggling work and organising an event, it was a challenging week - but nothing prepared me for the phone call I received from my hubby: he'd had a motorbike accident. Geoff told me that he'd hurt his ankle and shoulder...and then the line dropped out.

I had no idea where he was and no way to contact him! I was beside myself with worry, trying to contact him at all hours of the day and night. As the saying goes, 'the show must go on', so I had to continue to organise Happy Feat for the concert while worrying about what condition my husband was in.

Very generously, Guy had offered our Happy Featers the chance to stay and watch the rest of the concert after our number. After explaining that they also had carers, it was quickly organised for a parent or carer to be there with each Happy Feater. In total, it meant approximately seventy free tickets, amounting to an incredibly generous $5320 worth. How could we ever thank Guy, Dan, and his crew for this amazing experience!

Friday morning arrived, and there were several messages to let me know about an article in the local paper. There were details of Guy's concert, and then an equal amount of space given to the fact that Happy Feat were performing with him!

I made several phone calls to Dan, Guy's tour manager, to see if I could get our local videographers to film the performance. This was no small deal and meant having to acquire legal permission from Guy's solicitors and record company, organising media passes, and many other details I'd never dealt with before. Those four hectic days of planning were a steep learning curve for me as I had no idea what was involved in organising an event like this. The thought of our Happy Featers being included in such an event kept me going.

The meeting time for the concert was 4:45pm at the Townsville Entertainment Centre, a huge indoor venue. It was so uplifting to see our Happy Featers arriving in their performance costumes and being so excited. They had hundreds of questions, and because I'd never done anything like this before, I was flying by the seat of my pants - running on gut instinct.

Then came the dreaded words: "Leigh, Channel 7 News is here and would like to speak with you."

My first reaction was total panic! I wondered how could I get out of it?

I took some deep breaths. I'd do the interview if my Happy Featers could be involved as well. We did it!

It was soon time to prepare for the tech rehearsal. Everyone was ready except a group of nine Happy Featers, who still hadn't arrived. It takes a lot to rile me, but I was furious. It made things extremely stressful, and I had to hide my emotions and try to keep everyone calm. In the end, it wasn't until we were going on stage that the latecomers arrived, flustered, and upset. The last thing I wanted for my Happy Featers.

The band was also running late, so the tension was electric. To hasten their getting into position on stage, we split our team into two groups, entering from both sides. As we lined up on the stairs, one dancer freaked out at the loud music. I had to frantically grab a volunteer to support this Happy Feater and lead her away from the noise. Unfortunately, she was one of the main dancers at the front, so we needed a Plan B. Solution! One of the band members came to the rescue and gave her some earplugs. The show went on.

Our Happy Featers were all in position. The song began - and so did the magic. Their love of dancing and performing lit up the whole concert hall. Guy and the band were pleasantly surprised, or probably more accurately, totally shocked! In fact, Guy was so thrilled he filmed the performance on his phone as he sang with our Happy Featers.

It was high fives from Guy, then off stage, line up and back on stage again for another run through. Each time the Happy Featers began dancing, it simply wasn't important that they weren't in precisely the right position or doing the moves exactly as we'd practiced. They were doing it 'the Happy Feat way'- having fun and doing their best.

As we walked off stage again, I happened to look up at the band and saw their huge smiles. I knew they'd experienced the magic of Happy Feat. Guy was also beaming, and I whispered to him, "Our Happy Featers think they're the rock stars at this concert!" The rehearsal had gone extremely well, despite the stressful start.

Guy's wonderful tour manager, Dan, had been a dream to work with. He was super organised, as well as very caring and empathetic. Instead of our team having to find somewhere to wait until the performance and have dinner, Dan organised a private room for us so we could all be together. This was wonderful, as we could all support each other, and keep up to date as information and plans came through.

The time came for the parents and carers to take their seats at the concert, so our Happy Feat team gathered and made jokes while we waited to be called on stage. During the whole night, I kept marvelling at our incredible, caring, and amazing team of volunteers. None of us had ever done anything like this before, and we all just worked together to make it happen. There was no whingeing or negativity, just getting on with it, looking after each other and making sure everyone was OK.

The stage call finally came. It was show time!

Our Happy Featers were very professional, walking through the backstage corridors and lining up ready to go on stage. Seeing their excited faces in the semi-darkness made me realise I'd done it. Our Happy Featers were going to perform on stage with Guy Sebastian!

With the help of our awesome volunteers, the Happy Featers were quickly in position. The song began, and so did our dancers. They rocked the stage, and I wish I could have captured their expressions as they danced their hearts out.

All too soon the performance was over. Our priority now was to get everyone off the stage as safely, quickly, and quietly as possible, then get them to their seats to enjoy the rest of the concert.

During the concert, Dan spotted me in the audience and came and sat beside me in the aisle. I hugged and thanked him for giving our team an experience of a lifetime. He seemed quite moved and said, "I must ask you; how did Happy Feat begin?"

I said that I'd seen The Merry Makers and decided to do the same thing in my hometown. Even though I'm not a dancer, or formally trained to support people with special needs, one of my mottos was 'Believe and you can achieve'. He shook his head in wonder as we sat and watched Guy's next song.

After the concert, it was very moving to see the different age groups of people coming to congratulate our Happy Featers. We even had teenagers shaking hands with our dancers. I was excited at the thought of progressing even more with two of my goals: breaking down barriers and achieving acceptance in the community.

The magic just kept happening. I loved watching our Happy Featers being congratulated, their photos being taken with friends and relatives as they enjoyed their newfound stardom. The jubilation on their parents' faces said it all. After a lifetime in the shadows, facing

HOPE, GRIT AND GRATITUDE • 227

countless challenges every day, our Happy Feat families were finally seeing recognition for their family members' abilities and gifts.

While another Happy Feater basked in the limelight as his relatives lined up to take photos, I noticed Dan, Guy's Tour Manager coming to join us. I grinned at Dan, pointing to the Happy Feater playing it up to his audience.

Dan laughed. "Yes, I know. He's a rock star!"

I told the group that this was 'Dan the Man', the one who had helped make it all happen. We all cheered and gave him a Mexican Wave. Dan and I shook hands. When I thanked him again, he said, "No, thank *you*!"

That's what I call, 'The Magic of Happy Feat.'

My beautiful Merry Maker friends, Robyn and Bob, were staying with me at the time. In the car on the way home, they mentioned something about when everyone stood up.

"Hang on," I said. "What did you say?"

"Leigh, didn't you see? Happy Feat received a standing ovation."

It's amazing, but when I'm on stage, I hear nothing and see nothing but my Happy Featers. I'm so focused on making sure that they're OK, nothing else exists for me. Robyn went on to say: "That wasn't even the highlight for me. It was when Guy said the words 'Happy Feat' and the whole crowd gave the biggest cheer."

Wow. I was on the stage at the time and had no idea!

We arrived home at midnight. After a shower, I took my dinner and ate it under the stars. Smiling, I looked up at the star-speckled sky. It made me think of something one Happy Feat mum had said about comparing our Happy Featers to the night sky. She said, "When you look at the stars, some are shining brightly, others are twinkling beautifully, and others combine to make the unique Milky Way. All together, they make the most exquisite and incredible display." That was a perfect description of our Happy Feat team.

A quick check of my phone showed countless congratulatory texts but only one text mattered. Geoff let me know he was fine and able to continue with the motorbike rally. What a perfect ending to a perfect day.

In the days following the concert I heard many little stories about what happened both before and after the performance. One carer had stopped at a local café to get a coffee for herself and her Happy Feater before the concert. The young guy behind the counter asked if she was excited. When she asked what he meant, he grinned and said, "Happy Feat dancing with Guy Sebastian."

News had travelled! Another mum recounted that they were stopped several times to be told how amazing the Happy Featers were as they made their way to their car. One lady even got out of her car to come over and congratulate them. People were also tooting their horns, waving if they noticed a Happy Feater in a car on the way home.

Such an amazing experience had come from just reaching out to see if it was possible. Believe and you can achieve, indeed. As stressful and utterly mind-blowing as dancing on-stage with a national superstar had been, our next step out into the world was on a whole other level. Both Happy Feat and I would both be tested in ways I could never have imagined.

CHAPTER 32

The Special Olympic Games: The Journey Begins.

One single comment from a Happy Feat mum sparked an idea that changed everything for Happy Feat. I was talking with one of the mums. She mentioned that the Special Olympic Games (SOG) were to be held in Australia that year. Huh. You don't say….

After some research, I discovered the Special Olympic Asia Pacific Games were to be held in Newcastle on the first of December 2013. It had Happy Feat's name all over it!

How exciting would it be to take our Happy Featers on the trip of a lifetime? I began dreaming about how they would take part in the opening ceremony of the Olympic Games. Impulsively, I sent off an email to the SOG committee. I proudly introduced our Happy Feat team, promoting the idea of us participating in the opening and/or closing ceremonies. To our collective delight, they responded immediately! They were very interested in the possibility of including Happy Feat in the Games.

Such an event would require enormous amounts of work and organisation. There would be months of intense negotiating, marketing, fundraising - and many other challenges ahead, I was sure. I also knew it would be time and energy well spent.

Gathering our amazing film crew together for a meeting, I excitedly announced our extremely ambitious Special Olympic Games adventure! Ideas quickly began to flourish. Someone suggested a Happy Feat documentary, capturing rehearsals in the lead up to the Games, as well as taking our film crew on the four-day adventure. We even overcame the issue of filming during the performance: our film crew would also learn the choreography and join us on the field. Talk about multi-tasking! They would strap Go Pros to their chests, front and back, and cut discreet holes in their shirts to capture all the action! Our plan was now in place and the film crew were excited to be sharing another Happy Feat journey.

The SOG team supplied a list of accommodation in Newcastle but none of their recommendations were suitable for a group as big as ours. I spent many hours researching alternative locations and plans. Eventually I came up with the idea of staying at Camp Breakaway, a purpose-built facility that provides respite care for people with disabilities and their carers. It was about an hour away from Newcastle, which meant organising the catering, and coaches for transport, but it was worth the effort.

The SOG team weren't used to dealing with such a large group. They were only going to allow two to three volunteers backstage with us to help look after all 35 Happy Featers. After some tense negotiations, I organised for our team of volunteers to join us for the performance. That way they could help look after our Happy Featers before, during and after the event. Another challenge was conquered.

An intense marketing campaign was initiated; fundraising events and sponsorship programs were promoted to help fund the enormous costs.

Being guest speaker at various events played an important role in spreading the word and boosting our fundraising efforts. Despite my fears about public speaking, I had to 'put my big girl pants on' and 'Just do it.'

A Happy Feat SOG committee was set up. Anne Sanker was instrumental in organising comprehensive timetables, intricate plans, accommodation, information packs, catering, including special countless dietary requirements necessary for taking 70 of our Happy Feat team on a four-day adventure of a lifetime.

Donna, our 'treasured' treasurer was kept busy with the sophisticated and numerous accounting requirements. Our wonderful secretary, Kristin, who is also a solicitor, was invaluable in assisting with the liability/legal requirements, indemnity forms and paperwork.

Can you imagine the headaches and coordination required for organising seventy flights and luggage? I'm sure the flight company team were thrilled when it was all completed! I know I was!

Being over-protective when it comes to our Happy Featers, I even organised for a remarkable, caring, and super-efficient nurse to join us for the trip. She looked after our members' wellbeing and medication requirements and was a valuable member of the team.

Then there were the event tickets for the parents to watch the opening ceremony. Not knowing where our team would be performing, I stressed over what part of the stadium to purchase their seats so they could best see their stars. Gut instinct won over again, and I ended up purchasing seats...right in front of our Happy Feat performers!

Throughout 2013, it was fulfilling to watch our whole Happy Feat team of dancers, parents, and volunteers bonding, strengthening friendships, helping each other, and working together to prepare for our adventure at the Special Olympic Games in Newcastle.

Unfortunately, my little house of cards was about to come crashing down. Not everything was as peaceful as it seemed. After a painful episode of losing someone very special in my childhood, I had put a wall up between myself and others. At times, it was hard for me to be vulnerable with people I didn't know. That wall had been decimated by the innocence and beautiful souls of these people with disabilities, and I'd let them into my life and heart completely. I would protect them and promote how amazing they are with all my heart. As close as I thought I was to my Happy Feat family though, my next lesson was to teach me about the importance of boundary setting and letting go.

CHAPTER 33

Being Strong When Your Heart is Breaking.

It was the last night of term three of Happy Feat. We were finally introducing our choreography for the Special Olympic Games. All eyes were glued to the screens as we gave our team a special viewing of the two dances we'd be performing. First, it meant getting everyone in height order. That might sound easy, but it's not a simple task when you're dealing with 35+ constellations of special needs and a kaleidoscope of personalities. Some were patient, some were anxious, some were excited, and others were agitated and uneasy.

Eventually everyone was in some kind of line. The music began and so did the magic. Watching the concentration on their faces as they moved in unison, I had goose bumps all over. I was so proud of every one of our dancers, and in awe of how far they'd progressed since we'd begun not three years before.

This first rehearsal of the new choreography went reasonably well, and soon the night was drawing to a close. At this time of night, we do some of the slower dances to wind down. In the middle of 'I Still Call Australia Home', I noticed that Trudy was upset. Quickly going to her aid, I held her hands and quietly asked her what was wrong. Trudy looked up with her beautiful and innocent eyes. "Troy keeps coming around."

Mmm. Well, that seemed easy to fix. Troy was another of our Happy Feat dancers.

"That's OK, Trudy," I said. "I'll stop him coming around."

To this day, I don't know why I asked the next question. When I heard the answer, I felt as if a knife had been driven through my heart.

"Trudy, what does Troy do when he comes over?"

"He does dirty things to me."

That sentence will haunt me for a long time to come.

I realised I needed to quickly pull myself together. That meant taking Trudy aside while I worked out what on earth to do and give us some privacy so I could learn exactly what had happened.

I looked Trudy in the eye and found simple words for her to understand. "Trudy, you haven't done anything wrong. It looks like Troy may have made some wrong choices and I'm going to stop this happening. We love you very much and want you to be safe and happy. Does Troy do this when your other flatmates are there?"

Trudy shook her head, "No, he doesn't."

This, at least, was a minute piece of positive news against the backdrop of a very grave situation. I wanted to cry my heart out and shout with anger and frustration, but I had to remain calm. I said farewell to everyone, wearing my 'Leigh smile'. Everyone waved and wished me Happy Birthday and good luck for my upcoming holiday.

As Troy walked past, I asked him to stay because I wanted to speak with him. When the last of the families had left, I took Troy aside. As I went to talk to him, I quickly realised I was not trained for this type of serious confrontation. I didn't want to misstep and rush recklessly into such a sensitive matter.

Rather than bringing up the issue, I simply asked him for his mobile number. Sensing something was wrong, and being a master of changing the subject, he started telling me about his sore arm. Totally ignoring this, I asked him again for his mobile number. One of our volunteers looked at me with a stunned expression. This wasn't the usual caring and empathetic Leigh she knew!

Once again, Troy tried to change the subject by saying he was now feeling dizzy.

"What's your mobile number, Troy?" I asked again, ignoring the distraction.

Once he gave it, I checked it against the number in my phone and let him go.

I turned and walked away, feeling completely out of my depth.

Reaching the privacy of the carpark, I sat quietly and planned an appropriate course of action to take. Even though it was 9.30pm, I decided to immediately contact Trudy's carer.

Unable to reach her, I left a message asking her to call me urgently, no matter what time it was. I couldn't help worrying about leaving Trudy on her own.

Quickly going to Plan B, I rang the manager of the organisation who looked after Trudy. Relieved when she answered, I apologised for calling at such a late hour and stressed the seriousness of the situation. After sharing what Trudy had told me, I said I felt that it was a matter for the police. I needed her guarantee that she would involve the police and seek counselling for Trudy. Voicing my concern about leaving Trudy on her own with her flatmates currently away, I explained that I was going to her place immediately to ask if she'd like to come home with me to stay until the issue was resolved. The manager said to leave it with her and that she would ring me back.

Arriving at Trudy's place, I found her calmly doing her weekly budget. She said it was the most settled she'd felt for weeks. Sharing this information with someone she trusted had helped put her mind at rest.

I quickly rang Geoff to let him know I was dealing with a serious situation and not to worry – I'd be home later.

Once again, I reaffirmed to Trudy, as simply as possible, that she hadn't done anything wrong. Troy may have possibly made wrong choices, which had hurt her, but I was going to stop it happening. I also reassured her that we loved her and wanted her to be happy and safe. I asked her if it was OK with her if we called the police so that we could stop this happening. When I saw her eyes as she gave her agreement, my heart melted, and it made me even more determined to keep her safe.

There was a sigh of relief when the manager of Trudy's care organisation called back. Putting the phone on speaker, I was also relieved to see Trudy's face light up when she recognised who was on the line. That's a good start, I thought — at least she's in the right hands. The manager reminded Trudy that her carer would be picking her up the next morning for her planning meeting and that she would then take Trudy to her office to discuss this situation involving Troy. Trudy seemed content with this plan, and I felt reassured she'd have qualified people to help her through this delicate discussion.

As I made sure Trudy was safe for the night, checking her doors and windows were locked, my gut instinct was hounding me. As the president of Happy Feat, I felt it was my responsibility to report this situation to the police as soon as possible. I rang the number of the local police station displayed next to Trudy's phone and was advised to ring another number. Wanting to speak to someone in person, I tried another police station. Once again, I received a recorded message. When I finally got through to a female officer, I briefly explained the situation and she urged me to bring Trudy down to the police station.

By that time, it was 11:00pm. Trudy and I were both exhausted and I quickly explained that Trudy had a disability. The officer said that if the police were to come to Trudy's house, it could take hours. As it had already been arranged for Trudy to be with qualified people in the morning and having at least reported the matter to the police, I reluctantly admitted defeat. Knowing Trudy was safe and secure, I headed home.

It was nearly midnight by the time I arrived home, so I quickly had dinner, a shower and fell into a deep sleep until 5:00am the next morning. As soon as I woke up, I wrote a full incident report, noting exact times and dates. Then I emailed this report to our Happy Feat Secretary, a solicitor. I asked if it was OK to send it to the manager of the organisation looking after Trudy. To keep her safe, I was eager to send this information so that immediate action would have to be taken.

Then I called an urgent meeting with our small Happy Feat committee for 5:30pm that afternoon. It was Thursday, and Geoff and I were scheduled to fly out on holidays on Saturday. I certainly hadn't been expecting to be addressing such a critical and delicate situation so close to leaving.

At the time, I was under enormous pressure. Like anyone who works, I was trying to finalise everything before I went on leave. I was also managing our Special Olympic Games event, so I was completely unprepared for our holidays. Working 19–20-hour days continuously for weeks was definitely taking its toll - and if I didn't need a holiday before, I well and truly needed one now!

I tried to organise a meeting with Troy and his parents for that afternoon. Troy's dad had something planned, and Troy was supposedly visiting a friend in hospital. I told them I would be at their home at 9:30 the following morning, as I had something I needed to drop off before I went away. That 'something' was Troy's letter of suspension from Happy Feat and all associated activities. Pending the outcome of the police investigation, he could also be disqualified from Happy Feat.

After an extremely hectic day, it was time for our committee meeting, and I began by emphasising the strict confidentiality of this meeting. No Happy Feater's names were ever to be divulged outside this meeting. Reading my report, the committee members were devastated to hear the news and struggled to keep their composure. I told the members that I had forwarded the report to the appropriate organisation and how I had unsuccessfully tried to contact the manager all day to see how Trudy went with the police.

We were concerned for Trudy. I rang her during the meeting and was relieved when she answered the phone. She said she'd been taken to the police station, and she seemed comfortable with the outcome.

During the meeting, I also read Troy's letter of suspension to ensure that everyone agreed with this course of action. Then I had a dreadful thought. What if Troy was going around to Trudy's place instead of visiting someone in hospital? I decided to visit her myself after the meeting, just to be sure.

By the time I reached my car, it was already 7:30pm and my amazing daughter was preparing a family dinner for us before the holiday away. I was already late. I rang Trudy again to check that Troy hadn't visited. She was settled and felt safe. We went through a practice of how to handle things if Troy did visit.

"Trudy," I said firmly. "No matter what, do NOT open any of your doors to Troy. Say, 'Go away or I'll call the police!'"

We practiced it over and over, as I tried to get Trudy to say it louder and more forcefully. Then for some reason, it occurred to me to ask her if Troy also rang her repeatedly.

"Yes, he did," she said.

"Has he rung you today?" I asked.

"Yes, he wanted to come over and say sorry."

Once again, we practiced what to say and how to say it. Satisfied, I hung up and headed to Stacey's, thinking how very fortunate I was to have my wonderful family.

The next morning, I drove to Troy's place with a heavy heart. As I arrived, his dad met me at the door saying, "Leigh, I can't believe it. He won't see you."

"That's OK, I'll see him," I said, walking past.

As I stood at the doorway to his room, Troy was lying on his bed and opened his eyes. His father watched on.

"Troy, I'm sorry but I've come to give you this letter."

I proceeded to read the letter of suspension, and then went on to explain everything, so he well and truly understood the situation.

"Your membership at Happy Feat has been suspended pending the police investigation. That means you can't participate in any Happy Feat activities until this matter has been investigated. If it's found that you have broken any rules, your membership with Happy Feat will be disqualified and you won't be able to be part of Happy Feat again. Troy, I'm so sad this has happened."

He turned his head the other way and I left the room. His dad stopped me, asking about the Special Olympic Games. I returned to Troy's doorway and explained it to both of them.

"Troy, unfortunately this means you won't be attending the Special Olympic Games. We will refund any money you've paid."

When I asked his father about a bank account to refund the money into, I saw that he was very upset, so I didn't push the issue and told him that we'd send a cheque.

As I walked out, he said, "I don't know what else to do."

Normally, I would have stopped and tried to commiserate with him but under the circumstances, what could I do?

As difficult as the situation was, I drove off knowing in my heart that I had done the right thing.

It was my birthday the next day and lately I'd been too busy to catch up with my besties, Joy, and Katie. I'd planned to spend the day with them, and nothing was going to stop me. I tried to put the horrible situation behind me and went to meet up with them. I felt like I'd been hit by a bus.

That afternoon I was overjoyed to receive an email from Trudy's manager saying that they were relocating her. That was the very best news, and I knew I could go on holiday with peace of mind knowing Trudy was safe and protected.

Even during my holiday though, I couldn't stop thinking about Troy. I worried what was going to happen to him. Did he even understand why what he allegedly did was wrong? I had known him and his family for years with Happy Feat and had helped them so much in that time. I couldn't just discard him without a care, that's simply not in my nature.

When I returned from holidays, I decided to make enquiries about how to help Troy and his family and found someone to help. I rang Troy's father and told him about the counselling organisation I'd found who was ready to take them under their wing.

Unfortunately, the organisation ended up turning Troy and his family against myself and Happy Feat, threatening the validity of our suspension with legal action. I couldn't believe it! For over three years, I'd helped this family. They knew I was very protective of our Happy Featers' wellbeing, and in this situation, I had to protect Trudy, if not potentially other members. It hurt to see how quickly they dismissed everything I'd helped them with over the years!

There was no way they were going to force Happy Feat to take him back and put my members' safety in jeopardy. I had poured my heart and soul into our dance group and to think an organisation like this was going to try to bring it down. Well, they'd have a hell of a fight on their hands if they tried!

I must admit, it totally gutted me. I started to question how I did things. Perhaps I shouldn't give so much of myself to everybody. Maybe I should back off and not help people as much. Maybe I should distance myself from everyone and protect myself from the hurt.

My doubts and questioning went on for weeks while juggling work, family, and Happy Feat — not to mention organising all the details for taking 70 people to Newcastle for the opening ceremony of the Special Olympic Games! I found myself wanting to hibernate the second I didn't have to be out there doing my stuff. I just wanted to put a cocoon around myself and prevent any further hurt.

This was so out-of-character for me. I kept telling myself to put some cement on it and toughen up! All that mattered was that Trudy was relocated, safe and very happy and our team was protected, right? This situation with Troy and the care organisation cut me to my core, and I needed time to regroup.

Thankfully, some weeks later, I finally regained my mojo. I always take something good out of a bad situation. This taught me to be more street smart. I realised that even though I couldn't stop being me, I couldn't stop giving my time and energy to my Happy Featers, a protective wall had to remain. It was such a serious situation with so many different facets, and it was made even more difficult by not being able to tell anyone. I felt as if I was carrying a very heavy burden I couldn't share.

I came to peace with Troy's family's actions. The analogy I kept reminding myself of was the fact that I love my skippies, but I wouldn't approach one of the females who had an injured joey. She was sure to attack me to protect her offspring. This was the same situation: a family trying to protect their child.

Once I came to terms with these facts, I felt I was able to be me again. I regained my spark. As I've said before, I believe that everything happens for a reason. If something like this happened again, I don't think I'd do anything differently. I knew in my heart I'd done the right thing in protecting Trudy and getting help for Troy, even with the blowback from his care organisation and family. I could have forgotten about Troy and his family, saying that it wasn't my problem, but that's not how I was raised. They were now receiving the guidance and counselling that I'd helped organise. Sometimes I just wish my wonderful parents hadn't brought me up to do the right thing all the time. Life would have been much easier!

All of this was going on while Happy Feat was on the cusp of its biggest adventure yet. While organising for the Special Olympic Games on its own was like a marathon, everything going on in the background had made it so much more gruelling to get through. At last, we were ready for the big trip south. Surely, these last weeks were the worst of it, right? Surely, we had nothing but clear skies ahead. Right?

CHAPTER 34

The Special Olympic Games: Adventure of a Lifetime

Receiving the choreography only eight weeks before the Games was a huge challenge! It would be an enormous task for any dance group to learn choreography for two different dances in such a short period. While we had many parents and carers stressing, I kept reminding everyone to 'Believe and you can achieve', reassuring them that our Happy Featers were more than capable of taking on this challenge.

And they did! Every move synchronised as they danced with passion and determination. It was another remarkable achievement for our Happy Featers!

Having never attempted an event like this before, we tried to make sure that everything was organised and ready to go. Fundraising was complete, Happy Featers were allocated group leaders and notified what groups they were in. They were provided with packing lists, detailed timetables, even care-packages for their flight, as well as clear instructions so they knew what to expect. The more information provided, the more relaxed and comfortable everyone felt.

Finally, everything was complete - the accommodation, seventy return flights, two coaches, all catering and takeaway meals for the rehearsal and performance, costumes, hair and makeup sessions, stadium passes, forms and copious amounts of paperwork. Before we knew it, the exciting day arrived. There were no more sleeps. Today was the start of our biggest Happy Feat adventure so far.

Finalising the packing, I found that I was ready early. I picked up my brother, and a Happy Feat volunteer, Donna L, and we drove with great excitement to the airport. We found it hard to believe that after all these months of planning, we were headed to the Special Olympic Games!

Battling all our extra luggage and bags full of costumes, we made it to the check-in counter to confirm our arrangements. The airport staff were ready and eager to begin the group booking, we were prepared with our folders and group lists, so we thought we'd head to the café to enjoy a quiet coffee before everyone arrived. A group of Happy Featers had the same idea, however, and greeted us excitedly. OK: Plan B!

It wasn't long before everyone began arriving, huge smiles on their faces. Their excitement and energy filled the airport. Our Happy Feat team knew they were to report to their allocated group leader. When their whole group was present, they checked in as a group, proceeded through security to wait in the area we had agreed upon. This system worked efficiently for our large group, and we were soon all gathered and waiting together. Even the 40-minute flight delay didn't perturb anyone, as we were thrilled to be together and ready for our adventure.

Adding further to everyone's great excitement, our local superstar, Steve 'Pricey' Price, made a surprise appearance to wish us good luck. Everyone gathered around for chats and endless photo opportunities. Representatives from two of the local television stations also arrived, quickly getting caught up in the buzz. As they interviewed several Happy Featers, the others looked on, waiting for their turn in front of the camera. Shy little butterflies - NOT! Gathering everyone involved, we took a huge group photo, with lots of cheering and posing for the cameras.

Soon it was time to board the plane. Coming together in their allocated groups and being checked off the list, everyone boarded the plane efficiently and effortlessly. I was so proud of how smoothly everything had gone so far. It was only early days but so far so good!

The flight went well. I took photos throughout and checked that everyone was happy and doing well. The flight attendants commented on how well-mannered our group was as they went through the cabin offering coffee and tea. This was another opportunity to show the wider community how amazing our Happy Feat team is, helping break down barriers and stereotypes.

After disembarking, it was time for a toilet stop before proceeding to the baggage area. In the lead up to the trip, detailed weekly letters been sent out. Our team knew that they were to gather in their groups near the baggage carrousel while designated members retrieved the Happy Feat luggage. Yellow ribbons indicated which were the Happy Feat bags, then a secondary coloured ribbon indicated which team they were for. It was a brilliant and efficient system that made the process smooth and stress-free.

Two buses were waiting for us, along with our friendly drivers. The luggage was loaded effortlessly, the team boarded, and we were on our way to Camp Breakaway. There was a lot of singing, photos, and dancing in our seats. We uploaded photos to our Happy Feat Facebook page showing everyone having a ball.

At Camp Breakaway, we were met by Stephanie, the wonderful lady who had helped us throughout the whole planning stage of our adventure. Gathering in the community hall for a delicious dinner, we were taken to our allocated accommodation. Everyone was so impressed with the facilities and the standard of accommodation. It was like being in a five-star resort! I was absolutely thrilled that all the planning and hard work had paid off.

By 5:00am the next morning, I was awake, showered and enjoying a quiet cuppa in the community room. It wasn't long before I was joined by several volunteers and Happy Featers. We enjoyed catching up and having a laugh, getting to know each other better.

After breakfast, it was time to have some fun on the go-karts that were part of the wonderful activities available at Camp Breakaway. We spent hours laughing, taking photos and videos, and racing each other, getting up to all sorts of antics! I even talked some of the mums into having a turn themselves.

One mum had tears of laughter streaming down her face as she got off the go-kart and commented that she hadn't laughed so much in years. There were several moments when I felt quite emotional seeing everyone having so much fun, getting on and helping each other. This was what it was all about – the performance at the opening ceremony was just a bonus.

As if the go-karts weren't fun enough, we then discovered the play area where we all enjoyed a second childhood. A flying fox, swings and the jumping pillow were all hugely popular. Once again, after a little bit of encouragement, the Happy Featers and their mums had a ball on the jumping pillow, laughing like nobody was watching. Hearing our Happy Featers' and mums' squeals of joy as they simply enjoyed the freedom and sense of escape from their daily challenges - well, words can't describe those moments.

As we get older, we tend to think swings and other playground equipment are only for the young ones, but not me. I tell my kids, 'Just because I look old doesn't mean I have to act old!'

Finally, we dragged ourselves away from the fun to have lunch, followed by a rehearsal. We discovered that one of the dances we'd been practising for the last eight weeks had been modified by the SOG team; they had slowed the accompanying song down. Surprisingly, this didn't faze the team and we just practiced at the easier and more sedate tempo. Once again, our Happy Featers nailed it and were all in unison. Time for the dress rehearsal!

Seeing everyone in their costumes really brought home that we really were performing at the opening ceremony of the Special Olympic Games. After all these months of planning and the many challenges we had to overcome, it was finally happening. We were all thrilled to be part of such a huge and exciting event. We packed our picnic dinners, gathered in our groups, boarded the buses and were soon on our way to Newcastle.

Our excitement reached a crescendo when we saw the Hunter Stadium. This was a big moment: we were about to experience our first rehearsal for the opening ceremony. All the mums and Happy Featers were beside themselves!

Gathering outside the stadium, we waited for our SOG armbands. After ensuring we were extremely organised and efficient with our Happy Feat preparation, I was surprised to find that things were not running so efficiently on the SOG side of things. That was slightly concerning to me because when you're working with a group like ours, you really want things to run to plan to avoid undue stress.

Some of the volunteers and I took over the distribution of the armbands, discovering that they hadn't provided enough of them. Prepared, I produced my email documentation to show the approved number of performers, the number of carers allowed to be backstage and the authorisation for the remaining mums and carers to be seated in the grandstands during the rehearsal. They realised we were on the ball and meant business, and without hesitation produced the missing armbands.

We proceeded to our dressing room, while the mums went to take their seats in the grandstands. They were the only ones in the whole stadium and felt very special as they eagerly waited to see the Happy Feat team in action. The rehearsal was late starting, but our team waited very patiently. I have told them on many occasions that they're superstars now and when you're a superstar, there's lots of waiting involved. There was never any complaining.

Lining up in the tunnel, everything around us seemed chaotic and disorganised. Suddenly, we were called to start our dance, and our team frantically tried to get to the performance area in time - on the other side of the stadium! It was heart-breaking seeing the stress this evoked in the dancers, and it was degrading to have to practically drag our dancers onto the field to get them into position in very little time. We not only have members with special needs, but also have some quite elderly members, so moving quickly can be a huge challenge.

The rehearsal was a complete disaster. Seeing our Happy Featers dragged out onto the field was against everything I believe in; I vowed never to let that happen again! I was totally devastated. It was hard to have to hold it all together when I had so many people relying on me.

Eventually everyone got to the far side of the stadium, and it was an absolute shemozzle. Nobody knew where we were supposed to be, our team becoming agitated and stressed. I locked eyes with Rhi. I could tell we both could have just sat down there and then and cried our hearts out! After such a total disaster, we were told to go back to the tunnel and do it again, but the second time was no better.

Had I put my heart and soul into something that was going to be a total disaster of an event? As the leader, it was my responsibility to make it work, and make it as positive an experience as possible.

Returning to our dressing room, everyone was quite emotional and running on lots of adrenaline. Our volunteers, who had never participated in such a big performance before, were quite overwhelmed. Yet there were tears of joy as they recalled the feeling of entering and performing in the stadium - even though it was empty!

Inside, I was a mess. On one hand, I felt totally gutted at having to drag our beautiful Happy Featers onto the stadium. On the other, I was thrilled at seeing our volunteers' response. To be honest, I was also worried sick that it was such a shemozzle and so disorganised, especially after all our hard work.

Beaming from ear to ear, one of our Happy Featers came up to me to excitedly show me a move he'd managed to do tonight for the very first time. He straightened his arms above his head, and then moved them to one side. These might be simple everyday movements for you and me, but after his accident, and because of his limited use of one arm, this was a momentous feat! For him to have achieved this was like climbing to the top of Mount Everest. I was so proud to stand up there on top of that mountain right beside him. Any worry and anxiety I had experienced that night paled in significance as I watched him proudly showing everyone else what he'd just shown me.

Even if we gained nothing else from this whole experience, it was already a success. Our amazing film guys were there, keen to zoom in on me fighting back tears, but it was a very private moment for me. I didn't want anyone to notice me feeling fragile. Even after three and a half years of Happy Feat, I still marvelled at the difference it made in so many lives. I felt as if I had witnessed another miracle.

When Ashley was diagnosed with Leukaemia, I made the decision that I wouldn't cry. Happy Feat was teaching me how to show my emotions again. It was difficult, because for the past six or seven years, it was rare for me to allow myself to cry in front of others. At this point, while I was feeling low and exposed, we were given some news.

We were told we could go home - because two of our events had been cut. Despite going to the tremendous effort of getting our 70 members to Newcastle to perform two dances, participate in another event and then the finale — and this is what I'd told our team — we were now informed we were only doing the two dances.

I couldn't believe it! The news was shattering, and I was furious (something very out-of-character). I hate letting anyone down - and now I had to tell our team that we were only doing two out of the four dances we had prepared.

I took some deep breaths! It was another character-building time.

Trying to hide my emotions, I led our team back to the bus for the return journey to Camp Breakaway. Everyone was tired so the trip home was quiet. Most people went straight to bed after we arrived. Some of the volunteers sat up having a cuppa. Deep in thought, I sat quietly, trying to come up with Plans B, C, D and even E!

It was a waste of time trying to sleep that night. After only two hours I got up, showered, and desperately sought some inspiration.

How was I going to overcome these challenges? It wasn't only trying to get our Happy Featers across the stadium in time, it was also being able to participate in more than two dances. It was doing justice to the incredible work they'd done to learn the choreography so quickly, then having to learn another again at the slower tempo. We had come a long way for this.

I kept telling myself, "Leigh, you must fight for this. It's your responsibility to stand up and fight for their right to participate in this event like you were promised!"

You'll never believe it, but as I was getting the milk out of the fridge for my Milo, deep in thought, I found my inspiration! There was a quote on the fridge from Paula Radcliffe that I hadn't noticed before, and that I'll never forget. It said:

'Never set limits, go after your dreams, don't be afraid to push the boundaries. And laugh a lot – it's good for you!'

In a flash, I knew exactly what I had to do. I grabbed my To-Do-list. I needed to go straight to the top of the SOG committee and fight for the rights of our Happy Featers, pushing the boundaries if necessary. Perhaps not at 4:00am, though! Part of me wanted to give them a blast and tell them exactly how I felt - but I've learned that you get more bees with honey, so I regained my composure and took lots of deep breaths.

Next on the list - organising an important meeting with the volunteers to formulate a plan to get our Happy Featers into position for their performance. Once again, perhaps not at 4:00am, but soon! I have the most awesome, caring, dedicated, passionate and committed team of volunteers I could ever wish for. I simply couldn't have done it without them. Most have been with me since before Happy Feat began, and I'm so proud to work alongside them.

Taking my Milo outside, I sat in the middle of the grass. To my surprise, I ended up surrounded by ducks. As I sat formulating my plans, I marvelled at those ducks. One had a sore leg and was waddling around keeping up with the others, while another had an injured wing. I sat there admiring how well they had adapted and were doing everything the other ducks were doing.

Then the parallel to Happy Feat hit me! I grinned to myself as I thought how funny it must look. Here I was at an ungodly hour of the morning, sitting among a flock of ducks in the middle of nowhere, grinning to myself – but it was just the therapy I needed to recharge my batteries. I had to be ready for another very long and character-building day ahead.

This morning was to be very relaxed and low-key for everyone, and they had free time to do their own thing. After breakfast, I told the film crew that I was going to make the call to the head of the SOG committee. We tried to disappear somewhere quiet where I could concentrate, but I soon discovered one of our Happy Featers walking around a little secluded area with his phone. When I quizzed him, he said that he was just walking around, taking photos of the beautiful flowers. I was taken aback because he always tried to come across as a big toughie and here he was, mesmerised by the beautiful flowers. People are fascinating - there are always special things to discover when you least expect it.

Finally, the film crew and I found a quiet area so I could make this important call. I felt such a range of emotions: anxious, unsettled, and furious, yet determined. The lack of sleep probably didn't help, either.

I took some deep breaths, calming myself, then dialled the number. Ring, ring, ring. Message bank!

I reminded myself that you get more bees with honey than vinegar, so I smiled and left an upbeat message, asking the project manager to call me back. What an anticlimax. I really wanted to get it over and done with so the situation could be more settled, but it looked like another Plan B was needed, including waiting, and hoping to get a call back.

It wasn't long before my call was returned. I ran over to the film crew trying to calm myself down, reminding myself again about using honey to get the bees. I tried to be upbeat, saying how excited we were having come all this way. I said that I was just confirming with her that we were still doing the two dances, the finale as well as the circle that we'd been scheduled to do according to the latest communication.

Silence.

"Leigh, I'm sorry, but Happy Feat isn't in the finale."

Silence.

"Oh! Well, I suppose we still have the two dances and the circle."

Silence.

"The circle isn't happening now."

Silence.

"I can't believe you're telling me this!"

During the following tense discussion, something was mentioned about one of our favourite dance songs, 'What a Wonderful World', which would also be part of the ceremony.

"Oh great," I said. "That song is right after our two dances, so we'll just stay out there for that."

"No, it's not on straight after your two dances."

"Yes, it is!" I insisted. "That song was on as we were leaving the stadium after rehearsal last night. Great, so we'll stay out there for that. Isn't it good that we'll already be out there and won't have to go in and out of the stadium!"

She reluctantly agreed, though I didn't give her much of a choice. At least I had achieved three out of the four performances I was fighting for.

In our meeting after breakfast, the volunteers and I came up with a plan to get everyone into position on the field quickly and safely. During the rehearsal, I'd seen some of the other performers running onto the field. We decided that rather than all holding hands and moving out as one, those capable of running out could do so, with safety still being the priority. Those who needed to take a little longer could come out at their own pace and simply savour the moment. It was a huge gamble, totally changing our game plan for the opening ceremony, but we were now doing this 'the Happy Feat way!'

To make this critical change more fun, we gave our three groups a name: Abba, Garth Brooks, and Elvis Presley. We then allocated a volunteer to each of the Happy Featers needing assistance getting out to the field so that they could walk at their own pace.

The Abba group would go first. When it was time, they were instructed to get on the field as quickly and safely as possible. They would be followed by the Elvis Presley group, then the Garth Brooks group could take their time and lap up the attention, getting into position without any extra stress.

It was probably the biggest gamble I'd ever made in my whole life. There was a lot to gain, but there was also a lot to lose! We would have 30,000 people watching from the grandstands, plus camera crews beaming the event to people all over the world. And the size of the audience to our success or failure wasn't even my biggest concerns!

After practising a plan for several months, on game day, we were completely changing that plan for the team! I have never felt so much pressure in all my life. It's times like this I ask myself why I didn't take up mountain climbing, sky diving or something less stressful! Hang on, remember our chant, Leigh: "We can do anything given a chance!"

At Happy Feat, we constantly throw different challenges at our members, deliberately mixing up their routines. We've noticed that it has increased the dancers' tolerance for change, and they have become more comfortable taking on new challenges. Their success at Happy Feat increases their self-worth, so they now have so much more self-confidence. They feel safer at taking risks too, knowing that we always have their best interests at heart.

There are numerous theories. Some 'experts' don't believe people with autism and similar challenges should have their routines changed or be encouraged to go outside their comfort zones. Perhaps the experts should see the growth and incredible transformations of our Happy Featers! My wonderful hubby once showed me a quote that made him think of Happy Feat: 'Magic happens outside the comfort zone.'

My special Merry Maker friends were coming to visit me at Camp Breakaway, so with everything now organised, I greeted them with open arms. Watching them walk through the gates was like seeing my parents arrive, emotions just washed over me. Having been through it all with The Merry Makers, Robyn and Bob understood the complexities of running a group like this. This meant that I was able to openly share the stresses and challenges we'd been facing and what we'd just planned. Their reassurance and approval gave me the confidence that we'd made the right choice.

I quickly got ready and joined everyone for an early lunch. While they were eating, I got their attention. I had a very important announcement and they needed to listen very carefully.

"You know when we do big performances, and I say to be prepared for many changes of plans? Remember the Guy Sebastian concert and how many times our plans changed? Well, who still had a fantastic time?" Big cheers went up and everyone put their hands in the air.

"Well, we have to make a huge change to our plans for tonight but we're only doing it to make it better and more fun for you. You know that whatever we do, we only have your best interests at heart. I want to ask you in a few weeks who had the best time at the SOG, and I want you all to cheer in the same way. So, here's the plan."

I then went on to explain about the different groups, and not holding hands. When I said that the ones who needed assistance could come onto the field in their own time, there were sighs of relief.

I stressed the importance of safety, telling them that we'd hate anyone to fall over and hurt themselves. They must keep safety as the top priority when getting out onto the field. I felt relieved at how well everyone had handled the drama of changing our plan so close to the main event. This was a huge gamble, not having practiced it, but the alternative was unacceptable.

You should have seen the preparation and cooperation as everyone sorted and distributed our snacks and the picnic meals prepared by the staff at Camp Breakaway. If you got in the road, you'd get run over. Once again, the colours were a Godsend as everyone gathered in their groups, making sure all the meals were there.

Soon it was time to board the bus taking us to TAFE College for our hair and makeup. There were nine hairdressers and six makeup artists who had given up their whole Sunday afternoon for our Happy Feat team. Some had even travelled quite a distance! During every step of the whole SOG adventure, I was so blown away by the generosity and support of everyone around us, even complete strangers. The TAFE ladies asked me what we'd like for the hair and makeup.

I said that we were doing it the Happy Feat way, which meant whatever they wanted! If they wanted funky, give them the funkiest hairstyle you've ever done! If they wanted curls, give them the most beautiful curls you've ever done! The SOG committee had instructed us to have natural makeup and hair off the face in a ponytail or a bun. But after getting the run around from them, I'd had enough. I was following my instincts (and rebelling a bit as well!).

All the months of planning were worth it, just seeing our Happy Featers getting pampered, and fussed over. When they presented their fancy hairstyles to the rest of the team, there were more cheers and squeals of delight. The energy in the room was incredible!

I had flashbacks of these same Happy Featers on their first night, all shy and quiet. And look at them now! They had truckloads of confidence, were standing proud, beaming from ear to ear, and eager to perform in front of 30,000 people (and millions more via camera!). It was priceless.

We could have returned to Townsville at that moment still having had the adventure of a lifetime - but that was only one chapter and there was so much more excitement to come. I hoped that every sponsor realised the opportunities they've given our whole Happy Feat team, and how much it's truly appreciated.

As we thanked and said our goodbyes, the hairdressers and makeup artists had tears rolling down their faces. It was very moving. They'd also had the time of their lives and didn't want the experience to end.

Arriving at Hunter Stadium, excited and buzzing after our makeovers, it was a relief to see that the SOG members were a little better prepared for our Happy Feat team. Armbands were promptly distributed, and I proudly gave out the grandstand tickets to the mums and carers, telling them to go and thoroughly enjoy it all. They went off like a bunch of excited school kids.

We were fortunate to share our dressing room with a dance group from Grahamstown Public School. This amazing group of students could have taught the rest of the world a lesson on inclusion and acceptance! As they danced and sang while waiting to perform, they included and taught our Happy Featers the different moves and played games. They treated our Happy Featers with utmost respect and were so caring and gentle. We were having so much fun that I said to one of our volunteers, "Make sure we don't miss show time!"

When the Grahamstown dancers lined up with special books to get our Happy Featers' autograph, it was priceless to see one Happy Feater writing the most beautiful first letter of his name. Another of our elderly members proudly passed one book on as she casually took another. How quickly they adjust to fame! This for me was the pinnacle of inclusion and acceptance. I had to fight back tears as I proudly watched our Happy Featers signing autographs. It was another memory I will cherish for the rest of my life.

All too soon, it was show time!

Just imagine hundreds of performers lined up in the tunnel, waiting to burst onto the stadium to perform at the opening ceremony of the Special Olympic Games! There was a combination of excitement, nerves, adrenaline, tension, anticipation, and exhilaration. But as we've come to expect, our whole Happy Feat team was extremely professional, calm, and poised. I was so proud of each and every one of them.

On the inside, however, I was feeling extremely anxious. I hoped that our Happy Featers would make it safely to their correct positions, and that our highly ambitious and risky change of plan would work!

There were huge sighs of relief as our Happy Feat team reached their positions on the field safely; our plan had worked perfectly! We had totally changed the strategy we had been practising for eight weeks - and our Happy Featers stepped up to the mark, following the new plan without any hesitation or drama.

This was another truly momentous achievement. As our Happy Feat Chant says, 'We can do anything given a chance!' We aren't trained to deal with people with special needs, so this was also a huge feat for our amazing volunteer team. We accomplished this challenge with flying colours!

During the performance, it was the most heart-warming and wonderful experience to look around at each member as they danced their heart out. I knew the challenging journey that each Happy Feat member had travelled to experience this very moment. Even now, I get choked up with emotion when I think about how much every one of them had blossomed.

Here are some of their journeys:

One Happy Feater was born with an extremely serious heart condition and her mum (and specialists) said Happy Feat had genuinely extended her lifespan because she loved it so much.

One elderly member, who uses a wheelie walker, was standing ten-foot-tall with a cheeky look of excitement and concentration as she did the moves so gracefully.

A Happy Feater always helped another member with the dance moves during rehearsals. I decided to separate them because I wanted to give them both the opportunity to shine. Well, there they were, both shining like the brightest stars in the sky.

Another Happy Feater had never participated in anything else before joining Happy Feat. Now here he was, smiling and beaming for the whole world to see. He was having fun with his very own friends for the first time in his life.

One member whose mum had suffered a heart attack just days before we left, was out there shining like a diamond knowing his mum was watching from her hospital bed.

Another member, whose friends had told him he wouldn't last two weeks at Happy Feat, was now, three and a half years later, proving them wrong and dancing his heart out. He began Happy Feat using a walking stick, but now refused to use it! After the performance, he had tears rolling down his face and said, "How awesome was that?!"

A couple of the Happy Featers, who often didn't participate greatly during the rehearsals, were now doing every move with enthusiasm and precision!

One Happy Feater's mum told me that her child couldn't manage to do much before but was now showing the world that, yes, they were very capable and could indeed do something very special.

Another who'd been bullied all her life was out there leading our Happy Featers and showing the world how truly amazing she is! What disability?

A member who'd been in an accident and couldn't move one arm was now standing proudly with both arms stretched out, reaching for the sky. This was a miracle in itself!

A Happy Feater who was so introverted, shy, and frightened when she'd joined the group was now performing in front of thousands of people and loving every moment. In fact, I thought we'd have to drag her off the stadium!

Talk about the magic of Happy Feat!

As if that wasn't exciting enough, when all the other performers left the stadium, our Happy Feat team were the only ones left in the stadium for the song 'What a Wonderful World!' It was the Happy Featers' turn to shine!

This was only achieved because we weren't afraid to push the boundaries and stand up for their rights. Feeling very much on cloud nine, and with adrenaline pulsing through our bodies, we excitedly returned to our dressing room. The Grahamstown students were lined up cheering, clapping, and giving our Happy Featers a superstar welcome back to the dressing room. What a buzz!

During this whole adventure, we were very fortunate to have two dedicated members of the team capturing the magic. Will and Luke filmed many of our rehearsals leading up to this event, also joining us for the Newcastle SOG adventure. With no previous experience of working with people with special needs, this experience proved to be an inspirational and life changing experience for these young men. Luke commented, "I feel my life is more fulfilled after having this experience."

It wasn't just our film crew who were moved by the whole adventure. The comments below say it all:

"It was the best weekend for happiness, laughter, goose bumps, and happy tears."

"When I saw my son Dean and his Happy Feat team walk out onto the stadium, waving to the crowd, and then performing with Marcia Hines! Well, that was just the proudest moment for me and brought tears to my eyes."

"Despite being out of their environment, routine, and comfort zone, I saw our Happy Featers at their absolute best. They were joyful, generous, and obliging. I was glad to get to know them all just a little better, and by the end of our four days, I couldn't think of a group of people I would rather have travelled with."

"I'm so proud to know such an amazing group of dancers. All the hard work paid off in the smiles on faces of the dancers and audience –you could see how much fun they were having."

"Just witnessed Happy Feat believing and achieving."

"Every moment was a shining moment for me – there was not one minute that went by where I wasn't awestruck by how special our Happy Feat team is."

"Seeing all the teams pulling together to help set up, serve and clean up at mealtimes – it showed the great team spirit that we share."

"After the rehearsal we were all very emotional, but the Happy Featers comforted each other. The compassion these people have is unbelievable."

"I get teary every time I think about the trip and talk about our experiences there. It is a few weeks since we came back, but I am still highly emotional as it was such an opportunity to help others shine and show the world why our Happy Feat team and others like them should be given a chance and accepted with love into our community. They have such a loving and giving nature, we would all be better off if we had a Happy Feat person in our lives. I feel so privileged to have been a part of this wonderful experience and it is one of the best things I have done in my life."

Chapter 35

Sheer Terror in the Grand Canyon

After such a mammoth project like the Special Olympic Games, you might expect me to hibernate for the next twelve months, seeking a boring, uneventful year ahead. Oh no, not me!

Picture this...white-water rafting and hiking through the Grand Canyon for nine days? Was I crazy?!

Well, it all began with a random email I received back in July 2012. It was from an acquaintance in Utah, asking if anyone was interested in doing the trip two years from that date. There were only five spots left - and our names happened to be on the email list. Geoff called me immediately, saying, "I'm not sure whether we're supposed to be on this list, but I really think we should do it."

"Gosh," I thought. "Why not?!"

I'd never attempted white-water rafting or hiking in my life, but why would that stop me? Plan A was that in January 2014, only a month after the SOG adventure, we'd get serious about hiking training and preparing for the trip. But January came and when it rained continuously, we went to Plan B.

Then February arrived, and it rained even more. Plan C! We signed up with the local hiking club, attending a meeting with only three other members. The group was planning an all-day hike that Sunday which was aimed at experienced hikers - but being adventurous, we decided we'd have a go!

Sunday arrived and the reality was that we simply weren't prepared. Everyday living, family commitments, and hectic schedules prevented us from organising the correct footwear or clothing (two minor details!). So, Plan D came into action as we scurried to get our gear organised so we could attend the following hike in the nearby National Park. Then a fast-approaching cyclone entered the scene, and all national parks were closed until further notice. Now we were down to Plan E!

Unfortunately, Geoff and I had prior commitments for all future hiking dates on the calendar, so we were pretty much down to Plan S! It wasn't looking good. Maybe we weren't destined to do this trip. It was now the end of May 2014 and with only eight weeks until the trip, we still hadn't started our hiking training!

Geoff had planned a couple of motor biking weekends instead of hiking training, so I did something very out-of-character. I spat the dummy. That's it! If we couldn't commit to proper preparation for such a challenging and gruelling adventure, I strongly believed we should cancel the trip. By being unprepared, we could let the whole Grand Canyon team down and I would never do that.

After much discussion, we decided we would commit to getting our trekking gear and training hard for the trip. The following Saturday, we visited all the adventure stores in Townsville, eagerly trying on hiking boots and backpacks. That afternoon, we laid out all the gear, filled the Camelbacks with water and packed, so that each backpack had a weight of around 10kg.

At 5:00am Sunday morning, we looked like professional hikers as we set off from home for a four-hour trek. I commented on the weather being a bit chilly, and no wonder – it was only eight degrees! Whose crazy idea was this?

The hike was surprisingly enjoyable as we pointed out various wildlife and interesting things along the way. After about two hours, we found a tranquil spot on the riverbank and ate our breakfast with huge appetites. This beautiful spot was just up the road from home – why hadn't we discovered it earlier?

The organisers were regularly sending us information about preparing for the trip, and frequently stressed the importance of drinking plenty of fluids as it was going to be hot in the Grand Canyon. Naturally, I was anxious to make sure I drank enough water on our Sunday walk, and continuously sipped from my mouthpiece. After about three hours, I asked Geoff to check my Camelback as I thought it had a kink in it. No – I had already drunk four litres! Hmm, might have to back off on the water!

Over the next few weeks, we religiously trekked Castle Hill and other local spots with all our gear and 10kg backpacks. We certainly got some weird looks from other walkers dressed in shorts and singlets and only carrying water bottles, and here was Geoff and I in our trekking gear and all loaded up. Yep, that's those crazy Caldwells!

It was soon time to fly out. Saying goodbye to Stacey and her adorable new bubby boy was heart-breaking; I just didn't want to leave. The reality set in and I had tears streaming down my face as I finally walked to our boarding gate.

A few days in Las Vegas helped us to adjust to the right time zone and get over the long flight. The highlight of that stay was seeing an amazing water acrobatics show called Le Rêve (The Dream). I would have gone to Las Vegas just to see that show.

I felt so nervous as we took the shuttle to Flagstaff, Arizona, where we were to attend a briefing before our big hike on the Bright Angel Trail the next morning. I was anxious about the arduous hike and the white-water rafting, worried that we weren't fit enough to keep up with the daily hikes. There were so many unknown challenges that lay ahead.

Yes, we sure were out of our comfort zones! The briefing went well though, and everyone was lovely and friendly. Returning to our motel room, we completed the final pack before finally retiring at midnight, ready for the 4:00am alarm.

We were to meet everyone at 5:00am for a 5:30 start, however Geoff left his sunnies in the room so had to make a mad dash back to get them. Was this a sign of what was ahead? The adrenaline was running in overdrive. My backpack felt extremely heavy, and I was going to have to carry it on an infamous hiking trail for the next six hours in 40+ degree heat. Question to self, "Why the hell am I doing this?"

After lots of photos of the glorious sunrise, with tremendous scenery in the backdrop, we set off on our hiking adventure that had been two years in the making.

Initially the trail seemed well maintained and rose only gradually, and I was going to make the most of the good conditions while they lasted. I really enjoyed talking with the other members of our group, getting to know them as we trekked our way through the stunning scenery. Note to self, "Remember Leigh, drink plenty of water, and nibble on nuts and energy bars."

At each rest stop, we soaked our shirts, bandanas, and hats with water, had a welcome toilet break, and quickly had something to eat before setting off again. On the last hour of the hike, however, and no doubt because I was so well hydrated, I desperately needed to pee. With a growing feeling of urgency, I left Geoff and went ahead by myself. Around every corner I hoped to see the banks of the Grand Canyon or something even more exciting – a toilet! I tried to focus on the stunning scenery, and the gorgeous creek running beside the trail. Any other time the crystal-clear flowing water would have been welcome – had I not needed to pee!

After the longest hour of my life, I finally came around a corner to see some people swimming in the beautiful creek. There was a young girl standing in the middle of the trail, so I desperately asked if it was long to go. She said, "You've made it!"

It was at that time I saw the toilet behind her, and in my excitement and relief, I gave her the biggest hug - even though I was totally feral from five hours of hiking. She must have thought I was a fruit loop and worried that she would be spending the next nine days with this crazy lady! But oh, the sweet relief.

There was mayhem when we scrambled to transfer the gear from our backpacks into the big dry bags that would be stored on the rafts, then sort out the gear we would need in our dry day-bags, all the while listening and seeing the thunderous rapids right in front of us. It was too late to turn around and run back up the hill, the only way out was down the roaring rapids. My next note to self, "Suck it up, princess!"

Climbing onto the raft, my stomach was doing double backflips, and my heart was threatening to explode. This had to be one of the craziest adventures I'd ever attempted. I couldn't wait for it to be over. If only I could press the fast-forward button, I would have been out of there in a heartbeat.

We were very lucky to have Tess as our skipper. She told us where to sit, how to hold on and brace ourselves, and most importantly, what to expect. The very first rapid ride was rated among the most challenging in terms of difficulty and danger. Oh great! Where the heck is that fast-forward button?

With white knuckles, and breath held in, we catapulted through the rapids. Freezing water drenched us as we rode the waves like they were a wild bucking bronco.

"Geoff, remind me why we signed up for this adventure!"

Thankfully, it wasn't all wild rapids, and we soon had the opportunity to take in the scenery and magnificent canyons. We got a chance to learn more about Tess and the other guests on the raft.

I still hadn't let go of the fact that there was no mobile reception. Can you understand the significance of this? I was cut off from my kids, my family, and my friends, and that's what it was going to be like for the next nine days.

Before we left, I'd bought a cheap waterproof watch and was constantly checking the time wondering what time we'd stop for lunch, what time we'd be doing the next leg of a hike, what time the break would finish, what time, what time... But Tess kept reminding us that we were on 'river time' now and all those things would happen when they happened. There was no fixed itinerary; we stopped at random places for lunch, camped when we were tired, and hiked when we wanted to. We were now going to let the river take us to an unknown destination.

What a complete turnaround it was from the Happy Feat Special Olympic Games adventure we'd just experienced where everything had been planned and organised down to the last five minutes! Mmm, this would take some humongous adjusting. Hang on – this was going to take a total transformation! And to make matters worse (or was it a blessing in disguise?), my new el cheapo watch wasn't working.

So, at some unknown time and destination, we stopped for a delicious lunch, and I really enjoyed getting to know more of the guests on our trip.

Our very first camping site certainly left a lot to be desired. It was so hot that the only way to find enough relief to get to sleep was to totally saturate our bodies, clothes, bandana, and sheet - and have a container of water to wet everything again after the heat had evaporated every drop of moisture. Despite how exhausted we were, sleep that night was a waste of time. Did I say time? What time? I had no idea what time it was. Tipping water over my head throughout the night helped. It was useless trying to read with my head lamp because it was an open invitation to all the creepy crawlies in the area to come and party with me. And we were going to be doing this for another eight nights.

As you know, at home, we have a cuppa with the skippies every morning. The Grand Canyon offered a pretty good alternative, as the majestic mountains were kissed by the sun every morning. I had no idea what time it was when we woke up, but found myself thinking, "What does it really matter what time it is?"

It made me realise how obsessed we all are with time in the 'real world'. From that moment on, time became insignificant to me. It no longer mattered what time we had lunch, dinner, pulled up to camp for the night, went to bed, woke up etc. It just didn't matter.

That said, by the second day, I was still trying to come to grips with not having mobile reception. It was difficult to not be in touch with our kids or the outside world. Again - at home, I was used to being on the go for 16-20 hours every day and this totally different change of pace – just sitting on the rafts, not organising anything, not doing all the cooking, not managing a million things – soon had me feeling like a caged animal. I was itching to do a hike and burn some energy. How on earth would I handle another seven days?

By day three, I seemed to have settled into the Grand Canyon lifestyle. Setting up camp each night had become second nature and we soon had a little routine. Thankfully, the weather was a little cooler than that first challenging night. I had resigned myself to the fact that I didn't have phone reception or a watch, so I just needed to make the most of the adventure. I started to notice more of the magnificent scenery around me and was able to just be in the moment.

The serenity was short lived, however, when we were about to confront a series of life-threatening rapids! We realised how serious the situation was when we were instructed to pull the rafts over to the bank. Our guides had a long private in-depth discussion about what route we could take through the next rapids so that we came out alive! I remember standing on the shore and nearly panicking, thinking, "There's, actually a chance we could die!" My heart was racing, and I found myself searching the bank for an alternative route to avoid these rapids! "Geoff, why the heck did we sign up for this?"

The guides returned and gave us strict instructions about exactly what to do. There was no room to negotiate. Silently climbing back onto the rafts, you could feel the tension mounting as we pushed away from the bank to enter the most terrifying and dangerous rapids we'd encountered so far.

After what seemed like an eternity, we surfaced - drenched, but alive, and anxiously watching as one by one the other rafts came through safely.

"Well, that was as much fun as childbirth!" I thought.

One morning, we packed our own lunches and snacks, ready for a big day of hiking. Geoff's knee was playing up, so he and a few others stayed beside a beautiful thundering waterfall, while I joined others for a full day of walking. We were dropped off at a ledge along the way and set off uphill for our adventure.

It wasn't long before the trail became nothing more than a narrow ledge overlooking the canyon below. The others didn't baulk at it, so I gathered courage, held my breath, and did the same. The steady uphill climb was very challenging in the unforgiving 40+ degree heat but it was still enjoyable; the waterfalls and scenery were spectacular.

I really enjoyed the hiking challenge and getting to know the other team members even more. In one of the conversations, I had along the way, I happened to mention that I was new to hiking. The others laughed and thought I was joking. They were incredulous when I explained that Geoff and I had only been hiking for eight weeks, max!

We had nearly returned to where the others were waiting beside the waterfall, when I stopped dead in my tracks. We had arrived at a ledge so narrow you could hardly even stand on it, overlooking a vertical drop into the canyon – and we were expected to cross it! In fact, the drop was so far down that you couldn't even see the bottom of the canyon.

Again, I felt terrified for my life. My heart was doing backflips, and my terror paralysed my face and body. I couldn't move a muscle. In that moment, I totally understood why people roll up in the foetal position and rock back and forth in moments of high stress!

Words crossed my lips that I rarely uttered. "I can't do this."

I contemplated hiking back the six hours it had taken to get this far, just so I didn't have to cross this ledge. Luckily, I was surrounded by a group of caring and experienced hikers who helped me through my terror. Ted took my backpack so that I could lean my back against the rock wall, while Rebecca and Lorna talked me through it. The ledge wasn't wide enough for my whole foot to fit on it, half of it protruding into empty space as I took each terrifying step. I couldn't breathe, and I definitely could not look down into the abyss below.

Even as I made it to the other side, I couldn't sigh with relief. I knew I had to do it all over again - there was another lethal ledge ahead! Hang on, I didn't agree to this! I'd never been afraid of heights before, but there had always been safety barriers and nets for protection. Here, there was absolutely nothing to stop your fall and I was aware of the previous fatalities in the Grand Canyon. I was absolutely terrified to the core.

Arriving at the next terrifying ledge, I told myself, "Nike, Leigh, 'Just do it.' You're always the one encouraging others to believe they can do anything. Now it's your turn."

Believe and you can achieve.

Once again, I had to dredge up every ounce of courage, strength, and intestinal fortitude to get through this life-threatening challenge.

The only way out was quite simply to get to the other side. I sucked it up and inched across. I couldn't wait for the next terrifying seconds to pass. Finally, I reached the other side, and it was time to celebrate. I couldn't wait to return to the rafts. I didn't utter a word on the remainder of the hike; I was too shell-shocked and traumatised by what I'd just experienced!

When Geoff saw me, I ran into his arms (he must have been thinking I hadn't been away that long) and hugged the breath out of him while shaking all over and bursting into tears. I blabbered out the story about the two ledge crossings and my sheer terror. I was so relieved to have made it back to him... Alive!

Would I do this trip again knowing what was involved? Heck no! Maybe?

Nature had always been there for me when I needed to recharge and rest. This trip to the Grand Canyon had been something different. It pushed me and taught me valuable lessons that I had maybe been too busy to remember lately. To unplug and take time to make time, to cherish those quiet moments with loved ones and good company. To push through fear – even when every instinct made me freeze or want to go in the opposite – and maybe safer - direction. To put trust and faith in the amazing people around me.

Our Special Olympics adventure had been huge in terms of scale – the organisation, planning, fundraising, scheduling. Getting our massive team of dancers, volunteers, parents on flights to and from Newcastle, organising transportation, food, accommodation, the struggles with the SOG committee, our documentary crew – it was enormous in scope and size. Our adventures in the Grand Canyon had brought everything back to the personal. To the things that are truly important, which was about to brought home in the most painful way.

CHAPTER 36

We'll Keep Dancing for Lany

My day began with a text at 6:30am: "Lany back in hospital, not good."

Allana, one of our amazing Happy Feat family members had a serious congenital heart condition – so serious in fact, that her specialists said the joy of Happy Feat had extended her life! Over the last few weeks Lany had been in and out of hospital with a chest infection but still managed to come to Happy Feat and dance up a storm.

I rang Marion, her mum, and learned that Lany had pneumonia and her heart was struggling to hold out. I went silent, fighting back tears. Marion asked if I was still on the line, so I had to quickly pull it together.

The situation was very grave, there were family members flying in from interstate. I asked Marion if she'd like me to come up to the hospital and she quickly said yes. Before I hung up, I asked if she'd like me to put it on Facebook so that people could send their thoughts and prayers. She readily agreed.

I quickly got dressed, donning my work outfit for after the hospital visit. I was desperately wracking my brain for ways to help Lany get through this.

My beautiful hubby said, "Don't you think you should be wearing your Happy Feat shirt?" Oh, my goodness, yes! There's something extraordinarily empowering about wearing that Happy Feat shirt; you know you are making a difference in the world and people associate it with happiness and joy.

Marion had said she'd been singing Happy Feat songs to Lany so I thought I would take some Happy Feat music with me, but what could she play it on? I had an MP3 player, but I only knew how to turn it on and off. How on earth did you put music on it?

It wasn't a ledge above the Grand Canyon - so when push comes to shove, you just do it, right? I hooked the MP3 player up to my laptop, hoped for the best and started downloading the music. It hadn't finished by the time I had to leave, so I threw the whole lot in the front seat, hoping it continued to download on the way to the hospital.

I'd also grabbed one of the yellow Happy Feat costume shirts that had been sitting in my cupboard, in case Lany might like to have it in the room. It's funny, so many times I'd gone to grab the shirt and put it back with the other costumes but for some reason, I knew I had to leave it there.

Before rushing out the door, I quickly put together a photo and post for our Happy Feat:

> 'HELP!! We need your thoughts and prayers for Allana, one of our beautiful, amazing, funny and special Happy Feat family members. Allana is in hospital in a very serious condition. Please send all your thoughts and prayers to help Lany and her family get through this.'

Seeing Lany in hospital, I was surprised by how bright she looked. I had been expecting the worst. Lany smiled as I gave her a hug and held her hand. I told her we all wanted her back at Happy Feat - we had the Carols by Candlelight coming up. I showed her the MP3 player, saying that I'd brought some Happy Feat music for her to listen to. I put the earplugs in her ears and her whole face lit up as she heard and recognised the music. Marion and her friend remarked that she was definitely listening to the music, and it was the first time they'd seen her settled.

We call it 'the magic of Happy Feat'.

When another relative arrived, I moved to get out of the way to let them hold her hand. Lany wasn't impressed! After a few minutes, Lany became unsettled, and we wondered aloud that it would be funny if it was because the music had stopped. Guess what! That's exactly what had happened! We weren't game to look at each other as I quickly got the music going and Lany became settled listening once again.

I looked for a place to hang the Happy Feat shirt and Marion's friend suggested a place where Lany wouldn't have been able to see it. I grabbed a chair and balancing precariously, hung it up on the netting above the curtain where Lany would be able to see it. Marion looked at her friend and said, "Leigh can get away with anything!"

The little hospital room was feeling crowded as other family members arrived, so I headed off. Later, I returned to the hospital during the afternoon visiting hours, bumping into Lany's sister, Sonia, and some family members, also on their way to the ward. Sonia said they were now waiting for a bed in the palliative care ward.

Those two words shocked and devastated me. I asked if Lany was settled and comfortable and they told me the nurses had given her a bath and put her in a different position, so she was settled now. I also asked if Marion had seen all the wonderful responses of support on our Facebook page. Sonia said they'd been reading the comments out to her during the day.

Marion and Lany now had a huge extended Happy Feat family, and there were already over 40 comments and over 130 likes on the Happy Feat page. How comforting for them to know that everyone was rallying around them.

The next day, I was getting so many texts and messages, I rang Marion saying we had a wonderful problem. So many people who loved them and were worried about them, wanted to know how they both were, and I couldn't keep up with it. I asked Marion was it OK for me to put an update on our Facebook to let all her Happy Feat family know how they were. I prepared a carefully worded message, ran it past Marion to make sure it was OK then posted it.

That afternoon, I met one of the Happy Feat volunteers at the hospital, and we visited Lany together. I was armed with our Happy Feat photo book I'd prepared to give them for their Christmas present, together with our Special Olympic Games newsletter. We showed Lany the photos, laughing at the memories as she looked on intently. Next, we did the Happy Feat Chant and held her finger up for her favourite part, 'We are number one!' In so many photos we have taken of Lany she has her pointer finger raised as she does the Happy Feat number one pose!

Over the next few days, I kept in touch with Marion, giving her my strength and support to get through this, letting her know how much her Happy Feat family was there for her.

Just after 10:00pm on Tuesday night, Marion phoned to let me know Lany passed away peacefully. She said that, surprisingly, it was the most beautiful experience. Lany had all her family with her and after many sporadic breaths, Marion leaned over and whispered in her ear, "It's OK to let go Lany."

Marion said she felt relieved her beautiful daughter was at peace and no longer suffering or in pain.

At 5:00am the next morning, I had notification that someone had posted a message about Lany's death on our Happy Feat Facebook. I quickly fired up the computer and hid the message, not wanting anything to go up on Facebook until Marion had contacted all her family and had given the go-ahead. Knowing that Marion was like me and didn't sleep much, I texted her at about 5:45am to see how she was. She texted back that she only had a couple of people still to notify then would let me know.

In the meantime, I prepared the message for our Facebook page and sent it to her for approval. Marion was so touched by the message that she gave permission for me to post it immediately. The response was overwhelming and beautiful, heartfelt messages of support just kept rolling in.

I was quite anxious about Happy Feat that night. I was worried about how everyone would cope with the news that someone in our Happy Feat family had passed away. This was a first for Happy Feat. We'd lost one of our very special volunteers in the past, but we'd never actually lost a Happy Feater before, and it was hitting everyone very hard.

I prepared an action-packed program so we'd be so busy having heaps of fun that we wouldn't have time for anything else. I engaged the help of a special lifetime friend - who was also our nurse for the Special Olympic Games adventure - asking her to come along to Happy Feat. To my surprise, she advised against using euphemistic language like, 'passed away'. She explained that was confusing for our Happy Featers, I needed to be more precise and use simple language.

That night, two of our Happy Featers had made gorgeous cards for Lany's family and were making sure everyone signed them. When I had the group together, I said, 'You will notice that one of our beautiful Happy Featers, Allana, isn't here tonight. Ever since Lany was a baby, she's had a very sick heart. So, for over 40 years, Lany's heart has been very sick. That's a long time, isn't it? Well, last night, Lany's heart was so tired it stopped working and Lany died while Marion was holding her hand. She was surrounded by her family and so much love. How lucky was Lany to be surrounded by so much love, hey?!'

It was at this moment I saw several Happy Featers crumbling and starting to cry. Then, the most beautiful thing happened. As I saw the volunteers come from every direction to comfort those Happy Featers, love, care and empathy filled the room. I'll always treasure my memory of that moment.

As they were being comforted, I continued, "Lany wouldn't want us to be sad. She'd want us to be happy, keep dancing and having fun. So tonight, we're going to dance for Lany and do the Happy Feat

Chant soooo loudly that the people down at McDonalds will hear us. They'll be eating a Big Mac and say, 'Oh my goodness, that's Happy Feat doing their chant!'"

I'm sure it was the loudest chant I've ever heard! It was one our most fun and magical nights as our Happy Feat family danced for Lany.

On the morning of Lany's funeral, I arrived at the church early, armed with a helium gas bottle, truckloads of Happy Feat balloons and ribbon. One of my wonderful Happy Feat volunteers also turned up early to help blow up balloons, and we set about making the church colourful, filled with the Happy Feat theme (as Lany's mum had requested).

I felt very privileged to be able to share my thoughts during the ceremony. I had to be strong and confident (or fake that I was, anyway) so that everyone could feed off that strength.

"We've been really privileged to have Lany as part of our Happy Feat family from the very first day we began – 4½ years ago. Over that time, we've shared so much fun, laughter, camaraderie, and magical moments with Lany. Memories made of her dancing up a storm every Wednesday night and walking the red carpet at our Graduation and birthday galas. Pure joy as she performed at five Inclusive Community festivals. The awesome four-day adventure to the Special Olympic Games and many, many more precious times.

Lany absolutely loved dancing and doing the Happy Feat Chant. In fact, she loved it so much that she thought we should do the Happy Feat Chant during a performance at the WNBL semi-finals when the Townsville Fire were playing. It was a packed stadium and we had very limited time. The music began and everyone was dancing their hearts out...except Lany! She turned around and started telling us, in no uncertain terms, that she was not a happy camper. Lany wanted to do the Happy Feat Chant and she was standing up for what she believed in. How awesome is that! We loved that spirit!

Another thing Lany loved was her birthdays and every week, starting in January, she would announce excitedly "Birthday, my birthday!" One of our new volunteers had been speaking with Lany in February and asked us if it was Lany's birthday soon.

"Yep."

"So, is it this month?"

"JUNE!"

Every week, when Lany arrived at Happy Feat, she would line up for her hugs. We're really going to miss those hugs and that big, beautiful smile! Last week, our Happy Feat team danced for Lany and it was the most magical and memorable night that I will cherish for the rest of my life because we could feel Lany watching over us. Lany has touched the hearts of so many people.

We know she'll be up there dancing and doing the Happy Feat Chant to her heart's content! Rest in peace our beautiful Happy Feat angel."

CHAPTER 37

Remind Me Why I Do This?

While I was on holidays over the Christmas break, I thought long and hard about the launching of our Happy Feat documentary. Until that moment, I really didn't feel our team was ready, but I now felt the time was right. I emailed the videography team and suggested that we combine the launch with our fifth birthday celebrations in May. As this was another five months away, it gave them plenty of time to wrap it all up and produce it.

We had already investigated venues. Our biggest challenge was finding one with a stage big enough for our 35+ performers, plus room for 300 guests, and easy parking. Checking out one of the local colleges, I was lucky enough to see it set up for a school Graduation and declared it the perfect venue!

The next step was to choose a date. I'd been checking in with the Cowboys, noting the dates of their home games so we didn't clash with them. Then the fun began to find a date that Rhi was available (we couldn't have a function without our amazing dance teacher), if the hall was available, and to make sure there wasn't another significant event on the same date. After changing the date many times, we finally came up with a date that was suitable: Saturday the 4th of July, which seemed very fitting for the occasion.

Our weekly Happy Feat venue was unavailable during February so that only left sixteen Happy Feat nights to prepare, which really wasn't a lot. A committee meeting was held to plan for the event and a team was chosen for the costumes and other planning. I was thrilled to have delegated the costumes to others and so would only be involved in the final decision-making. Knowing nothing about sewing and costumes, I was happy not to be involved.

As we had new display homes opening for our business, work was hectic and very stressful. New display homes meant decommissioning the current display homes, and it was my responsibility to catalogue and sell all the display furniture, as well as juggling everything else to get the new homes ready for our sales team! The pressure was threatening to engulf me, and I was getting by with only four hours sleep to get everything done.

In terms of planning our birthday event, I felt I was beating my head against a brick wall! No matter what I did, there seemed to be a constant source of overwhelming obstacles preventing me from getting things crossed off my list. Our volunteers saw me resorting to 'Plans B, C, X, Y and Z' as I tried to get things accomplished.

Time was marching on, and yet nothing had been organised for the costumes. I realised it was a case of 'if I didn't do it myself, it wasn't going to get done.' In my very limited spare time, I visited local stores and searched the internet at 3:00am looking for suitable costume material. It had to have the 'wow factor', be reasonably inexpensive, and be available in large quantities at very short notice. The costume process had become an absolute nightmare, so I finally delegated some of the tasks to the parents. This was an eye-opener as several people I thought would step up to help, simply didn't. This was incredibly disappointing for me when I was putting in so much effort for their children.

I certainly didn't need all this drama and stress in my life - anyone else would have given up years ago. Trying to remain positive, I concentrated on the wonderful parents who were genuinely happy to help, and appreciated the effort I put in. Reminding myself that I'm a strong person, I was able to press on and get it done.

Eventually, I discovered a supplier in America and, after several middle of the night phone calls, managed to source some stunning fabric for the skirts. I was surprised at how quickly the material arrived – it even arrived quicker than some of the material ordered in Australia.

When the costumes were made, I didn't want any of the parents to see them. This was partly because I was so upset by the behaviour of some of them - and partly because it would be nice to surprise everyone on the night. But another challenge presented itself!

When I saw the leotard and skirt on one of the Happy Featers, I was so disappointed that I walked away and wanted to weep. After being assured they would all fit well, the leotard was more like a baggy shirt and the skirt looked ridiculous with the frilly petticoat. I had to put on my happy face and continue with the nightly program. To cheer myself up, I walked around singing under my breath, "I get knocked down, but I get up again!"

I eventually caught Rhi's attention. I quietly asked her what she thought of the costumes. She felt the same way I did. We went backstage and spoke to the dressmaker. To my relief, she agreed to alter them all so they would fit as we had originally requested.

Despite this small win, I was totally over the whole event and wanted to cancel everything, walk out the door and never return! Time and time again, I had to dredge up every last bit of strength to carry on. I went home late that night and played Billy Joel's song, 'You're Only Human (Second Wind).' It has got me through many low periods, picked me back up and helped me get on with it.

After many months of stress and heartache, finally the Happy Feat fifth birthday event was here. It should have been an exciting experience to launch our documentary and celebrate another milestone, but sadly, I couldn't wait for it to be over.

First thing Saturday morning, our faithful team of passionate volunteers, as well as a couple of wonderful Happy Feat families met at the venue. There were tables to be set up, costumes to be sorted, signs to be displayed and the hair and makeup area to be organised – just to name a few tasks. But our team worked together brilliantly, and we were finished setting up in no time. This meant we were all able to do our own thing until meeting back at 4:30 pm for the hair and makeup experience.

This was a huge highlight of the whole event for me and anything that happened afterwards was just a bonus. The buzz in that little room was contagious and the atmosphere was indescribable. One of the Happy Featers looked in the mirror after having her hair and makeup done and exclaimed, "I didn't realise I was so beautiful!"

Everyone in the room choked back tears. For me, that moment was worth all the blood, sweat and many tears of the last months, and strengthened my belief that with just a bit of effort, (well, admittedly in this case, it was truckloads of effort!), we can all make a big difference in someone's life.

Seeing another Happy Feater really excited about her dad coming to watch her perform was another special moment. All her life, her dad had only really participated in events for her siblings, nephews, and nieces, so this was a very exciting moment for her. Watching the guys getting spiffed up was also wonderful. They too wanted to feel special as they were pampered and pruned, and their beaming faces said it all.

Escorting some of the Happy Featers back to the venue with their hair and makeup done, I made a big scene getting everyone's attention and introducing our stars to the group as we entered the room. Cheers went up and there were huge rounds of applause as our Happy Feat family made them feel like superstars. Later, I had to laugh when I escorted other Happy Featers back to the venue and they asked if I could introduce them to everyone again. Mmm. Were they becoming Divas? So what!

It was soon time for everyone to get into their brand-new sparkling costumes. To see their huge smiles and excited faces as they twirled and danced was almost worth all the stress and heartache these costumes had caused. On the inside, I was still reeling from the hurt and disappointment, and never wanted to be involved with costumes again.

The excitement was building as the Happy Featers lined up on stage ready for their curtain call and the atmosphere was electric. Our Happy Featers weren't nervous at all, just very excited. Couldn't we all learn a lesson from this! It was time for them to wow the audience and do what they love doing: dancing and performing.

For our new Happy Featers, it was an experience like they'd never had before, but our veteran dancers guided them through the experience. Happy Featers who had been cared for all their lives were now carers themselves, as they nurtured our new members.

Our brilliant production manager had everything timed to the very minute. At exactly 7:30pm, our wonderful radio superstar, Pricey, welcomed everyone and introduced our Happy Feat superstars. Even though Pricey is a big deal in the Townsville community, he understands when it comes to Happy Feat, he plays second fiddle, as it's our Happy Featers who are the stars. I was so impressed by the time, dedication, and passion Pricey put into his role of MC. I had sent him individual photos and a little blurb on each of our Happy Featers and he took the time out of his super-busy life to learn and memorise every bit of information so that he was able to identify each Happy Feater by name. This gave our members such a thrill to think that Pricey knew their name.

After sending him the documentary sneak peeks that we'd be presenting on the night, he rang and left a very emotional message to say how touched and excited he was to be part of the Happy Feat event. I learned later that he also rang his partner as he recalled watching our amazing documentary and becoming overwhelmed with emotion. Happy Feat has the unique ability to touch the hearts and souls of people, give warm fuzzies as well as a dramatic and unexpected reality check in peoples' lives. As someone once said, "You leave Happy Feat a better person."

The curtain went up. The bright coloured lights shone on our Happy Featers standing still, striking poses in preparation for our first dance, 'Titanium'. The music and magic began and our Happy Featers came to life, dancing with passion and joy. The energy and adrenaline were contagious, the crowd clapped in time, everyone beaming with happiness. The opening set was a perfect combination of light, shade, building to an emotional peak, highlighting their tremendous ability.

A huge round of applause erupted when the curtain dropped and Pricey returned to the stage. It was time to introduce our first documentary sneak peek. I was the last person wanting to be out in the limelight; as far as I was concerned, it was our Happy Featers moment to shine. They were more than capable of recalling and introducing the highlights of our Special Olympic Games adventure shown in the documentary preview.

Each Happy Feater was very carefully chosen to introduce the various parts of the documentary. First on stage was Wayne, who on the outside could appear to be a rough diamond but had a gentle soul. He'd been told by his friends that he wouldn't last two weeks at Happy Feat but here he was, some five years later, proving them all wrong. Pricey and Wayne were involved in the local motorbike club and often caught up on their regular bikie get-togethers. Although Wayne was unable to ride himself, through Happy Feat, he'd met a beautiful couple full of community spirit who'd ride the 30 minutes out to where he lived so that he could join them for each bikie adventure.

Wayne painstakingly made his way onto the stage to introduce the first documentary sneak peek. It was important for the audience to see the effort it took him to simply walk out on stage, something we all take for granted. After a serious hit-and-run accident, Wayne had been told he'd never walk or talk again but after much determination and hard work, he was able to get around with the help of a walking stick. However, it wasn't long after he began Happy Feat that he discarded the stick as he felt it cramped his style and inhibited his dancing! So, Wayne walking out on stage gave everyone a reality check. The things we took for granted were challenges he faced 24/7. Yet despite those challenges, he was still able to dance to the intricate and sometimes fast-paced dance routines. After Wayne and Pricey chatted for a while, reminiscing about their motorbike and Happy Feat adventures, the first of the documentary sneak peeks was played.

The clip received an enthusiastic round of applause before, once again, the curtain went up for our Happy Featers to wow the audience with our 'Blast from the Past' bracket of dances. They stepped back in time, dancing some of the original routines we'd begun with five years ago. It was important to show the audience the basic dance moves we'd started with, then highlight the sophisticated and more complex choreography we progressed to.

The next clip from the documentary showed the fun we'd had on the go-karts at Camp Breakaway. Abbey was our next star to do the introduction, and she had the crowd laughing as she charmed Pricey with her cheeky sense of humour. This was an excellent opportunity to showcase the wonderful characters and huge personalities of our Happy Featers.

To introduce the sneak peek about our Happy Featers getting their hair and makeup done for the Special Olympic Games, I chose Marion Pope, Lany's mum, our amazing Happy Feat mum with a beautiful soul. Lany's excited face featured in this clip as she lapped up the experience of getting her makeover and being treated like a superstar. Marion's strength and determination are a true inspiration. I battled tears as she spoke to Pricey about Lany, and how much they both loved Happy Feat. As the lights dimmed to play this clip, I snuck on stage in the dark and hugged Marion. I don't know who was supporting who!

The night was a huge success. The crowd erupted as the final curtain came down. I loved seeing the Happy Featers interact with the audience after the show and having their photos taken like rock stars!

A little surprise awaited us as we were cleaning and packing up the tablecloths. Someone had gathered the confetti on the table and painstakingly created a little masterpiece with the words 'Happy Feat' and a great big heart!

Yes, it's the simple things in life that matter.

CHAPTER 38

Another Incredible Guy Sebastian Experience

At the beginning of November 2015, I discovered that Guy Sebastian was returning to Townsville for another concert. Immediately, I zapped off an email to his wonderful tour manager, 'Dan the Man'.

After a couple of weeks not hearing anything, I followed my gut instinct and sent the same email again. Dan responded immediately.

"At a recent meeting when Townsville was mentioned, Guy said that we should do something with you chaps again. Will be in touch after the craziness of this week is over."

Can you believe that? Guy wanted to perform with our Happy Featers again!

As exciting as this was, it created some major dilemmas: First and foremost, Stacey was getting married on our property at the beginning of April 2016. I wanted to concentrate on this and not have to even think about Happy Feat. Secondly, it had been a challenging and emotionally draining year.

I'd been in survival mode for many months and was suffering from burnout like I'd never experienced before. How was I going to pull it together when I just didn't have any energy left in the tank? My mum was really worried about me, and after another concerned lecture from her, I explained, "How could I let our team miss out on an opportunity of a lifetime just because I'm burned out! I need to dig deep, go on auto pilot, and demonstrate my Nike motto, 'Just do it'."

We had performed Guy's hit 'Don't Worry Be Happy' with him last time. This time, my gut instinct was screaming at me to organise the song, 'Like a Drum', which we'd learned some time ago for a community flash mob. We'd never even finished the choreography and hadn't practiced it for over twelve months - it was a little crazy to think we could pull it off.

It was also the end of the year; things were very busy. We really didn't have time for anything else. I remember saying to Rhi, "I really hate asking you, but are you able to finish the choreography and have it ready to teach... tomorrow?!"

I always tried to avoid putting unnecessary pressure on Rhi, but I just knew we had to dig deep to accomplish this huge feat. We didn't even know which song we'd have the privilege of performing with Guy, so I was going purely on gut instinct.

What's more, we only had two Happy Feat nights left for the year, a seven-week break over Christmas, then just another two Happy Feat nights before the concert. Most people would have said it's too hard, you'll never do it, don't put yourself through the stress. Rhi and I agreed that we had to make it happen.

I don't know how she managed to produce the funkiest, most fast-paced and fun choreography in only one day, but... 'Believe and you can achieve'. We felt so blessed to have such a phenomenal dance teacher leading us on this journey.

You should have heard the Happy Featers when I announced that they'd be performing with Guy Sebastian AGAIN! I thought the roof was going to lift off. There were squeals of delight, lots of jumping and flapping – and that was just the parents! – only joking. In fact, a mum of one of the newer Happy Featers came up to me looking concerned and said, "Leigh, what if the audience don't do anything, what if they don't even clap?"

It took me a few moments to realise she was serious.

"Oh, my goodness," I said, trying to reassure her. "There's no way that would happen. Did you not hear what happened when they performed with Guy last time? 3000 people gave them a standing ovation!"

Her look of sheer relief reminded me that these families have been ostracised their whole lives. They just weren't used to this positive response from the community. It's one of my biggest rewards that Happy Feat has been instrumental in changing this.

Our Christmas break-up required an intensive rehearsal of the new choreography; however, Santa's visit and the distribution of presents made it another special night. It's interesting to see how terrific ideas develop. Some of the mums had already recorded the different dances for their Happy Featers to practice at home. Tonight, it was suggested that we film Rhi doing the dance, and then send it to our Happy Featers to practice with over the break. What an awesome idea!

A couple of months later, only two weeks before the event, we received the news that Guy wasn't even doing our song 'Don't Worry, Be Happy'. If we hadn't insisted and made the effort to learn the dance 'Like a Drum', our Happy Featers would have missed out on the opportunity to dance with Guy. It goes to show how important it is to follow your gut instinct.

On the night of the performance, it was very dark as we lined up to go on stage for the rehearsal. Even though this could have been daunting, our Happy Featers seemed as cool as cucumbers.

Working with dancers who have autism, putting them in unfamiliar situations can be distressing. However, our Happy Featers feel safe, knowing that we will look after them, that they're supported. They've become very accustomed to having to adapt to different situations, and that night, they simply proceeded to the stage raring to go.

During our Wednesday night rehearsals at Happy Feat, Rhi and I stand on the same level with the dancers. Seeing Guy's concert stage setup, we decided to see how it would go if we stood below the stage, out of view from the audience. Once again, this change could easily have thrown our dancers into a panic, but it didn't faze them one bit.

Talk about changes, though! The music began, and I freaked out: it was a different version from the song we'd been rehearsing to!

"Take a deep breath and get on with it, Leigh!"

The Happy Featers never cease to amaze me with their acceptance and willingness to take on any challenge. I am so very proud of each one of them. Unfortunately, we only had time to practice the dance once before heading back to our special waiting room.

There was an excited hustle and bustle as a steady flow of Happy Featers had their hair and makeup done and ate their dinner. With our loyal film crew capturing these moments, we snuck in a couple of informal dance practices. Before long, it was time to take the team to their seats so they could enjoy the concert before their big performance. We sat in separate groups on either side of the stage, to make it faster for our Happy Featers to get into position.

At the beginning of the support act, I escorted several Happy Featers to the toilets. As Charlene, one of our Happy Featers, was washing her hands, a lovely lady looked as if she wanted to say something.

I initiated the conversation by saying, "I hope you're enjoying the concert." To our surprise, the lady, Rhonda, said she was only at the concert because of Charlene. Apparently, Charlene had served her at a local café and had told her about performing with Guy Sebastian. She had even sung her a song. Rhonda was so moved that she bought two tickets: one for herself, and one as a birthday present for her sister, who lived in Cairns.

Blown away by this story, I asked if she'd seen Charlene's Channel 7 News interview. Charlene proceeded to tell her word-for-word what she'd said in the interview. I asked what her surname was so that I could keep an eye out for her on our Facebook page. A little hesitantly, Rhonda said, "Charlene, I actually have quite a famous son who is a Cowboy." Charlene absolutely loved the North Queensland Cowboys, so she was over the moon. I'm always amazed by the number of people affected by our Happy Featers – even people we don't know about.

If only she'd known Charlene's horrendous, heart-breaking story of survival and triumph.

When this extraordinary Happy Feater was young, she suffered a brain acquired injury after being horrifically abused. She'd been dragged behind a motorbike, had cigarette burns all over her legs, and had been locked in the bottom of a fridge for indefinite periods. Because of this incarceration, the doctors said she'd probably never walk again.

Yet here she was, shining like a bright star, about to perform on stage with Guy Sebastian.

Another extraordinary person is Guy Sebastian himself; he is so special and has such a genuine caring heart. This was evident by the fact that he changed his whole concert for Happy Feat. Can you believe it? He swapped around the whole run sheet so that Happy Feat could be part of his grand finale.

Dan, his tour manager, wasn't convinced it was such a good idea. It meant major changes and preparation for his crew as well, but it's what Guy wanted. He could easily and deservedly have soaked up all the attention in the grand finale on his own - but he has such a beautiful heart, he wanted to share that moment with the Happy Featers.

After an incredible first half of the concert, at last it was time for our dancers to line up ready to go on stage. Everyone was extremely excited. When Guy was introducing Happy Feat, he said, "I had so much fun with these guys last time that I'd love to take them on tour with me!"

During performances, it's really weird, but I literally don't hear or see the audience. So, I only heard later that when Guy mentioned Happy Feat, the crowd cheered so loudly that it was like a huge roar.

Plan A was for the Happy Featers to quickly take their positions, but they had different ideas. They wanted to shake hands and introduce themselves to the band members instead! As Charlene took her position, she yelled at the band members, "By the way, I'm Charlene!"

I love the spontaneous magic that happens. Guy couldn't believe the number of Happy Featers coming on stage. He even said, "Gee Happy Feat has grown! They keep coming!"

Although the crowd was standing right in front of me, I saw nothing – I still don't understand it. Maybe I was just in the zone. My one and only concern - our Happy Featers. I got a visual check on each one of them to make sure they were doing well, and we had the volunteers side-stage ready to step into action if required.

The music began - and our Happy Featers absolutely rocked the stage! I loved seeing their beaming faces as they danced the moves to perfection. It was amazing that even the Happy Featers who hadn't done much in the rehearsals, performed every move perfectly when they were in front of an audience! Later, I was told that the crowd were on their feet dancing and singing and the energy in the room was electric.

All too soon, the song was over. Guy was high fiving each one of our dancers, who were lapping up every bit of attention and limelight. We left them on stage for as long as possible before taking them down to the waiting crowd.

It didn't take long before I noticed a mum with a teenage daughter waiting to speak to someone. The mum told me that she wanted us to see how much Happy Feat had moved her daughter. Giving her a hug, I told her, "Tell me what you're thinking."

She struggled to put it into words, but managed to say, "It was such a great experience that I will remember for a long time. These people have so many challenges but are so happy and have touched me in a way words can't describe." I hugged the girl again and told her it was what we call, 'the magic of Happy Feat'.

Back in the dressing room, Dan came in, asking for just Rhi and I to follow him. Dan had said several times that he'd organised for us to meet Guy, which was lovely. Without all our Happy Featers there though, it just wasn't the same. It was our Happy Featers who really wanted to meet him, and I couldn't help feeling guilty that we were having this incredible experience without them.

Guy was lovely and down-to-earth. He was so kind and thoughtful - he'd worried about how our dancers would cope with the last-minute changes to our song introduction.

This concert with Guy illustrated how far we had come as a group, and how much I had grown too. From coping with the fresh changes as they came, finding ways to make challenging situations work for us, Happy Feat and I had both grown. Our dancers knew we had their backs enough to cope with changes unthinkable when we first started. While I wouldn't say that I was getting used to stepping out of my comfort zone, for Happy Feat and its dancers, I was able to move mountains. Or step into the limelight alone if I had to.

Importantly, we were learning to cherish each amazing moment, each amazing achievement, as we claimed our spot in the limelight, and in the community. As Happy Feat was growing in popularity and acclaim, I was about to have some breath-takingly hard lessons to remind myself how fleeting it all could be.

CHAPTER 39

In the Blink of an Eye

The day started like any normal Monday. Stacey had dropped off our gorgeous grandson, Flynn, on her way to work, so that he and I could have lots of fun and adventures. We were enjoying a morning filled with laughter and silly moments when the phone rang. Normally, I didn't answer the phone while Flynn was awake as it was our precious time together, but for some reason I felt the need to answer this call.

After having a mammogram, the previous week, a 'nonspecific' area of concern had been discovered and they had rung to ask me to return to the clinic the next day. How your day can change in the blink of an eye!

I was so fortunate to have Flynn that day. He made me laugh and stopped me dwelling on the worry that was lurking in the back of my mind.

While Flynn had his afternoon nap, I busied myself in the kitchen. Looking out the window, I stopped in my tracks. There, sitting on Flynn's sun shirt, sat a large butterfly. Butterflies are so special to me and when I see one, I feel a sense of calm and know that everything will be all right. I immediately texted Geoff and a friend to share this moment with them.

Usually, I'm a dreadful sleeper and am regularly up doing Happy Feat emails at 2:00 or 3:00am but surprisingly, I slept well that night.

Walking into the waiting room the next morning, the atmosphere was tense, and everyone looked extremely worried. I sat quietly, but when I returned to the room after the first series of my tests, I thought, "I desperately need a coffee!"

Not being the most technically minded person, it was quite entertaining trying to work out the coffee machine. I joked with Pam, one of the other ladies I'd just met, who also desperately needed a coffee. She told me how worried she was, so I shared that it was my third call back after a mammogram and that the first two had been totally fine. That completely broke the tension in the room and got everyone involved in the conversation. It wasn't long before we were all laughing, joking, and even taking selfies!

Each time one of the ladies was called in for a procedure, we wished her good luck and cheered her on. On this occasion, I was again extremely fortunate to get the all-clear. For some reason, my instinct was telling me it wasn't going to be good news for Pam.

At this point, everyone else had gone home except myself, and Angela - another lady I'd just met and who already felt like a long-lost friend. I really should have gone back to work, but I decided to wait for Pam. If it was bad news, I didn't want her to come out to an empty waiting room with no support. Angela and I waited together.

Time ticked by and we couldn't help feeling worried. The doctor walked past and stopped to ask why we were still there. We told her we wanted to make sure Pam was OK and she asked how we all knew each other. Surprised by the fact that we'd only just met that morning, the doctor said we were fine to go in to see Pam.

Entering the room, we found Pam trembling uncontrollably. Recognising that she was in shock, I quickly gathered blankets to wrap around her. Hospitals were my second home, and I knew where to locate them. Geoff and I had been in that position when they broke the news about Ash. We both had been shaking from head to toe, chilled to the bone.

Pam told us that after a long day of prodding, an ultrasound had found breast cancer. When the doctor told Pam the diagnosis, she began trembling with shock and thought, "Gee, I wish Leigh was still here!"

When the nurse asked, "Would you like me to get your friends?", Pam replied, "I came here alone." It was at that moment that Angela and I arrived in the room.

We had already decided to drive Pam home in her car (she would be in no state to drive). Then Angela's hubby, Peter, would collect us later to drop me back at my car. What I didn't know was that Pam had driven her daughter's Getz - and it was a manual transmission. I hadn't driven a manual car in years, so we all laughed as I kangaroo hopped and occasionally ground the gears driving out of the hospital carpark that day.

Imagine my horror when I asked where we were driving to and discovered I'd have to drive up a hill as well! If anyone had heard the laughing and banter on that trip home, they'd never have guessed the severity of the situation, nor that we'd only just met that morning!

Angela's hubby soon picked us up. Embarrassingly for me, Angela shared the story of how horrible the waiting room was until I walked in. She said that I had made everyone feel at home and totally changed the atmosphere. I felt so self-conscious!

I always try to take something good out of a not-so-good situation, and the most wonderful thing about this whole experience is that the three of us have become 'bosom buddies' and 'forever friends' with a special bond like no other. These two wonderful friends have had such an impact on my life that I can barely remember what life was like without them.

It was such an amazing and unpredictable end to a very long day.

Chapter 40

Life is like a Box of Chocolates.

After a challenging, horrible week dealing with lots of issues, I worried about how I was going to bring positive, happy energy to Happy Feat that night. Amazingly though, when my Happy Feat shirt goes on, it's like when Batman dons his suit and becomes a superhero. I could already feel my spirits lifting as I opened the venue, cranking up the music as I began to set up.

Seeing our Happy Featers beaming as they arrived, ready for a big hug and to get their name tags, filled my heart with happiness. Laughter, joy, and positive energy filled the hall, and we soon began our dancing.

People don't realise how much thought and time goes into planning each evening: I make sure the night starts with upbeat songs then continues with a blend of free dances, drink breaks, learning time, and then slower songs to calm them down before going home.

Lately I'd been trying to sneak in two-minute breaks to catch up with the parents, to talk to them about their Happy Feater. The first mum I spoke to that night, Kelly, was relatively new. I wanted to tell her how much I loved the way her son Tom came up to me at the start of each night with the biggest grin as if to say, "I'm here for my hug and I'm so glad to be at Happy Feat!"

Kelly laughed and said she'd noticed him doing that. When I went on to ask if he was always like that, she burst out laughing and said, "Heck no! Only at Happy Feat!"

I felt so honoured think that Happy Feat could have such an effect on him. It was always amazing to see the little changes in the confidence and personality brought out by the group.

Amid the dancing, I spotted someone very special in the audience. Lany's mother, Marion, was there to catch up with her Happy Feat family. I was thrilled to see her laughing and having a wonderful time with her Happy Feat friends.

As I was dancing alongside Gary, one of our Happy Featers, he had a mischievous look on his face - then pinched my bottom! I immediately thumped him on the shoulder, saying in my cranky voice, "That's inappropriate, Gary!"

Then in the same breath, I continued, "Hands up, then out to the side."

One of our volunteers had witnessed this whole scenario and burst out laughing. She said to me later that in one breath, I chastised Gary for pinching my bottom then immediately continued helping him with the dance. You just never know what's going to happen next at Happy Feat!

A few days later, I was heading to a Rotary luncheon. I'd been asked to speak at months earlier, but little did I know what a crazy, challenging time I was going to have in the week leading up to this event. I desperately tried to psych myself up. I was still scrambling with what I was going to say, when I took a wrong turn and found myself stuck in traffic.

Mmm... I certainly hadn't allowed for any extra time getting to the venue. Sitting at the traffic lights watching the minutes disappearing, I couldn't help but laugh at the week's events and thought, "Well, if being late is my biggest problem today, I'm going to have a great day!"

Pulling up to the venue, I smiled and thought, "Of all days, this is when I need the parking fairy!"

Feeling positive and hopeful, I drove towards the entrance and happened to find a park right at the entry. "Thank you, parking fairy!" I thought as I zipped into the space.

Dashing up the stairs and into the boardroom, I quickly backed out when I saw a room full of men. "Sorry, I must have the wrong room!"

To my surprise (I really mean 'horror'), the gentlemen reassured me that this was where I was the guest speaker! Faking an air of composure and serenity, I walked into the room and calmly took my seat. I had to stop myself laughing when I thought, "If these people only knew what challenges I'd been dealing with for the last week, they'd know I was anything but calm!"

I joked with them and devoured my lunch, realising how hungry I was, and then scrambled to get in the zone for my speech. All too soon, I was given the cue to start.

When it comes to Happy Feat, I just speak from the heart, my passion and enthusiasm taking over. Being very down-to-earth, I just tell it as it is, and always find myself enjoying sharing the magic of Happy Feat no matter how nervous or terrified I feel in the lead up.

The Rotary members seemed to be interested (though perhaps they were faking it like I was faking composure!) and I was surprised to be asked so many questions afterwards. Some of them even discreetly wiped tears away after the short video of our team performing with Guy Sebastian. Happy Feat just has that effect.

The following month, we were privileged to have the Cowboys' cheerleading squad joining us for a very special treat. I'd zapped around the city sourcing forty sets of pom poms for our Happy Featers and we were set for a very busy night.

Early in the evening, I saw Tyson, a Happy Feater who we'd watched grow from a boy into a wonderful young man. Quietly, I said to him "Tonight we're going to have some special visitors that I know you're going to love! It's a secret, so don't say anything to the others."

His whole face lit up, and I could see the excitement and anticipation building.

That night, we were initiating three of our Happy Featers who'd successfully completed the four-month probation period and were being presented with their Happy Feat uniforms and backpacks. They couldn't wait to put their Happy Feat shirts on and had the biggest smiles as they proudly showed them off to their friends and volunteers.

We were also introducing the first of our funky Christmas carol dances, and this important practice had to be done before our guests arrived. The Happy Featers loved the choreography, having heaps of fun doing the moves.

There was some confusion as we began distributing pom poms - and the anticipation started to build. We fobbed off the questions and curious looks. Next minute, the Cowboys theme song rang out, their cheerleaders bursting into the hall. Seeing the Happy Featers' reactions was just priceless. Tyson ran over, picked me up and spun me around as he thanked me!

Pom poms shook and hips wiggled as our Happy Featers followed the cheerleaders' choreography, joining in the fun. Following the dancing, we took the opportunity for photos with the girls and our team lined up excitedly. I noticed two of our very shy Happy Featers were mooching around, not quite confident enough to join in the photos. I gently encouraged them to get involved. At first, they were quite awkward - but when I gave them a set of pom poms, they quickly joined in and had a ball.

I had to smile as another Happy Feater quickly ditched his girlfriend to gather around the young cheerleaders, looking all goggle eyed. And he wasn't the only one —our Happy Featers loved being surrounded by such beautiful girls— both inside and out. These young ladies had given up their time to make a difference in our Happy Featers' lives. They quickly discovered that they loved meeting our members and had so much fun, that they benefited from the whole experience too!

Happy Feat has taught me to go with the flow, and that you get even more joy and positivity from the joy and positivity you bring to a situation. But every day brought a new challenge, something new to juggle and make plans for. We were heading towards our biggest end of year performance and Christmas break-up. What new challenges were coming our way?

Chapter 41

Carols by Candlelight

The first sign that we had a 'character-building' night ahead was receiving an alert for a 'severe thunderstorm warning with large hail, heavy rain, and damaging winds'. It was 2:00pm on the afternoon of our Carols by Candlelight performance and I was just about to have a shower to get ready.

"No way! Can't it just be simple?" I exclaimed, but quickly admonished myself for having a pity party.

Investigating further and discussing the likelihood and timing of the storm with Geoff, we both thought it would probably be over by the time the show began. As Happy Feat were meeting at 5:00pm, I was worried we might be right in the middle of it. I quickly set about texting the whole team: "Carols is definitely on. Meet at 5:30 instead. That's why they have the huge marquee."

My phone was flooded with messages from that moment on. I quickly got dressed, gathered plenty of blankets to spread on the ground, as well as umbrellas, raincoats, towels, and a change of clothes, and set off to pick up one of the volunteers. This turned out perfectly, as she was able to answer the stream of text messages received as we made our way to the venue. All the while, ominous clouds gathered, and chain lightning and thunder surrounded us.

Arriving at the mammoth marquee, I set up the blankets for our Happy Feat group, then made my way to the meeting place to wait.

Very excited Happy Featers arrived, and it soon became apparent that our meeting place wasn't going to be big enough, which called for Plan B. The council had allocated us a room on the first floor, and we decided to gather there instead, but the only way up was in a very small lift. It wouldn't have been so bad with only a few people, but I was concerned about how long it would take to get 70-80 people down the lift and over to the stage in time for our performance. In the end, the room was an unsuitable option.

After diplomatically voicing my concerns to several council representatives, they directed us to an area big enough to cater for our large group at the back of the stage. Unfortunately, it wasn't under cover and, with the clouds looming overhead, I knew this plan was going to be short lived. I looked around to find a suitable area myself, checked with the council reps, and we went to Plan C! I tried to make a joke of it, telling our Happy Featers that we were going on another adventure to find a place undercover in case it rained.

It's amazing that our Happy Featers never seemed fazed with the changes in plans; they were just happy and comfortable being with our Happy Feat family.

Our volunteers gathered to work out the next part of our game plan. To make things easier, we decided to seat our Happy Featers in the order they would go out onto the stage. Time ticked by, we kept a close eye on the run sheet and who was on stage so that we would be well and truly ready when it was our stage call. After a quick check with the volunteers, we agreed to get our team lined up with the less mobile Happy Featers on stage but out of the audience's view. The excitement grew and their beaming smiles showed they were raring to perform and do what they loved best.

Our 'showtime' call came, and our dancers were on stage, lined up and in position in record time. The music began and our Happy Feat team lit up the stage, as the audience cheered and clapped loudly. Even though they'd only had five or six weeks to learn the choreography, they danced as if they'd been practising for months.

On one side of me was Gabrielle, who had been so shy and introverted when she started Happy Feat – but was now dancing enthusiastically and loving the limelight. When I looked to the other side, I had to hold back my tears as I watched another Happy Feater's face beaming as she danced her heart out. After being shown love, empathy, and delicate care after her rescue from abuse, Charlene had become one of the most amazing, intuitive, and considerate human beings I'd ever met.

The music ended all too soon. As always, no one wanted the magic to stop. The audience cheered and clapped even louder; many even rose to their feet for a standing ovation. If only they knew the story behind each Happy Feater, they would be even more blown away by the power of their human spirit.

Leaving the stage, the whole Happy Feat team was bursting with joy and pride as they hugged each other affectionately. They excitedly relived each moment together before reluctantly returning to their area amid the audience to watch the remainder of the show.

It was early December in North Queensland, and the weather was sweltering. We fanned our Happy Featers, making sure the team was drinking plenty of fluids. I became very concerned about one of our elderly Happy Featers when I heard what had happened after the performance.

Two of our amazing volunteers had been helping this Happy Feater back to her place when her wheelie walker overbalanced on the uneven ground. They had done everything possible to stop the walker from tipping her onto the ground and were totally devastated when she fell. After helping her to her feet and checking her thoroughly, she'd declared she was fine, and they continued their way back to join the group. When we asked her how she was feeling and if anything was sore, she said she'd like to go to the toilet. The challenge was not only getting her through the crowd of people but steering her wheelie walker as well.

Norman, one of the volunteer's husbands came to the rescue. He hovered protectively behind her in case she stumbled, while I went ahead to clear the way as she pushed her walker. When we made it clear of the crowd, the Happy Feater sat on the wheelie walker and a volunteer pushed her while Norman held onto the walker and walked backwards so that he could always keep an eye on her.

To our horror, even with such close supervision, the wheelie walker wobbled precariously and threatened to topple her once again! Norman grabbed her in time and set her upright. We were all shaken up and quite stressed by the time we got her to the toilet. While we were there, we saw an ambulance parked in the distance. I made the call to get her assessed by a paramedic as an extra precaution. I ran ahead to ask them to drive the ambulance over, so we didn't have to make the arduous journey.

The two ambulance officers were fantastic and made sure our Happy Feater was alright. After declaring her fit and well, they wanted to help us get her safely back to the group. Not wanting to battle the maze of people again, we decided to set her wheelie walker up on the flat ground of the bitumen road on the other side of the marquee. After getting her into position undercover, we left her in the wonderful care of our volunteers. One of the ambulance officers followed me back to the group to get the dancer's contact details from my phone. I thanked her once again, and she made her way back to our Happy Feater for one final check before returning to the ambulance.

I started fanning and checking the other Happy Featers to make sure they were keeping their fluids up. Another of our wonderful volunteers had grabbed me something to eat, so I finally sat down and caught up with one of the mums. She asked me if I found performances stressful. I replied honestly, that for some reason, this event had been extremely stressful.

I'm over-protective at the best of times but with the oppressive heat, I was extremely concerned for our team's wellbeing. This mum could understand as she and her son had a particularly serious heart condition, and they too were struggling with the heat.

It wasn't long before the storm clouds opened, lightning lit up the sky and everything fell into darkness as the power went out. There was a moment of chaos until everyone found their candles. The microphones had been rendered useless, so the audience began singing along with the performers on stage.

Many of the audience started to leave, and the mum, who I'd been speaking with earlier, came to say goodbye. For some reason I asked if she was OK. She gave me a surprised look and said of course. There was no need to worry.

I watched as she walked off, but my gut instinct started ringing the alarm bells. I ran over, quickly caught up with the family and walked beside her.

Suddenly, she faltered, and I held onto her as she collapsed to the floor. I quickly motioned for her daughter to look after her, and I started running at breakneck speed directly to the ambulance officers. Because of the earlier situation, I knew exactly where they were and made a beeline straight to them.

"One of our mums has collapsed," I said. "She has a serious heart condition. Come quickly!"

I turned and motioned for her to follow. The ambulance officer set off after me, then while she attended to the mum who had collapsed, I reassured other members of the family. We all made our way outside the marquee to get some fresh air. Cold water and ice packs were handed round while we waited for her husband to bring the car up.

Having seen everyone safely on their way, I drove some of the volunteers home before heading home myself. Feeling totally drained and a little frazzled, I poured myself a glass of wine and slumped onto the lounge. Sleep wasn't going to come easily that night as I was still reeling from the events and replaying them over in my mind.

Very few people would be aware of what had eventuated that night... and it was just as well.

After the challenging gig at Carols by Candlelight, Rhi and I were left feeling deflated and a little disillusioned. Setting up for our Christmas break-up, Rhi and I even had a sooky la moment together and questioning whether we could get through the night.

Sheer exhaustion, worry about the health of a family member, the relentless pressure, and lack of sleep were all contributing to the meltdown I felt coming. I decided to go for a shower at the venue, thinking that would give me a second wind and freshen me up in mind and spirit.

On a whim, I'd bought a Christmas elf outfit to wear that night and as I got dressed, I thought to myself, "I owe it to our Happy Featers to give them 200%, no matter how lousy I feel."

There were cheers and laughter when everyone saw my ridiculous outfit, and I made a beeline straight to Rhi. Whispering in her ear, I said, "You are about to see the best Logie performance of your life. We're going to have an awesome night!"

Every day I thought how very blessed we were to have Rhi, our wonderful, amazing, extremely talented dance teacher! Rhi had been with us since day one, and we couldn't have done it without her commitment, dedication, and skill. She had led our Happy Featers on this journey, sharing the very low lows as well as the very high highs.

Greeting our Happy Featers as they arrive is always fun – seeing their beaming faces lifts anyone's spirit. Taking one look at Penny, one of our newer Happy Featers, I said, "Gee, Penny, I just love seeing your huge smile. Tell me, were you like this when you began Happy Feat?"

She proudly replied, "No way! All through primary school and high school I was bullied, and I've never had friends. Now I have lots of friends and I'm just so happy!"

Well, if I was feeling fragile before, this nearly brought me undone. A lump rose in my throat, and I could feel the tears well up as I gave her the biggest hug ever. Yes, that's why I keep doing what I do.

The night began with a loud and enthusiastic rendition of our Happy Feat Chant, then we started busting some moves to the music. I was stopped in my tracks, though, when I looked over to where the parents were seated. Looking very fragile but watching on excitedly, was Jill, an 86-year-old mum of one of our Happy Featers. It took my breath away that she had made the mammoth effort to come. Not only because she was elderly, I'd also been told she'd been very ill. The tears made their presence felt once again, and I had to fight them back as I gave Jill a very warm, gentle hug and told her how excited I was to see her. It brought back memories of the very first time I saw Jill, and her daughter Theresa. None of us could believe Theresa's 's transformation since joining Happy Feat.

"Pull yourself together, Leigh!" I chastised myself, quickly wiping away a tear.

It was great for everyone to simply be able to dance and have fun after the intense rehearsals for Carols by Candlelight. Tonight was all about dancing, having fun, and enjoying the magic of Happy Feat. What the team didn't know was that after supper we were going to turn the lights off, put some special music on and be treated to a performance by some local belly dancers!

When the lights went out, our team looked at each other wondering what on earth I had come up with this time. There were gasps as the belly dancers made a grand entrance, one of them wearing an elaborate chandelier on her head while another was dancing with a colourful scarf. After the special demonstration, we excitedly told our Happy Featers that the group had generously brought a stunning belly dance skirt for each one at Happy Feat! Whoops of delight rang out and they all lined up to get their jingly skirts on.

The music began, and everyone started shaking their hips and twirling like some Bollywood movie. Once again, I stopped in my tracks. There on the dance floor, shaking her hips like a 20-year-old, was Jill, dancing with her daughter. When I regained my composure, I went over to one of the volunteers, grabbing a belly dancing skirt before running back to put the skirt on Jill. Seeing her moving her frail body in time to the music as she shared a rare and fun moment with her daughter was priceless.

The end of the night came all too soon. There were warm hugs and loud chatter as our team bade each other farewell and Happy Christmas. As we do after each Happy Feat night, all the volunteers gathered outside the hall, resting their weary feet, and sharing the countless magic moments of the night.

One volunteer vividly recounted how she witnessed a new Happy Feater speaking for the first time! So far, he'd been extremely shy and introverted however he was now saying a few words and making them laugh.

That same Happy Feater lines up before and after Happy Feat each week to give me a hug. He patiently waits until everyone else has had their hug, and his family can't believe it, as this is so out-of-character for him. I feel incredibly privileged!

Before leaving, I gave Rhi an enormous squeeze and said quietly, "I might have mentioned that I'd put on a Logie performance, but the moment I saw their faces, it wasn't a performance, just sheer uninhibited joy!"

Our Happy Feat journey had started small, but was now a large family of committed dancers, parents, friends, and volunteers. Throughout the highs and lows, we had become stronger together as a group, as well as a professional organisation. Like being oblivious to the audience when on stage with our Happy Featers, I was mostly oblivious to the growing attention we were starting to get in the wider community.

At a time where all I wanted most was to retreat and be with my family, I was stepping into the spotlight as Happy Feat was being recognised by the community, breaking down barriers and changing lives.

CHAPTER 42

Australia Day 2017

Opening the mail on the last day at work before the Christmas break, I came across two interesting and very official looking envelopes: one addressed to me and the other to Happy Feat. I curiously opened the first letter and had to read it twice before registering its significance.

I had been nominated for an Australia Day Award!

Unable to move or speak, I sat trying to comprehend the letter in front of me.

No, it didn't look like a joke. As I opened the next letter, I saw that Happy Feat had also been nominated for an award! I thought, "Wow, isn't that the pinnacle of inclusion and acceptance into the community!"

Regaining my composure, I shared the letter with Donna, who both worked for our building company and was our Happy Feat treasurer. It was amusing watching her expression go from curious and baffled to elated and over the moon.

Sadly, the day before the Australia Day Awards, we were to attend the funeral of a young lad, who had been a Happy Feater some years back. I'd known both of his parents when they'd worked for our company for about 15 years - they were like family. At the funeral, while I had to be strong for our Happy Feat family, deep inside, my heart was breaking.

I was also worried sick about my dad, who had been raced to hospital. Talk about high highs and low lows that week. My dad in hospital, the funeral on Wednesday and the Australia Day Awards the very next day. What a roller coaster of emotions!

Waking up on the morning of the funeral, I knew I had to dig deep, to find strength from somewhere. I had never attended a morning gym session before, but I felt that it was something I needed to do. Leaving home at 5:30am, my thoughts kept wandering to the funeral, and how I was going to get through it. After my gym session, however, I had a spring in my step and felt ready to take on the world again.

When our Happy Featers and their families arrived at the Crematorium, I comforted them and got them seated. The funeral incorporated some of our upbeat Happy Feat songs and the young man's friends and family shared many funny and amusing stories, which seemed to lighten the atmosphere. The family had asked the Happy Featers to do the chant, so we gathered rather awkwardly in front of the coffin and went through the motions of the chant.

I really regretted not having planned a speech; I just had too much happening that week and didn't have one ounce of headspace to think about saying anything at the funeral.

After the funeral, Mum and I went straight to the hospital to see Dad. Hospital isn't the best place to try to lift your spirits, but spending time with my precious dad, hugging him, laughing, and seeing his smile really was the best medicine.

Dropping Mum back home to my brother's place, we were greeted by Sam, a lovely neighbour from across the street. Although I'd never met him before, he wanted to shake my hand and congratulate me on the Australia Day award. Being a little baffled, I quickly reminded him that we were only nominated and hadn't won.

My alarm bells started ringing and a mild panic set in as Sam smiled and carried on about how much he loved Happy Feat. I mean, really, who'd have thought we'd even be nominated for an Australia Day award!

Because I didn't think there was any way we'd win, I hadn't made it a priority to gather my thoughts to prepare a speech. How on earth could I think about it when I was reeling from the funeral and worrying about my dad?

Sleep was a waste of time that night as I sat staring blankly at the computer at 3am, willing myself to come up with something amazing. Even to come up with something ordinary would have been a start, but there was just...nothing.

"Well," I thought. "Whatever I do, I must at least fake that I feel confident and comfortable getting up and giving the speech!"

Words came more freely after that, and by 5:00am I felt satisfied that what I had written was better than what I started with. I went back to bed and slept soundly 'til 6:45am. I know that's not much sleep, but it was better than nothing!

Knowing that our Happy Featers always arrive early at events, I was anxious to get to the venue with plenty of time to find a park and suss out what was planned. I happened to run into one Happy Feater and her mum as they were getting out of the car, so we walked together and enjoyed catching up. It was rewarding seeing our Happy Featers and their families so excited and bursting with pride as we gathered for the event. Luckily there were plenty of seats available for our Happy Feat crew, as we certainly had a large fan club that day!

At events like this, there is always plenty of pomp and ceremony with lots of speeches. I was so proud of our Happy Featers for their composure and patience throughout the event, but the minute Happy Feat was announced as the winner of the 2017 Cultural Award, they let loose! The magic of Happy Feat rose to engulf the crowd.

Our Happy Featers won many hearts that day as they high fived and shook hands with Queensland Premier Annastacia Palaszczuk, the Governor of Queensland, His Excellency the Honourable Paul de Jersey AC, Mayor Jenny Hill, and every other dignitary sitting in the front row!

The crowd roared as our Happy Featers proudly stood on the stage bowing and geeing up the audience. It was a joy to behold. John G had such a Tarzan grip on the award, that when Mayor Jenny Hill tried to turn it around the right way, there was no way he was letting go!

I couldn't help thinking back to when we first began Happy Feat, when we really had no idea what we were doing. Everything we learned was by trial and error – and there were plenty of errors! Having started with twenty-five Happy Featers we now had nearly double the number of stars! It was almost impossible to imagine now, but how timid and introverted so many of our Happy Featers had been when they first joined the group.

Today's Happy Featers were large as life, absolutely bursting with confidence. I can't even begin to put into words how proud I was of everyone that day. When we set out, one of the goals was for our Happy Featers to attain acceptance and inclusion in the community. Seeing our Happy Featers at the Australia Day Awards ceremony was another indication that this huge goal had certainly been achieved.

Immediately after the ceremony, the Premier came to our group to congratulate us and shake all our hands. Annastacia told me how thrilled she was that Happy Feat had won the award, saying that she loved seeing them. Apparently, she had once been Minister for Disability Services, so I said, "No wonder you get it!"

Annastacia's photographer asked for a group photo, and our Happy Featers promptly got into place as they were now seasoned photo gurus!

After the ceremony, I went straight up to the hospital to visit my dad. He was so proud of what I'd achieved with Happy Feat and loved hearing all about it. I knew it would cheer him up and make his day.

HOPE, GRIT AND GRATITUDE • 325

It was quite overwhelming reading the messages that followed:

"This award could not have been given to a more deserving recipient. Thank you, Leigh, for starting this truly life changing program."

"You are an inspiration to us all and we are so proud to say we know you."

"Congratulations to you and all your wonderful helpers, Leigh and for all the dedication and hard work that you put in behind the scenes!"

"It truly is a wonderful opportunity that you are giving everyone who participates in Happy Feat. We're so very excited and proud of all the Happy Feat family. Your continued love, respect, and effort for people with a disability to be part of the community is magnificent."

CHAPTER 43

Pressing the Pause Button.

As a private person, I'd kept the seriousness of my father's condition a secret from everyone for a long time. Very few people knew what we were going through. After the Australia Day Awards, my wonderful dad's health deteriorated. He and my amazing mum and family were my priorities, I didn't even have the headspace to add to my journal. Although I felt like I was running on auto pilot, I continued to run Happy Feat.

During this time, we had some of the biggest performances we've ever undertaken, and I have no idea how I managed to get through it.

Our Happy Featers had their third performance with Guy Sebastian, their first ever 'Dance for Daniel Ball', another performance at the Cowboys home game and another at the Townsville Arts & Cultural Festival. These events were all organised at a crazy time, usually 2:00–5:00am, so I was certainly lacking in much-needed beauty sleep.

I was working with Guy Sebastian's new management team for this concert, and they weren't familiar with previous Happy Feat performances. As this was going to be an 'intimate style' concert, we didn't have the room for our Happy Featers to perform. We couldn't bring ourselves to admit it just wasn't going to work so we had to do the best we could. Our Happy Featers were so privileged to dance with Guy once again.

Our team were also honoured to meet Denise and Bruce Morcombe for the first time when they did the opening performance for the Daniel Morcombe Ball. In fact, we were all having so much fun with the photo shoot beforehand, that we were all late for the Ball!

On a Wednesday night, only days before Dad passed away, I left the hospital to drop the keys and laptop into Happy Feat. I wasn't going to stay. I just didn't have the energy to face everyone. I arrived at the hall to find no one was there, so I began setting up myself. I learned that quite a few of the volunteers couldn't make it that night so, without much choice, I put on my Happy Feat shirt, my 'happy face', and got through the night without anyone having any idea what was happening in my family.

From the very next morning, for the next few days I hardly left Dad's bedside. My family and I were with him as he took his last breath. With our family trait of being extremely private, there was no announcement in the paper, we held a private funeral, and I didn't tell anyone at Happy Feat.

My father was very well known and respected throughout the Townsville and Burdekin districts - the funeral would have been bigger than Ben Hur. But that's not what Dad or our family wanted - or could have coped with. We needed time to heal from our enormous loss before we could share it with anyone.

CHAPTER 44

You've Got the Wrong Person!

Our whole family had been through a tough time with Dad's declining health and his passing. After a few months, we decided we needed to get away at the end of the year - to spend some valuable family time together. We settled on a snow skiing holiday in Canada. Although we knew our grandchildren were probably going to be too young to make the most of it, we all just needed to escape, spend time as a family, and have some much-needed fun.

There were many times when it would have been easier to say it was too hard, to forget about the holiday. The end of the year is always a crazy time with Christmas, closing the office over an annual industry shutdown, winding up Happy Feat for the year all happening at once. This year was even busier with so much to organise for our holiday, but I was the driving force behind this adventure, and we were going – no matter what!

Zapping through my junk email at work, I was tempted to just delete everything - but something made me double check first. To my surprise, I came across some sort of award nomination email. I thought I'd probably better save it as I didn't have the time to read it immediately.

It wasn't until several weeks later that I finally went back to it and immediately felt sick in the stomach. Why? As my friends know, I'm painfully private. This may sound totally bizarre, considering how 'out there' I am with Happy Feat, (and writing a memoir!), but I absolutely detest the spotlight, or anything that results in being in the limelight – like awards.

When I'm out of the public eye, I love nothing better than being with my family and friends just being totally daggy and relaxed.

This book only evolved after being captivated by the incredible transformations of our Happy Feat dancers and being totally bewildered by how it was all happening. Random notes and an amateur journal began capturing a kaleidoscope of exciting adventures. These were raw, emotional, and character-building life experiences, some hilarious escapades, and those moments where you pinch yourself and ask, "Did that really happen?"

Never did I think I would ever share these experiences with anyone because I'm so private.

That was until I had an 'Aha moment', and I realised my journey could inspire others to follow their dreams, and to get up every time you're knocked down. Two critically important messages.

If sharing my story encourages others to get that mattock out, or bulldozer if necessary, and knock down all those negative obstacles standing in your way, then I will 'put my big girl pants on' and get over my privacy fixation.

As Napoleon Hill famously said, 'Believe and you can achieve.'

If this ordinary, down-to-earth, blonde can do it, anyone can!

So, you can imagine my horror when I discovered I'd been nominated for Citizen of the Year. With a big award ceremony on Australia Day! Seriously?! There were thousands of people more deserving of this award than me!

Who was the culprit? It said in the nomination email. Oh no, I couldn't believe it. It was one of the most inspirational, caring and community minded people I knew. I loved him to pieces, but boy, was he in trouble!

I jumped in my car and drove to his partner's place, saying, "Help! Look what your boy has done! You both know I'm not into awards! He's in deep @$*#!"

Seeing the very sheepish look on her face, I knew he wasn't the only guilty one. Then a huge wave of relief came over me when I realised, I wasn't even going to be here for Australia Day; I would still be in Canada. Yeehaa!

I was really embarrassed about being nominated. I only told a couple of close friends and Happy Feat families, asking them to go along on the day so that when they read out the nominees, I wouldn't be a 'Nelly no-friends'. The reality was it was a 'rent-a-crowd', but that's OK, right?

It was Australia Day in Australia - and our family had just returned from an awesome day on the Canadian ski slopes. We were relaxed after getting our adrenaline rush and doing what we love, being together. I decided to be with my friends 'in spirit', enjoying a nice relaxing spa out on the deck, overlooking the snow. I would even toast the occasion with a glass of Baileys. My phone was close by and started to ping with messages.

Glancing over, I immediately burst out laughing. I was so loud that Ashley opened the window, asking what was so funny. I showed him the photo of a Citizen of the Year medal with my name on it. How clever Janelle was with Photoshop. I kept chuckling as I nonchalantly went back to my spa and Baileys. What a brilliant joke...so creative!

When a video came through, I almost didn't look at it until I'd finished my spa but finally decided to have a quick peek. Not believing what I saw, I watched it again, then a third time. I called Ash to have a look to see if they could have faked that as well.

A huge grin covered his face as he said, "Congratulations, Mum. That's unreal!"

A quick message to my friends confirmed to my horror and shock that I'd won the award. But why? There were thousands of people who deserved it so much more than me. It just doesn't make sense! I was even more embarrassed.

My phone went off again, but this time it was Stacey with some concerning news. She was going to find a doctor for our baby granddaughter, Mia. She wasn't well, and Stace was worried about her for our long flight home the next morning.

The award was immediately forgotten as I got dressed and went with them to the doctors. Armed with medicine and the reassurance that Mia would be fine to travel, we went back to our units to begin the sad task of packing to go home.

It wasn't until we were all seated in the shuttle bus at five o'clock the next morning, that Ashley announced to the others about the award. They congratulated me warmly, if briefly – after all, my family know better than anyone else that I'm not into awards. Then it was immediately back into my favourite roles as Mum and Grandma, being silly, laughing and pointing out interesting things to my beautiful grandies on the trip to the airport.

For me, the highlight of receiving the Citizen of the Year award was seeing the photos and videos of my amazing Happy Featers and volunteers, basking in the limelight that day. It meant everything to me to see those who are normally on the outside being included in the celebrations and being recognised for their achievements. The expressions on their faces, their pride in themselves, and the decorum they displayed certainly made winning this award meaningful. Their faces say it all.

CHAPTER 45

The Dance for Daniel Ball - Take 2.

From the beginning, gaining acceptance and inclusion in the community has always been an important goal for our Happy Featers. It had been such a long journey, with so many obstacles and challenges to overcome. To see our recognition growing - in the Cultural Award, in the audience responses - was just amazing. When our team was invited to perform for the second time at the opening of the Dance for Daniel Ball, a fundraising event for the Daniel Morcombe Foundation, we were just blown away with excitement.

We had all followed the heart-wrenching story of the Morcombe family whose 13-year-old son Daniel had disappeared while waiting at a bus stop near his home on the Sunshine Coast in 2003. There were many traumatic years that followed, full of the anguish of not knowing where he was or what had happened.

It was an honour to support Bruce and Denise Morcombe. Their mission is to educate young people about staying safe in physical and online environments, and to support young victims of crime.

Our Happy Featers had been privileged to open the show for the Dance for Daniel Ball back in 2017. Our team wowed the crowd so much that many who attended said that our Happy Featers were the highlight of the evening!

Rhi was busy preparing for her wedding in July, so we hadn't planned any Happy Feat performances or events for the year. We wanted Rhi to use her spare time on her own special event. Feeling this event was too good to miss, however, I hesitantly ran the idea past Rhi in early April. I assured her that I totally understood if she preferred not to do the performance, but Rhi gave an enthusiastic YES! to support the Morcombe family, so the planning began.

Thankfully, we already had the costumes from our 2017 performance, but our new members needed to be fitted and have their costumes made. Having over 40 performers means that managing our clothing and costumes is a mammoth undertaking. To give you an idea, for this one costume alone, we have over 180 items of clothing and accessories (and we have several costumes).

These days, we're very lucky to have incredible Happy Feat mums looking after the wardrobe. And as if this wasn't enough to juggle, they also wash every item after each performance to maintain their quality and longevity.

For the Dance for Daniel Ball, I was thrilled to work with the same team as the previous Ball. They understood the logistics involved with organising our team of nearly 100 people and were always eager to accommodate our requirements. Knowing how much our Happy Featers loved the NQ Cowboys, they quickly organised for our Happy Featers to meet Gavin Cooper, a NQ Cowboys player, and ambassador for the Dance for Daniel Ball.

Little did our Happy Featers know that while they were busy dancing and rehearsing one Wednesday night, Gavin and Tenille Cooper, and their adorable kids, gathered outside in the carpark to surprise them.

When the Cowboys' anthem rang out loudly in the middle of a drink break, everyone stopped what they were doing, looking baffled. You should have seen their faces when they rushed to greet their Cowboys hero as he walked through the door.

Gavin was wonderful. He made each Happy Feater feel as if they were the only person on the planet. Their faces were priceless as they posed with their hero, while their excited parents also savoured the moment.

As if that amazing experience wasn't enough, the Dance for Daniel event came with another bonus! We were invited to a photo shoot with Bruce Morcombe at The Ville Resort. Nobody knew how long Bruce would be available for, so the event was organised at the last minute. It was on a weekend, and I only had a limited time to gather a handful of Happy Featers together.

I arrived at the venue, lugging bright yellow Happy Feat shirts for everyone to wear, having quickly ironed them before I raced out the door. I beamed with pride watching the Happy Featers confidently introduce themselves and shake Bruce Morcombe's hand. It was such an amazing opportunity for our Happy Featers and their families.

When we get together, there's always plenty of laughter, and yes, we're even a bit silly – but gee we have fun. It was so good to see Bruce Morcombe getting caught up in the banter and laughter, forgetting all the cares of the world. I didn't think he'd had too many photo shoots like that one!

The organisation that goes into a performance is mind-boggling. Most people have no idea of the time and intense effort that goes on behind the scenes - even the best-laid plans often have to be changed at the last minute. I still remind our team that every performance is 'like a box of chocolates'. We never know what we're going to get. There are always plenty of on-the-spot decisions to be made.

The day of the big performance finally arrived. Our wonderful costume director, her son, and I arrived early. We needed the extra time to organise the costumes, making sure everything was ready to go. It's always nice to then have the time to take a breath, centre ourselves, and catch up with a laugh before everyone arrives and the chaos begins.

The plan was for carers and parents to collect the costumes when they arrived at our dressing room and then help their Happy Feater get changed. Sometimes we organise hairdressers and makeup artists to pamper the dancers but as the Ball was on a Friday night, there simply wasn't time. For this performance, they had to arrive stage ready, with their hair and makeup already done. I love seeing our Happy Featers' excitement before a performance as they often help each other, take photos, or just catch up for a chat.

We've taught everyone that we don't get 'nervous', we get 'excited'. Happy Feat is all about doing your best, having a go, and having truckloads of fun!

It was soon time for one of our volunteers, Donna, and I to chaperone the small group needing to take the lift to the performance venue downstairs. As we were making our way to the waiting area, we came across Denise & Bruce Morcombe, Kellie, Gavin and Tenille Cooper and two local radio presenters who were on their way up to the Happy Feat dressing room to greet the performers.

I escorted them back to our room. It was fantastic to see our Happy Featers' reactions and applause when the special guests arrived. Countless photos were taken, and I was thrilled to witness one very memorable event.

One of our dancers absolutely loathed having his photo taken when he first began Happy Feat, and even became highly agitated if there was a photo shoot. This continued for several years. When I saw him proudly posing for a photo with Denise Morecombe, I had to catch my breath. I shared this wonderful story with Denise, and she was delighted. They say magic happens outside your comfort zone.

The meet and greet was over way too soon. Gathering the dancers, we headed downstairs to prepare for the big performance. On cue, the Happy Featers entered the venue, smiling and waving, even high-fiving some of the guests — true superstars - as they made their way to the dance floor. In the middle of the dance floor sat a vacant chair, sticking out like a sore thumb.

Months earlier, one of our Happy Featers had become upset when she thought she'd miss out on this performance after having foot surgery. You should have seen her face when I reassured her that she could still perform. Sitting on that chair, she danced her heart out.

It still amazes me to see how the Happy Featers switch into professional mode whenever we are performing. They centre themselves and appear very calm, as though they've been doing this all their lives. Perhaps the reality is that they've been waiting all their lives for these moments.

After getting into position, the music began. This was their time to shine. During the performance, I kept a close eye on two of our younger members as this was their first time on stage. My concern was unnecessary though. They danced every move with grins from ear to ear.

I've always remained aware of how daunting it can be to dance in front of hundreds of people. But our team are seasoned performers now and think nothing of an audience of hundreds after performing in front of 30,000 people at the Special Olympic Games. Even so, there is always the potential for meltdowns, and we watch our group like hawks (or perhaps more like over-protective mother ducks!).

It was a difficult performance for Rhi and I as we struggled to hear the music, and it was distracting when some audience members continued talking. As soon as the performance was over, I started to gather our dancers, being mindful not to delay the event program, and was a little bewildered when our volunteers seemed to be stalling. No problem, I would take charge and get everyone moving myself.

But this time, we were going to Plan B. What I didn't realise was that Bruce and Denise had awarded the highly coveted 'Morky Award' to Happy Feat!

It's well known that I detest awards and recognition and do everything I can to avoid this attention, so everyone was sworn to secrecy. When the award was announced, I was adamant that our team should go on stage to receive it, and there was an awkward moment when I quietly refused to go. Not wanting to offend Bruce and Denise, however, this time I graciously admitted defeat and stepped forward to receive the accolade

Afterwards, Bruce and Denise asked our team to remain outside so their photographer could take photos with the Happy Featers. They are such a wonderful couple. I was touched that they left the Ball just so they could get photos with our dancers. To be invited, and be so warmly welcomed, by a family as nationally loved and respected as the Morecombes and their nationally renowned organisation was such an amazing opportunity to celebrate and showcase the achievements and skills of our Happy Featers.

CHAPTER 46

Ride Like a Girl

In the spring of 2015, I was overflowing with emotion, pride, and inspiration to see Michelle Payne win the Melbourne Cup, and be greeted by her brother Stevie, her strapper. Seeing Stevie skilfully and confidently take control of Prince of Penzance, the exhilarated, jittery, winning horse in front of thousands of excited people was a huge feat - and showed the nation that having down syndrome doesn't stop you from achieving your dreams. Watching Michelle embrace her adoring brother, it was clear that the two had an unbreakable bond.

When I heard that Rachel Griffiths was making a movie about Michelle's life, I couldn't wait for its release. Knowing how much I wanted to see the movie, Geoff read me an article from the local paper announcing that Rachel Griffiths was going to be in town for a special screening of the movie and a Q&A session afterwards. Thinking it was on a Happy Feat night, I resigned myself to having to miss out.

Not long after, Geri, our volunteer manager messaged to see if I wanted to go.

"Hang on – what night was that? Are you serious?!"

It wasn't a Happy Feat night so I could go! Knowing the tickets would sell quickly, I interrupted the meeting Geoff was in to see if he wanted to come too, then immediately purchased tickets.

On the night, while catching up with Geri in the foyer, I suddenly had a WIN News microphone in front of me. Looking like a deer in the headlights, I searched the crowd and thought, "Why didn't you pick any of them?"

As one of my mottos is 'fake it 'til you make it,' I spoke as if I was 10 feet tall and bulletproof. Geri also jumped in, saying that we were with Happy Feat and loved seeing Stevie in this story. Relieved when interview was over, we were treated to a welcome glass of champagne and took our seats.

While the house lights were on and the audience was chatting, I casually went down to the front of the cinema, leaving our Happy Feat documentary and photo book on the table set up for the interview with Rachel. I know, it was very cheeky, but if there's one thing I've learned through this whole journey, it's that you must make the most of every opportunity.

I absolutely loved the movie! It resonated with me on so many levels: Michelle's unwavering determination and perseverance, her love of her family - and watching her recovering after a serious accident brought back painful memories of when I was recovering from Guillain-Barre.

Another part I loved was when Michelle was with her dad after just winning the Melbourne Cup, she placed the cup on the mantelpiece and they both went about their business without any fuss. This struck a chord with me as quite often after a huge Happy Feat event, such as performing with Guy Sebastian, I'd come home, say it was great then have a shower and make a cup of tea. I love that it's no big deal with my family – it's just something Mum/Leigh does. Seeing Stevie showing everyone how talented and amazing he is and that having down syndrome doesn't have to stop you from doing anything was another very familiar scene.

When it was time for the Q&A with Rachel Griffiths, I was determined to get out of my comfort zone and say something. My stomach was churning, and to say I had butterflies was an understatement. They were more like eagles! It would have been easy to sit there, enjoy it and not put myself through the angst, but I put my hand up, and that was the point of no return. When I was called on to say my piece, I said:

"When I wanted to start a dance group for people with special needs, I was told I'd never do it, it can't be done and you're crazy! But I did it anyway and I now teach everyone to believe, and you can achieve. I want to thank you for your determination, for never giving up and for also teaching everyone to believe and you can achieve. And thank you for creating the best movie I've ever seen!"

I was particular about not mentioning Happy Feat because it wasn't about that. Rachel was a little lost for words initially, then spoke about Stevie's part in the movie. The next moment seemed surreal. The MC for the night happened to be Gabi, one of the local radio announcers who had joined the Morcombes in the Happy Feat dressing room before our performance at the Dance for Daniel Ball. Gabi must have seen the Happy Feat paraphernalia on the table and said, "Hang on, is that Happy Feat? I love Happy Feat, they're awesome!"

Geri quickly stood up, proudly yelling out, "Yes, it's Happy Feat!"

Rachel then asked if we were on Instagram. Geri and I looked at each other and said no, but that we were on Facebook. Rachel said that she didn't do Facebook but would look us up. I felt quite embarrassed, as I was conscious it wasn't the 'Happy Feat show', and I hoped they would return to talking about the movie. When the next question was asked, I leaned over to Geri and said, "Well, that was well and truly out of my comfort zone!"

Returning to the foyer at the end of the show, there was a queue for photos with Rachel Griffiths. Geri and I looked at each other and said, "Heck yeah! Why not?!"

Our phones were at the ready and we introduced ourselves to Rachel, saying, "We're from Happy Feat".

Then Geri invited Rachel to come to Happy Feat the next time she was in Townsville. We took several photos with her and were thrilled to see Rachel's PA holding our Happy Feat documentary and book.

On the way home, I texted Geri, saying, "Did that really happen?"

I love the saying: 'magic happens outside your comfort zone'. But it wasn't to end there. When we got home, I had a message on our Happy Feat Facebook page:

"Hi Happy Feat, I'm a journalist at WIN News Townsville, and I also just attended the 'Ride like a Girl' premier. Would you be free to do a story with us about your dance school and why it's important to have people with disabilities like Stevie more recognised in Australia? Thanks, Lucy."

Even though it was late, I replied saying that we'd love to do a story. While I don't like publicity for myself, for "Leigh Caldwell", from the Blood Bank documentary to our growing Happy Feat film archive, I knew positive things for Happy Feat would come from this. I invited her to join us at the last night of the term the following night.

Lucy said she'd love to come but didn't have a camera crew available as they were attending the Cowboys' Ball. I let her know that our son Ashley was coming along to do some filming, and bingo! It sounded as if they'd be able to work together to produce the story.

The next night Lucy arrived. Our Happy Featers loved meeting and welcoming her. She asked if she could interview me and some of the parents. None of us particularly wanted to do it, but our Happy Featers were lining up to be interviewed! Shy little butterflies aren't they?! See what I mean when I say that they're so confident now, they're ready to take on any challenge? They did a brilliant job, and I was super proud of them.

The story doesn't end there! The next day, Geri sent me a copy of Rachel Griffiths' Instagram post. It was a beautiful photo from her Happy Feat book with the words, 'So thrilled the Happy Feat dance crew came to our Townsville premiere and loved the film.'

With more representation onscreen and off, showcasing the abilities and amazing personalities of people like our Happy Feat group, I could see the growing acceptance and inclusion of people with disabilities in our wider community, if not our country! After all, our dancers had shown me time, and time again that it was really true – 'to believe, and you can achieve'.

CHAPTER 47

Meeting an Aussie Icon

It was another moment where my work team wondered what I was up to, as I danced around the office like an excited two-year-old. They soon learned that I'd just received an official invitation to a civic reception held by the Mayor of the City of Townsville - and the Chair of the Australian Broadcasting Corporation, Ita Buttrose.

Ita Buttrose had always been an inspiration to me. I'd followed her journey over the years and read her autobiography, so it was an honour to be invited to meet her. I excitedly shared the news with our Happy Feat costume director, who said she'd love to do my makeup for the event. She knew I was hopeless when it comes to makeup and don't usually bother with it.

I arrived at the function feeling excited (and rather glamorous) after my makeup session – only to find it bustling with dignitaries and unfamiliar faces. Walking into that event on my own, and not knowing anyone, was a bit scary and intimidating. But I reminded myself, "Leigh, you can do this. Be confident and fake it 'til you make it!"

Making my way to the bar and joking with the staff, I ordered my orange juice. Now what? Searching the room for a familiar face, I was relieved to see a local councillor who had been involved in several Happy Feat events. I walked over and stood quietly as the group was in deep conversation. It was a relief when I was introduced to the others and included in the chat. I instantly connected with a woman called Diana, and we found ourselves discussing many things we had in common until the official part of the ceremony began.

I always enjoy listening to Mayor Jenny Hill's speeches and once again, she broke the ice and made everyone feel at ease.

Then the fabulous Ita Buttrose took the stage and spoke with grace and passion. She had the audience enthralled as she delivered her important message.

Diana was quietly telling me who the different speakers were, when I exclaimed, "There's Michael Clarke from the ABC."

Diana asked me to point him out, as she had never met him, even though she'd done many phone interviews with him on the radio.

"We'll soon fix that!" I whispered. "After the speeches, I'll introduce you to him. He's wonderful."

As soon as the official part of the ceremony was over, Diana and I headed over to Michael and waited patiently while he spoke to one of his fans. He recognised me, and we were soon hugging and catching up on the gossip. I introduced Diana to him, and they were thrilled to meet face to face after all this time.

After keeping an eye on the queue of people waiting to speak with Ita, we eventually made our way over to join it. Being a social butterfly, I spoke with a gentleman and young girl who looked to be his daughter, who were in front of us.

During our introductions, I said that his face and name were familiar. After joking that I didn't get out much and they locked me in a cupboard, he burst out laughing and continued grinning to himself. I later discovered that he played a significant role with the Cowboys. When it was their turn to meet Ita, I grabbed the young girl's phone and took plenty of photos to capture the special moment for her.

My turn arrived and I excitedly announced (well, 'blurted out' was more like it), "Ita, I want to thank you for inspiring women around the nation to be strong, determined and showing them, they can achieve anything."

Ita was speechless but remained poised, elegant, and classy – everything I wasn't! I went on to introduce myself and presented her with our Happy Feat documentary and photo book. Ita was interested to hear that the Happy Featers had performed with Guy Sebastian at three of his concerts and was keen to see our documentary.

Although I wasn't keen on attending the ceremony to collect it, I feel truly grateful for all the privileges associated with receiving the Citizen of the Year award. While my focus was, and always will be, to find opportunities for the Happy Feat group, meeting Ita Buttrose was just one of my personal highlights, and is a memory I'll always cherish.

CHAPTER 48

The Mayor's All Stars Concert

It all began when I heard from an amazing woman with a big vision. Sally, our local radio announcer, performer, and entertainer, was putting a proposal to Mayor Jenny Hill to hold a fundraising concert for the annual Christmas appeal. Townsville was still recovering from a catastrophic flood event earlier in the year, and there was going to be a huge demand for hampers and support this Christmas.

"My vision is for your super dancing rock stars to be the feature act in my pre-event foyer function," Sally wrote in an email to me.

Part of my reply was, "I'm not really sure how or where forty Happy Featers would fit in the foyer to perform. Are you having anything on stage? Our Happy Feat stars performed on stage at the Civic Theatre for the Premier's Flood Appeal in 2011 and received a standing ovation."

Well, that was the beginning of the Mayor's All Stars Concert Adventure.

The focus of the event was community resilience, mates looking after mates, never giving up, leaning on others, having one another's back, cheering people on, and most importantly, the best medicine of all: lots of laughter.

Well, this is what Happy Feat is all about. And so, the organising began.

When we considered what to perform, it really had to be 'The Greatest Showman's' amazing song, 'This is Me'. I don't know what it is, but this song brings out so much energy and emotion and our Happy Featers dance their hearts out every time they hear it.

Unfortunately, Sally already had this song pegged for a remarkable soloist with a powerful voice who would 'blow the roof off' with this song. It was disappointing news, but my gut instinct kept telling me that our Happy Featers needed to perform this song for the audience. Then I had an idea.

"Sally, I know you have a powerful solo singer in mind for 'This is Me'," I wrote, "but can you imagine it twice as amazing by having our Happy Featers perform as well?"

She loved the idea, but we certainly didn't want to take the limelight away from such a talented singer. We decided that we would only go ahead if the singer was 100% happy with the idea. It wasn't long before it was agreed to and organised. We felt extremely privileged to be performing with such a talented singer. "Sandy is so excited and honoured to be performing with Happy Feat and I can't wait to come along with her to meet the troops," Sally wrote.

A rehearsal was set up, and Sally and Sandy were soon meeting and chatting with our Happy Featers. When the backing music began and Sandy sang her first few notes, you could hear gasps from our team; we immediately knew this was going to be a knock-out performance. The Happy Featers danced their hearts out and displayed such feeling and emotion, as I looked around, tears were flowing down many faces, including my own.

In the lead up to the concert, there were countless changes of plans as over 30 acts were juggled and fine-tuned. At one stage, our Happy Feat team was scheduled to be the closing act before interval and then the opening act afterwards. Imagine our excitement, then, when we learned that our Happy Featers would now be opening the show - as well as starring in the finale!

As with the Million Dollar Memo, I come up with my great ideas while I'm doing something else: mowing the lawns for hours or taking a shower. A couple of weeks before the concert, I had a shower thought, "If we're opening and closing the show, there'll be time to do a costume change. Our dancers can have two costumes!"

With trepidation, I rang Donna W, our costume director, and hesitantly put the idea forward. We had classy red and black costumes from the Dance for Daniel Ball for the finale, and the costumes from our fifth birthday gala in turquoise and black would be ideal for the opening act. This meant having to urgently check all the skirts to make sure we had enough sizes to fit our performers.

I reiterated that if it was all too much, we could easily give it a miss and just wear the one costume. Donna should have clocked me over the head, but instead, this dedicated, thoughtful, meticulous, and incredibly special lady immediately jumped into action to get the costumes prepared.

For the past several weeks, Donna L, my amazing treasurer, 'right-hand-man', weekly DJ, and special confidante had been out of action with a health scare which had really rocked my whole world. I'm tough and very positive, but I was extremely worried about her. The stress of waiting for results - as well as the extra pressure of her absence, at work and at Happy Feat - was taking its toll.

As I've said, I am a private person, and because I choose to wear a happy face and just try to be positive, people often have no clue about the pressure I'm under and the amount of work that goes on behind the scenes. That week at Happy Feat, when Rhi arrived with her mum, I opened up and secretly confided how worried I was about Donna L and that I wasn't coping very well.

I didn't get much of a response, so I chided myself for sharing my vulnerability and got on with things. We were still setting up however, when Rhi came up to me, shaking all over and in tears. I sat her down beside her mum, my stomach doing somersaults, frantically worried that she might have some life-threatening illness.

As my arm was around her and I was trying to console her, Rhi announced that for the past several months, she'd been struggling to come up with new choreography. She felt as if she had nothing left.

She'd come to the decision that after nine-and-a-half years committed to Happy Feat, she'd like to finish up at the end of the year. It's crazy, but even with the extremely significant consequences this would have, I was so relieved that she wasn't seriously ill. I couldn't have handled that news. If that had been the case, I would have fallen in a heap on the floor and cancelled Happy Feat that night.

I thanked her for the many, many years of total commitment, for her dedication and sharing the blood, sweat and tears with me. We'd get Ashley to video any dances we didn't have, so we had a complete library of Rhi's dances for our Happy Featers to continue dancing to each week. Rhi looked bewildered, and I reminded her that I'd learned to go to Plans B, C and D when Ashley was on treatment and that was exactly what we'd do now. I also reminded her of the line in our Happy Feat Chant, 'We can do anything given a chance.'

Apparently poor Rhi had spent several weeks not sleeping properly, distressed, and worried sick about having to tell me. She was a little stunned about how well I took the news. Her wellbeing was my priority; we could deal with anything else.

As I still needed to set up and prepare for the night, I put on my happy face and continued preparations before the Happy Featers arrived. I was too busy to think any more about the situation. Nobody knew what I was dealing with as we danced, laughed, and had another awesome night at Happy Feat.

Two days later, our adorable mum, my brother Bruce, and I were on a plane to Brisbane to celebrate Mum's sister's 90th birthday. This seemed a welcome respite from everything I was dealing with - until my 'Mighty Mouse' mum, trying to show her agility and independence, raced ahead of us and tripped, falling face-first onto the concrete! Though Bruce and I were only one step behind, we couldn't catch her in time. With blood oozing down her face, a big chunk out of her hand and rather dazed, she sat on the path while Bruce and I desperately assessed her. I asked him to go inside for help as I comforted Mum.

Even though we hadn't seen our cousins for many years, it felt like it had only been yesterday as they arrived at the crazy scene, taking it all in their stride. Pressure was applied to stop the bleeding, and we carefully moved Mum inside while having a laugh and making her feel better.

Seeing Mum and her sister, Sue, together after all these years was magical. Even though Mum now had ice applied to her rapidly swelling cheek and bandaged hand, it didn't stop the two of them from busily catching up on all the news, happily reminiscing about old times. Bruce and I fussed over Mum, applying ice packs, giving pain relief, and watching her like a hawk. So much for having some respite from the worries of the world!

The following week was the last rehearsal before the concert and our Happy Featers totally rocked it. Understandably Rhi had a lot on her mind. If she forgot some of the moves, our Happy Featers gave her heaps! They were quite chuffed to feel 'better' than their teacher and continued dancing anyway. When it happened again, one of our beautiful Happy Featers said, "Rhi, what's going on? You did it again!"

Really – what disability!

At our volunteer meeting at the end of the night, we were about to wrap up and head home when Rhi reminded me that she wanted to let the volunteers know about her plans. When she did so, disbelief and shock followed. I desperately needed to take the pressure off Rhi so I put my arm around her, giving her a reassuring hug.

I explained that our beautiful Rhi was just a young girl when she first came to Happy Feat, and now she was a married woman, looking forward to the next phase of her life. I also mentioned that Ashley now had all Rhi's dances filmed so our Happy Featers could continue as usual.

Soon it was the Monday night tech rehearsal at the Civic Theatre. After an intense day at work, I made sure I got into the zone before everyone arrived. We gathered in the foyer and started with our Happy Feat Chant. I reminded everyone there was no need to be nervous, all we needed to do was have fun, have a go and do our best. The event organiser gave a quick briefing before we had a very hectic rehearsal of our opening and closing performances. Then we all rushed home for an early night.

Time for the Main Event! Everyone arrived early, and as we were the opening performance, the Happy Featers immediately got into their costumes and lined up for curtain call. It's amazing to see our Happy Featers go into performance mode, their sheer concentration, minimal talking, and very professional behaviour.

To get their energy up, we began with the Happy Feat Chant, then it was time to move quietly through the dark and cluttered backstage corridors. Getting everyone into position was quick and effortless as they'd practiced the night before – and it certainly helped having the huge curtains closed in front.

When that curtain went up, and the music began, every Happy Feat member danced their heart out. Quietly changing positions throughout the performance and constantly scanning our team, I checked to make sure there were no meltdowns, and that everyone was fine. I loved seeing their smiles as they became super confident, moving with the music. Then, we seemed to blink, and the song was over. It was time to move backstage and wait for our finale performance. Their faces were beaming as the adrenaline pumped, however everyone remained quiet and professional all the way back to the dressing room.

Over the years, we've taught the Happy Featers that being superstars means there's a lot of waiting before and after their performances. Some were happy to watch the concert live streamed on the big screen, and others gathered to colour in or play cards. What a great bonding experience.

Our weekly Happy Feat night finishes at 9:00pm. Tonight however, we weren't scheduled to perform until 10:00–10:30pm. This was a challenge as most members would have been well and truly in bed by that time. So, closer to show time, I was on a mission to perk them up, and get the energy and enthusiasm ready to wow the audience. Together with some joking and clowning around, the chant always does the trick. Everyone was now dressed in their second special costume, and they all looked like movie stars.

Once again, it was time to navigate the dark corridors backstage. By this time, all were comfortable with the various obstacles – true professionals. Nobody whined about how late it was; the dancers were a dream to work with.

Because we had amazing singers accompanying us for the finale, they too lined up, taking their positions behind our Happy Featers. The curtain raised, the music and singing commenced and our Happy Featers transformed into the most magical performers, dancing with emotion, depth, passion, and in synch. As I looked at each of their faces, the words of our chant came to mind, 'We can do anything, given a chance.'

At the end of the song, the remainder of the cast gathered on stage and mingled with our Happy Featers, and everyone took their final bows together.

Ashley captured our two performances on film, and it was so moving to be able to watch our superstars in action on the stage. Being on stage I'm in tune with the performance and the dancers, looking to troubleshoot if necessary. To just relax and enjoy the performance myself, was truly special. Each Happy Feater danced their heart out, glowing with confidence, synchronised, and looking very professional.

Our Happy Featers are showing the world their amazing abilities and demonstrating our motto, 'Believe and you can achieve'. Imagine if I had listened to the people who thought I was crazy? If I hadn't persevered through disappointments, the sometime long hard hours, and occasional heartbreak? I wanted to show the world how phenomenal and beautiful people with disabilities are. That nothing can hold them back when they believe in themselves – and have a team that believes in them too.

We'd performed with Guy Sebastian three times. Performed on the Townsville Civic Theatre stage three times, even earning a standing ovation in our first year! We'd been invited twice to perform at the Dance for Daniel Ball, organised by an organisation known and loved Australia-wide. We'd performed in front of a televised audience of millions for the Special Olympics. What on earth could be Happy Feat's next adventure?

CHAPTER 49

Born To Try

For many people, the number 13 is unlucky. Not for me.

On the 13th July 2020, a very significant adventure began as I 'put ideas out to the Universe.' As my friends quite often ask, "OMG, what have you been up to now?"

Unable to sleep one morning, I sat by my computer and researched Delta Goodrem's agent and contact details. Delta was performing her Townsville concert in April 2021, and I thought I'd explore the idea of our Happy Featers performing with her. After all, they'd already performed with Guy Sebastian at three of his concerts so this truly demonstrated our motto 'Believe and you can achieve'.

Having followed Delta's truly inspirational journey, I've always loved and admired everything about this incredible, compassionate, down-to-earth talented young lady. Experiencing Ashley's diagnosis and my own Guillain-Barré syndrome, I've felt a deep connection to Delta's struggle with Hodgkins Lymphoma and the devastating nerve damage she suffered during an operation. Throughout the whole ordeal, Delta showed true grit and determination, something else I can relate to.

Call it cheeky, but one thing I've learned over the past ten years is if you don't ask, you don't receive. I had 'put it out to the Universe' on that lucky 13th day of the month and, as I crossed my fingers and toes, I hoped the Universe would deliver.

Only ten days later, after relaxing and enjoying the variety of acts on Britain's Got Talent, I debated whether to read the very late email that had just arrived in my Inbox.

The first words stopped me in my tracks. Immediately I looked at Geoff with shock and disbelief.

When he kept asking what was happening, I held up my hand, speechless, then continued to read.

"Hi Leigh,

Many thanks for your inquiry.

My name is Tina Kennedy, and I am Delta's manager. Your inquiry was passed along to me.

I loved the video you sent along of Guy with the Happy Feat team.

I'm certain we can do something similar with you when we head to Townsville in 2021. This is my direct email, so please do stay in touch with me and we will work out something wonderful together closer to our show in Townsville.

Congratulations on the extraordinary impact you're making in so many lives. Tina xo"

Not really knowing what to do next, I began a crazy happy dance all around the lounge room, still lost for words. My poor hubby looked on with that familiar, bewildered expression "What's she been up to now?"

Passing him the phone, I shared the amazing email from Delta's manager.

Having been married for over 37 years at that time, my poor boyfriend had become accustomed to my antics, and I don't think he was all that surprised.

Being late at night, I immediately sent a message to our amazing new dance teacher, Jarrah, my volunteer manager Geri (Jarrah's mum), and my second-in-charge of Happy Feat, Donna.

Being so excited, I thought, "Blow it, I'll ring them for a group chat instead!"

Ring, ring, ring, ring...nothing. What an anti-climax. I wanted to share this incredibly exciting news but there was no response.

Luckily, it wasn't long before Geri rang back, and we talked even later into the night as I sat on the couch on our patio.

"Geri, you're not going to believe what's happening right now."

"Leigh, you're so full of surprises so I'm not even going to guess."

While we were chatting, an inquisitive, cheeky possum climbed onto the couch beside me - a little too close for comfort!

Little did I know, the email from Delta's manager that night was the beginning of an exciting but turbulent two-year adventure.

Sadly, just after receiving this exciting news, we had the devastation of having to suspend Happy Feat due to the serious Covid-19 pandemic developing. This hiatus continued for the remainder of the year.

During that time, I had the heartbreak of having Happy Featers pleading with me to begin Happy Feat again. How could I explain this serious situation to them when I didn't even comprehend it myself?

For many members, Happy Feat was the highlight and one moment of happiness in their life. Not only were they stripped of this pleasure, but they were also forced into isolation and a frightening, mysterious new world of Covid-19.

Delta's concert was scheduled for April 2021, and I had the dilemma of pushing forward with the adventure when I had no idea when Happy Feat would even resume. The fact that we were unable to rehearse for the concert, was a concern - but I constantly reminded myself of our inspirational motto, 'Believe and you can achieve.'

Continuing with the planning, I booked a function room at The Ville for our Happy Featers to gather before the concert.

The next major decision was what song to choose for the performance.

We couldn't decide between Delta's two phenomenal songs, 'Born to Try' or 'Paralysed', so I contacted her team, putting it to them to decide.

Tina soon responded that Delta would be very touched to see these two songs added to our repertoire. Mmm…we'd still have to work on that decision.

Tina also requested that we hold off on making any announcements because they were continuing to work with governments and officials on the tour and might have to move the tour. They were hopeful this wouldn't happen, but they also had to manage everyone's expectations given the pandemic. She asked that we continue to stay in touch.

As the song choice was a vital factor in any performance, I agonised over this weighty decision. Gut instinct eventually steered me towards 'Born to Try' so Jarrah prepared her stunning choreography during the break.

By November 2020, Covid-19 was running rampant throughout Australia. Tina sent the following update: -

"Our promoter team has advised that we hold off for the moment. We are confidentially working on back up / plan B options, and we have a number of philanthropic initiatives associated with the tour and we have all in a holding pattern for the moment. It won't be until Jan where we have a clearer indication on the go ahead or reschedule. Let's continue to hold and remain in touch on movements."

January 2021 arrived with a slight sense of optimism tinged with the anxiety of trying to cope with this crazy new world of Covid.

At the end of January 2021, Tina sent an update that the tour was likely to move from April. Their team was in discussions with health officials. Even if the concert date was postponed, it may be postponed again depending on Covid and guidelines. She stressed the importance that nothing was made public given the many moving parts.

At the beginning of February 2021, there was boundless excitement, relief, and joy as Happy Feat began after a ten-month hiatus. Having to introduce a myriad of critical strict new rules, regulations and distancing didn't seem to faze our team. We were all so thrilled to be able to return to Happy Feat. While we were now socially distanced and more accustomed to hand sanitiser, the happiness and joy of Happy Feat continued.

That very first night back, we introduced our Delta Goodrem dance in among several other new dances to continue the cloak of secrecy. If the concert were to proceed in April, it meant we only had eleven nights to rehearse our new dance.

After only three night's practice, our son, Ashley, - now a videographer - put together a sneak peek of our Happy Featers rehearsing 'Born to Try' and I proudly sent it to Delta's team.

Tina immediately replied with this beautiful message, "Thank you so much for sending this along. Delta and I were so touched to receive. We love so much this incredible work you've done on 'Born to Try'. We'll likely have time in the show to run this song. We're still working on moving dates to October. Still a work in progress. Will keep you posted. Thank you for sharing this."

April 2021 was also the time our special long-time friends were getting married in Tasmania (over 3000km away). Unfortunately, the wedding had already been postponed from October the previous year due to Covid, so now we had the dilemma of whether to attend this event plus all the preparation for Delta's concert if it were to go ahead in April. Setting priorities and valuing friendships, we made plans to attend the wedding followed by a brief holiday in Tasmania. This was made even more enjoyable and relaxed after Delta's concert was postponed until October 2021. The pressure was off!

Touching base with Tina in May 2021, I smiled when she replied, "I'm sure the routine is looking spectacular. Well done to everyone involved."

She went on to say they were releasing a new album and had number of roll out initiatives in place. They were also planning to announce a tour/ Delta Goodrem Foundation campaign at the top of June which would need to lead the promotions and then they could take it from there on additional announcements.

By the end of July, even though Queensland was sheltered from the devastation of Covid and strict lockdown measures, the rest of the nation was suffering enormously. I decided to send Tina and her team some of my 'treasures' (inspirational quotes) that I keep on hand to help me through character-building times. It seems very cringy now, but I ended with a sentence including Delta's song titles:

'Keep climbing' because you will all be 'sitting on top of the world' again real soon.

Tina must have appreciated the thoughts as she soon replied, "Many thanks, Leigh. It's certainly a wild ride we're all on. So much uncertainty and hopefully there will be a handle on the situation soon. Continue to stay safe & well."

By the end of August, the inevitable happened, Delta's proposed tour for October 2021 was postponed until March/April 2022.

Camping with friends that weekend, I remember having trouble sleeping and checked my phone during the night. I discovered another late-night message from Tina. "Hoping this finds you well. You may have seen late yesterday that we have been forced to move our tour due to the Covid situation across Australia. It is so disappointing for all of us, and we know the fans, too, coming to the shows. No doubt it is very disappointing for the incredible Happy Feat team who we know have been working so hard. There's no guarantee we won't have to move it again - which would be devastating. We are optimistic, though, that by March things will have gotten into a new normal.

Let's continue to stay in touch."

This must have been devastating for Delta and her whole team, but it was the right decision to make in such uncertain times. I was so grateful they only postponed the concert and didn't cancel it all together.

In the following months, after hearing further reports about the continued harsh lockdown in the southern states, I decided to send Tina the link to our Happy Feat documentary. Warm fuzzies and inspiration go a long way in healing the soul.

It didn't take Tina long to get back to me and I treasure her message.

"I was deeply moved by the doco. In particular how and why you started Happy Feat. What you are doing, touching the lives of so many people of all ages is truly inspiring. You are making a difference in this world in the most special way. Cannot wait to meet the team on tour. Have a blessed weekend."

At the end of January 2022, with only just over two months until the concert, I emailed Tina to touch base. Not even sure that our Happy Featers would be performing with Delta, I still had to push ahead with the planning. Our hair and makeup teams were put on standby though because it was all still top-secret, I couldn't share any details.

Confidential plans were made with the manager of the Townsville Entertainment Centre to provide space for our team, and I prepared the costumes for fittings as our wonderful costume director was out of action with serious health issues. What was I going to tell our Happy Featers when they queried what we were preparing the costumes for? There was no way I could lie to them, so I shared that we'd been asked to perform at a charity ball. This was certainly true, but I was evasive about any further details.

Cheryl, my beautiful sister-in-law, came all the way from Bowen to fit the costumes and make any necessary alterations. There were so many times when I could have given up hope, but I just kept reminding myself, 'Believe and you can achieve.' Besides, I couldn't give up after two years of planning.

It wasn't until only six weeks before the concert, that I had any real indication that my plan would come to fruition.

"How many Happy Feats do we have doing the performance? We are not able to have them on stage given the number of people we have on stage in the band and the square metre rules etc...but it looks like we may be able to have them in front of the stage and down the front aisles.

As a first step, please send me the number of dancers we have, and we'll continue to work through it."

I immediately replied with an estimated number of performers together with three important questions. When could we share the news? To schedule hair and makeup etc, what time was 'Born to Try' on the Runsheet? And requesting a media pass for Ashley to film the adventure.

The countdown was on! Only fifteen sleeps to go!!!!! Still no announcement!!

At 5.01pm on the 22nd March, I received the email that had me sobbing with relief, joy, and excitement combined. It didn't matter that I was in the middle aisle at the supermarket! The tears flowed and unable to contain my excitement, I even did a 'happy dance' in front of the herbs and spices.

Tina's email said, "We're almost there and just want to thank you wholeheartedly for your patience. These have truly been unusual circumstances in navigating the new world of touring, protocols, restrictions, distancing rules, masks etc.

The show commences at 8pm and Born to Try is the last song of the night at approx 10pm (confidentially).

We have a Covid compliance officer on the tour and due to the restrictions of the number people on stage he and the Townsville venue have come up with a plan for the Happy Feat team to be at the front but not stage - they are going to move the front row of the seats back to allow for the Happy Feat team to spread out across the front.

We are happy for you to share with your teams.

I know it's not ideal as Delta would so love to have them join her on stage, but I hope you understand this solution."

How amazing was Tina and Delta's team! They had gone over and beyond for the past two years to make this all happen and yet, here they were, apologising for our members not performing on stage with Delta. Our Happy Featers would be over the moon just being in the same venue as Delta let alone performing while she sang.

Forgetting the shopping list, I ran to my car to send urgent messages and make the urgent calls I had waited two years to make. Anne Sanker, our events manager immediately went into action preparing detailed information to distribute at Happy Feat plus a multitude of other tasks.

The next night at Happy Feat, we began the program like every other night. After practising the dance for 'Born to Try', I got up on stage and asked a random question.

"Who watches TV?"

Looking perplexed, they put their hands up and yelled out.

"Then you would have all seen the show, The Voice. Well, one of the judges on that show sings that last song you danced to, 'Born to Try'."

At that moment, our DJ projected a picture of Delta up on the overhead screens.

"You will all know Delta Goodrem" I began. When I went to continue, the reality of all my effort over the last two years came to the fore and I became quite emotional.

Quickly gathering my composure, I continued. "Well, Delta is doing a concert here in Townsville and our Happy Feat team will be performing with her!!"

Jaws dropped, looks of total disbelief, and loud, excited squeals reverberated around the room.

"I love Delta Goodrem!" "I can't believe it!" "Wow, we're going to perform with Delta Goodrem!" "I remember her from Neighbours!"

Eventually getting back to the programme, we did the Delta dance a couple more times. The remainder of the night was filled with a buzz and heightened level of excitement.

With only ten sleeps before the concert, I had a panicked thought. I remembered the concert music is always different to the iTunes music we practice to. Previous experience had certainly made this event easier. I remember the terrifying rehearsal at Guy Sebastian's second concert. Rhi and I had been out the front leading our team with the choreography - but when the music began, it was totally different to what we'd been practising to! Having to be in synch with each other, I quickly followed Rhi's movements. On the outside, I was calm and professional, inside was another story!

Sending a quick email to Tina requesting a copy of the concert music, I was soon listening to a very different version of 'Born to Try'. With only one more Happy Feat night before the concert, our team would be busy learning a new version of the dance. But whatever we throw at our Happy Featers, they absolutely blitz it.

As with all final rehearsal nights before a big performance, there was constant quick thinking required and there seemed to be chaos and turmoil wherever I looked. Not having any decent sleep for many weeks didn't help the situation and I desperately tried to hide my stress and frustration.

This was the first performance where every one of our Happy Featers would be in the front row. Many Happy Featers felt more comfortable with the security and shelter of the second or third row. They no longer had this option.

I too knew that feeling. For the past 12 years, I had NEVER chosen to be in the front row, preferring to flit discreetly between the Happy Featers who looked to be struggling in those rows, standing between them to give them encouragement, strength, and confidence.

During the rehearsal, myself and several volunteers tried standing behind those members offering encouragement inconspicuously. I felt totally out of my comfort zone, frustrated, and upset that I had let my team down by not being able to work my usual magic.

I can't count how many times Rhi and I had gone home crying after the final rehearsals. But, knowing from experience, it would all come together on the night…it always did.

A comprehensive four-page letter was distributed to all performers and team members, detailing the full schedule and what to expect on the night. The very next morning, with only five sleeps to go, this plan had to be totally rewritten.

In the middle of moving furniture and preparing our two new display homes for the grand opening, I received Tina's exciting update. Offering our Happy Featers even more exciting opportunities, we were prepared to overhaul the whole schedule to incorporate these extraordinary experiences.

Tina emailed the following proposed run sheet:

>4:15pm: Happy Feat standby to enter close to stage.
>
>4:20p - 4:25pm: One run through with Delta. Happy Feat positioned on the floor in front of the stage (due to Covid)
>
>We are happy to provide seats to watch the show - will they be sitting in their costumes?
>
>8pm: Show starts
>
>Approx 10pm: We will pull the Happy Feat from their seats and standby for performance at approx 10:10pm.

Wow, our Happy Featers would get to rehearse with Delta! It was such an honour. We've found that when they're able to do a rehearsal, our Happy Featers are more settled, comfortable, and relaxed. So, to do the rehearsal with Delta...wow!

That week, for the media requirements, I organised for two of our Happy Featers to do the interviews. Like our chant says, 'We can do anything given a chance!' Talking with them on the way, it struck me with how comfortable they were doing the interviews and performing at the concert. They were encouraging each other, saying how excited they were to have these opportunities. The Happy Featers did such an amazing job that I just stood back and let them shine, while feeling incredibly proud.

During the week, Pricey, our local radio superstar interviewed Delta and told her that Happy Feat were a 'big deal' here in Townsville. In fact, he said, "Up here, it's like HAPPY FEAT supported by Delta Goodrem!"

I thought that was super cheeky, but Delta took it like a true champion.

In an interview with the ABC radio not long after, I learned that she said she was the "warm-up act for Happy Feat!" How priceless is that?

PERFORMANCE DAY – No more sleeps!

On the afternoon of the performance, I arrived at the Entertainment Centre feeling excited but surprised with how calm and relaxed I felt. The meticulous preparation and hard work had been completed and it was now time to enjoy the adventure.

Our Happy Featers arrived for the rehearsal, bursting with excitement and big smiles all round. Being on a mission to make sure this whole experience was fun for everyone; I joked around and acted the fool...something they're all very familiar with.

Having placed their names on the floor to mark out their line-up positions, it was soon time to take their spots and get ready for their exciting rehearsal with Delta. We were only allocated five minutes for the whole rehearsal, so it was critical that we got them into position quickly in front of the stage.

Josh and Kristy were either side of me as I lead our team out into the concert hall. The stage was set with Delta's piano glistening in the lights, musicians were checking their instruments - and our Happy Featers were revelling in the whole experience.

The music began. Our members quickly adapted to this surreal backdrop as they began dancing. When the song finished, Delta came to the front of the stage and spoke to our Happy Featers, looking from above.

I loved the moment when she said, "Hang on, I'll come down there."

Our Happy Featers quickly surrounded her with love and excitement. She was so caring and down-to-earth, even recognising Josh from a TV interview! When Josh went to give Delta the special gift we'd prepared, it was a little hard to hear him with the musicians continuing their soundcheck in the background. Delta sang out to the band to stop what they were doing so she could hear him properly. How respectful and courteous was that?!

I'd created a special card for her with pics of every one of our Happy Feat performers and the phrase, 'Life isn't measured by the breaths we take, but by the moments that take our breath away.'

Delta read the words aloud, loving all the pictures and special Happy Feat photo book we'd included with her present. It didn't take long for everyone to gather when she suggested a group photo. Time seemed to stand still as we basked in her beautiful aura and the relaxed, comfortable atmosphere. It felt like we were just catching up with a special friend.

As Delta had paying guests arriving for her Sound Check followed by the meet and greet, we had well and truly run over schedule. Reluctantly gathering our tribe, we set off back to our room and the waiting eager parents and support workers.

The Happy Feat families were to return home, shower, have dinner and get into costume before returning at 6.15pm. My caring, wonderful Events Manager and Joy, my forever friend, were on a mission to look after my wellbeing and keep an eye on me. I don't usually eat much before a performance, but they insisted I get some fuel in the tank. So, the volunteer team gathered for a quick meal and catchup at the venue close by. We're usually too busy to just chat so it was a great way to recharge the batteries before the big night ahead.

Gathering back at the venue, it wasn't long before the Happy Featers returned for their hair and makeup pampering, bursting with excitement. My dedicated hair and makeup team had endured the top-secret 'cloak and dagger' period where we had to prepare everything behind the scenes, without anyone knowing. Seeing the looks of sheer joy on their faces as they transformed our Happy Featers into superstars, it was easy to see all the effort was truly worthwhile.

After such a long, challenging journey to make this happen, I was thrilled to meet the amazing person who was equally determined to bring this dream to fruition. Meeting Tina, Delta's manager, was a highlight for me, knowing the true grit, determination, passion, and heart-breaking disappointments we had endured along the way.

Once again, Tina felt like a long-lost friend, and I loved any time spent with her.

Seeing Tina meeting our Happy Featers, interacting and getting caught up in the moment, she quickly became part of the Happy Feat family. Just when I thought things couldn't possibly get any better, well - they did!

Tina announced that she had free tickets for any of our Happy Feater's families, friends etc. She wanted them to also experience this memorable event ahead.

Sharing this exciting news with our team, I became emotional and overwhelmed with this generosity and thoughtfulness. I hugged Tina and asked her to make the announcement instead. Oozing love and respect, Tina announced, "Pick up your phones, ring your families, friends, and get them to join us. I'll have free tickets for them all."

A loud cheer went up as our members excitedly reached for their phones to make the calls.

Feeling a little fragile, I began chatting with one of the wonderful mums. It wasn't long before a lady approached, obviously very emotional, and wanting to speak with me. She shared that she couldn't take her eyes off me during the rehearsal because she could see the genuine love and devotion that I have for my Happy Featers.

My first thought was panic as I'd rather not be in the limelight for the performance, it's my incredible Happy Featers she should have been watching instead. Not knowing the woman but having noticed her throughout the afternoon, I gently took her elbow and said, "I'm sorry, but who are you?"

Hearing the words come out of my mouth, I was mortified. It sounded so rude!

She just smiled, saying, "I'm Delta's assistant and I have a child with special needs."

Continuing, she shared, "I see so many people in the industry treating it as a job, a means of income. But what I see in you is a genuine love and care for these people. I want to clone you and take you back to Sydney."

Well, if I wasn't feeling fragile and overwhelmed before, I certainly was now! Fighting off another sooky la la moment, and wanting to hide my increasing vulnerability, I asked a random question, "Do you have a DVD player?"

Seeing her look of bewilderment, I went on to say, "I want to share our Happy Feat documentary with you. We took seventy of our team to Newcastle to perform at the opening ceremony of the Special Olympic Games and produced an award-winning documentary." She was astounded that we'd taken on such a mammoth project but was thrilled when I handed her two DVD's.

The amazing people you encounter on adventures like this is one of the many highlights!

Hearing a heightened buzz in the room, I looked over to see Pricey, our local radio superstar had called in to say hello. His fans quickly gathered followed by lots of laughter and photos.

As Pricey's beautiful partner Barbie and her team had been busy doing our Happy Featers' makeup, I went over, gave her a hug and said, "Here you are doing all the work and Pricey just walks in the door and they're swarming over him!"

We had a good old laugh as we enjoyed watching our Happy Featers relishing the moment.

Ashley caught my attention at that moment, asking if he could film a 'piece to camera' with me. Finding a quieter space in the next room, he began filming. It was funny that he only asked one question and for the next ten minutes I went on to share the whole exciting Delta experience which spanned a two-year period. Looking at him to see if there was anything to add, he grinned and said, "That's a wrap!"

It was soon time to take our seats and enjoy Delta's part of the concert. It wasn't long before I saw one of our Happy Featers in the audience below. I went down to speak to Sam and his beautiful mum Meg. I couldn't help thinking how wrong it felt that Sam wasn't performing.

A week before Delta's performance, one of our volunteers had pointed out that at our last two performances, the loud music had upset Sam so much he'd become stressed and 'had a moment.' As all our Happy Featers were in the front row with this concert, there was nowhere to hide if we had a similar situation.

Sam works at our business, and I'd watched him mature and blossom over the years. So much so, I'd suggested to Meg that he work independently at our office without a support worker, and I would keep an eye on him. This worked so successfully that Sam now works independently at all the businesses he works with.

After speaking with Meg and talking about how much Sam has grown over the last few years, she suggested that they'd just get tickets and enjoy the concert instead of Sam performing. I couldn't help feeling upset at this situation.

When Delta was performing during the concert, I couldn't help watching Sam dancing in the space behind his seat and having so much fun. I went up to our volunteer and pointed out Sam, dancing his heart out and not even bothered about the loud music. Our volunteer said she'd also been watching Sam.

I returned to my seat, but my gut instinct was doing backflips and I couldn't stop thinking about Sam not performing with us.

Returning to the volunteer, I announced, "Sam needs to perform with us."

"He can't. He doesn't have a costume."

"I don't care. Sam needs to be performing with us," I announced with unwavering conviction.

"I'll ring our costume lady to bring his costume here," was the wonderful volunteer's response.

"No, I have all the costumes at my place. I don't care that he doesn't have a costume, he needs to be performing with Happy Feat and I need to make it happen somehow," I declared and returned to my seat.

The wonderful volunteer soon came and shared that the rest of the volunteers agreed with me and one of them had offered her Happy Feat shirt for Sam to wear. Problem solved!

I went to the other volunteer and asked her to find my shirt in the dressing room, change into it and bring me her shirt.

Sitting beside our amazing Events Manager, I knew I couldn't share what I was about to attempt. Everything we'd planned was so professional and meticulously organised. What I was about to do was such a high-stake gamble and totally unpredictable that it had the potential to go pear-shaped. In fact, very pear-shaped!

Without knowing the 'back story', I thought Anne would have vetoed this mission…and rightly so. Not having time to explain, I decided it was best to say nothing when queried what I was up to when a Happy Feat shirt was placed in my lap. I was going ahead with the mission anyway and had too much respect to go against Anne's wishes had she asked me not to proceed.

It was soon time for all performers to return to our dressing room, line-up and prepare for our performance. I was very quiet, hyped up, and focusing all my strength on what was ahead of me…whatever that was. It wasn't even because of the performance ahead, it was because of the extremely risky, impromptu, gamble I was about to undertake.

The performers had their lipstick touched up and as Barbie tried to apply my lipstick, I kept telling her, "Barbie, I'm about to do something totally radical, extremely risky and it could all go very pear-shaped! But my gut instinct is yelling at me that I must do it!"

Barbie had seen what I'd achieved over the years, and truly believed in me. Instead of asking what I was about to do, she simply said, "Well, if your gut instinct is telling you, then you must do it."

I took my position at the front of my team, with Josh on one side and Kristy on the other and juggled the Happy Feat shirt on my arm.

Anne came up to get the shirt out of my way but, with a Tarzan grip on it, I firmly told her that I needed the shirt.

Entering the stadium, I frantically searched for where Sam had been dancing all night. He wasn't there.

Had he gone home? Gone to the toilet and would miss this amazing experience?

It was at that moment I saw him dancing near the front row where we were about to line up. Thank you, Universe, for delivering!

Quickly positioning Josh and Kristy in their allocated spots in front of the stage, I went to Sam and asked if he'd like to perform with us. I was so focused on this mission, that I totally forgot about the thousands of people in the audience and the huge, daunting performance ahead. When Sam's whole face lit up and he beamed with excitement, I knew this was worth the huge risk I'd just taken. In a panic to get his Happy Feat shirt over his other shirt, I fumbled and got it upside down and back to front.

Being so fixated on my mission, I didn't even realise Delta's manager, Tina, was behind me and about to question what was happening. What I discovered later was that Joy had quickly and calmly stepped in and reassured Tina that Sam was a Happy Feater.

Eventually getting it sorted, I realised that the music was starting. I had intended to take Sam up the other end of the line with me to keep an eye on him and deal with any issues if they arose. Quick thinking and feeling confident with my mission, I placed Sam in line and promptly took my position. It was at that moment; the lighting was turned up and Sam was in the spotlight just like all the other performers.

At rehearsal, we'd learned that, for our members to be seen on the huge screens overhead, we needed to position them between the two cameramen located in front of the stage. This meant our team had even less room, but it was worth it for the audience to see them in action. Placing an additional Happy Feater in the limited space meant they all had to shuffle up a little, but they did so without being asked. That was another quick decision. Do I place him on the other side of the cameraman, and he won't be on the overhead screens because he wasn't in costume? Hell no, I didn't care about the costume! All that mattered was Sam was given the opportunity to perform just like all our other Happy Featers.

Feeling apprehensive and unsettled, it was time to put my 'happy face' and 'big girl pants' on and get on with the performance.

The stage positions were ever changing as we lost a few performers to ill health, so I was now in between two different members than first rehearsed. Seeing another member struggling, I quickly moved to her side and tried to calm her down and yet still encourage her at the same time. She had always refused to spin around as part of the choreography as I believe it made her lose balance. Instead of trying to encourage her to turn around, I let her do her thing then encouraged her with the rest of the choreography.

Happy Feat isn't about doing the moves perfectly, it's about having a go, doing your best, and having fun.

For performances, we rarely see the audience because they're usually in the dark. But for this one, being in front of the stage with the front seats moved back a fraction, we were still close to the audience. For our seasoned performers, they relished this situation, and enjoyed the spotlight. For many of our Happy Featers, with this being their very first time in the front row, it was quite daunting. It certainly was for me.

Being in that front row was totally out of my comfort zone and I was desperately trying to hide the fact that I was freaking out! I kept reminding myself about my 'happy face' and 'big girl pants!' What's that chant say...we can do anything given a chance?!

Instead of our Happy Featers watching our dance teachers to follow the moves, I could see some of them were distracted by being so close to the audience. But, as I teach them, performances are like a box of chocolates, you never know what you're going to get.

When you're dealing with challenges like autism etc, all these last-minute changes and unexpected situations have the potential to cause extreme anxiety and unpredictable behaviour. Having ZERO formal training to deal with this, I run entirely on gut instinct and motherly love.

As I've said before, we purposely mix up their routines and throw different scenarios into the mix. This means they now have so much confidence that they feel comfortable knowing whatever happens, we're right there with them. We have their best interests at heart.

When the music finished, apparently the crowd cheered but it wasn't until I saw several people in the front row standing for a standing ovation that I desperately fought back a flood of emotion. After 12 years, another dream had come true. I was witnessing acceptance and inclusion once again for our Happy Featers.

Delta was phenomenal. As she came to the front of the stage, she high fived every Happy Feater as they walked off. To make sure each member had this honour, I grabbed them and moved them forward. There was a bit of 'man-handling' during the event, but there's an old saying, 'If you snooze, you lose!'

I spotted Sam's mum among all the chaos at the front of the stage. When we saw each other, we gave each other the biggest hug, both knowing that one of the biggest feats had just been accomplished! I learned later that Sam's family and friends now refer to it as 'Leigh's Maverick Move.'

Arriving back in the dressing room, we noticed an important looking group of people waiting expectantly for us. Whispering to our volunteers, I asked, "Who are they?"

I heard a surprised, "That's Delta's backup band, Sheppard!"

Still reeling from the shock and realisation of what had just transpired, I asked our volunteer to announce them to our Happy Featers so they could acknowledge the band and make a fuss they so rightly deserved.

The next moment, we all stared in disbelief as we watched Delta, her whole band and all the singers coming into our dressing room! A loud cheer went up as our Happy Featers quickly jostled into position next to their idol. I knew that one of our dance teachers wanted a photo with Delta, so I grabbed her and yes, you guessed it, more 'man-handling' as I thrust her into position near Delta.

It was priceless hearing the singers tell our Happy Featers how amazing they were and how much they enjoyed performing with them. Cameras were clicking everywhere as we all wanted to capture this moment forever.

It wasn't until I was speaking with Ashley after the event, that he shared a golden moment that could easily have been missed. While filming, he captured one of the band members saying, "Yeah, we haven't had applause like that before!"

When the Happy Featers were heading off, my beautiful 'bosom buddies' called in to congratulate me and say how much they enjoyed our Happy Featers' performance. Having been sworn to secrecy, they had followed the whole Delta journey with me over the past 18+ months and wanted to be there to share the big finale.

Still chatting as we walked outside, we had a gentleman approach us and apologise for interrupting. He went on to introduce himself as the Covid Marshal for Delta's concert and to thank me for everything I've done for the disability world.

Being quite emotional, he shared that he'd been in the navy for 21 years and when he was young, had an uncle who became a quadriplegic when injured in the special forces. The love and respect he had for his uncle was evident as he proudly announced that his uncle had gone on to represent the UN and was also making an enormous contribution to the disability sector.

Wow, I find people truly fascinating.

As we got to the carpark, I told my friends that I was thinking of gate-crashing one of the Happy Feat families who couldn't participate due to a serious health condition. They were also family friends so it was even more shattering that they couldn't be part of this memorable event.

I checked the time, 11.25pm. "Don't be ridiculous Leigh! You can't drop into someone's place 11.25pm!"

I certainly felt like celebrating and checked out some bottle shops on the way to grab a bottle of wine. You could tell I'd never done anything like that before because I was surprised when they were all closed.

Pulling into the family's driveway, I was grateful they didn't have a vicious dog on guard. I hesitantly knocked on the patio door and yelled out. Nothing. Being very cheeky and brazen, I went around the front of the house and knocked on their bedroom window and held up the light on my phone, thinking I could be shot here, or the police arrive with sirens blazing. I could see the headlines in the Townsville Bulletin, 'Performed with Delta Goodrem then spent the night in jail!'

Next minute, the curtain was very slowly pulled back and I quickly announced, "Greg, it's Leigh from Happy Feat! Everything is OK, I just wanted to celebrate with Donna!"

Rubbing his eyes, he mumbled something about getting her.

Donna appeared at the patio door immediately panicking that something serious had happened. Quickly explaining that I wanted to celebrate with her but there were no bottle shops for me to come bearing gifts.

I was soon sitting at their kitchen bench with Greg fossicking around for a bottle of wine, and Donna heating up a big bowl of homemade vegetable soup because she knew I wouldn't have eaten much. Yes, that's true friendship isn't it.

As we relaxed on the back patio, I admitted that I wasn't sure whether to drop in or not. I didn't want her to feel sad as I went through all the magic moments, but she quickly reassured me and was eager to hear every detail. With both of us not being big drinkers, it only took half a glass of wine for us to be totally relaxed…something I hadn't been for many weeks.

At about 2am, I sheepishly rang my adorable hubby and asked if he could pick me up from Donna's place. It meant a 20-minute drive into town for him, but he didn't even hesitate. I'd been forgiven as we'd been married 39 years, and this was the first time he had to rescue me.

After two hours sleep, I was up responding to emails and social media. In the following days, we were so proud when Delta posted: -

"I'm extremely grateful for all your hard work you all put in to do such an amazing performance with me on my tour! Love you all! Thanks for lighting up the stage tonight everyone."

Another post was accompanied by a wonderful film clip that captured special magic moments of the night.

"I had the great honour of performing with the incredible group, Happy Feat, and what beautiful souls and talented performers they all are! As your card for me said, 'Life is not measured by the number of breaths we take, but by the moments that take our breath away.' Thank you for spending the night with us and lighting up the stage."

I loved hearing my cousin comment on how touched she was to see Delta and her team with our Happy Featers embracing and personifying inclusion. Another goal achieved.

I was planning to create a special photo book to thank Delta and Tina, so I asked our Happy Feat team to share their special moments to include in the book. When Josh, one of the Happy Featers shared his experiences, I was brought to tears.

"Can you believe that we've done this!? Can you? This experience was indescribable. The feeling of everyone clapping, cheering us on, made me happy and proud of us. It was so moving that Delta's manager still wanted to have us, even though Covid made it impossible to do it twice before.

From the bottom of my heart, I just want to say a MASSIVE thank you to Delta Goodrem, Sheppard, and especially her manager for providing all of us a wonderful time. As we say on the Happy Feat logo "Believe and you can achieve", and I truly believe that we've achieved our new stardom. Also, thank you Leigh, for this incredible experience."

After sharing this with Delta's manager, I was overwhelmed by her response. "What a gorgeous note from Josh! Please pass on to him our deepest gratitude. Meeting Josh and all the Happy Feat team and families was such a gift for all of us to receive."

Chapter 50

That's a wrap.

As you can see, the Happy Feat journey has been a diverse collection of exhilarating adventures and spine-tingling moments, that make you stop and think, 'Did that really happen?'

Watching our Happy Featers' confidence flourish, to experience their wonderment when they achieve things they didn't think possible, has truly been a huge highlight and continuous motivation for me.

Being able to provide them with a guaranteed 'happiness-fix' and bring sheer joy into their lives is fulfilling beyond words. This euphoria is contagious and reverberates through everyone around.

My journey has also been scattered with heart-wrenching, devastating periods. Having the motto of 'always taking something good from a not-so-good situation', has taught me that everything happens for a reason.

I had no idea that going through Ashley's traumatic treatment and experiencing Guillain-Barre syndrome would teach me numerous, untold character-building skills that empowered and prepared me for the Happy Feat journey.

Being able to constantly change plans in a heartbeat, to never give up, knowing to take time-out to heal, having the strength and resilience to pick myself up every time I was knocked down, learning the importance of humour and being able to laugh, all became extremely useful skills.

Gratitude also played an important role. No matter how horrendous the situation became, I always knew there was someone having a worse time than me and I could always find a truckload of things to be grateful for.

Being optimistic, positive, and having hope were other critical tools. When others thought it was impossible, I truly believed I could make it happen.

So, what's the next impossible, exciting adventure?

You've seen that with hope, grit and gratitude, anything is possible.

Watch this space because I'm reaching for my To-Do list!

ACKNOWLEDGMENTS

I have been very blessed to have so much support during the creation of this book.

My hubby, Geoff, has been indispensable throughout this process. Nicknamed Mufasa, 'the wise one', he has been my mentor, guiding light, therapist and pillar of strength. When I invented countless reasons not to proceed with my book, Geoff's patience, understanding, and wisdom inspired me to be brave and share my story.

My parents have been my biggest fan club and taught me valuable and cherished life lessons. Although they are no longer with me, I am comforted knowing they are proud of me no matter what and are always with me in spirit.

Stacey and Ashley, my wonderful children, thank you for all your love, support and for generously sharing me with my other family, Happy Feat. Like my parents before me, you can count me as your biggest fan club!

My brother and special friend, Bruce, thank you for your steadfast love and support.

As for taking my random notes and embarrassing, amateur journal and transforming it into a book, I have two very important editors to thank.

Whilst sharing countless cups of tea, Julie Johnston provided valuable coaching, direction, and encouragement.

Michelle Boaler's passion and unwavering belief in my story inspired me to continue the sometimes frustrating and terrifying process of creating a book to share. Michelle took my written words, joined the dots, and added finesse where required.

For all my friends and wonderful people in my life, I am truly grateful.

'Believe and you can achieve.'

www.ingramcontent.com/pod-product-compliance
Lightning Source LLC
Chambersburg PA
CBHW070933230426
43666CB00011B/2419